Wheels on Ice

WHEELS

ON ICE

Stories of Cycling in Alaska

Edited by **JESSICA CHERRY** and **FRANK SOOS**

University of Nebraska Press   Lincoln

Acknowledgments for the use of previously
published material appear on pages 267–68, which
constitute an extension of the copyright page.

The University of Nebraska Press is part of a land-
grant institution with campuses and programs on the
past, present, and future homelands of the Pawnee,
Ponca, Otoe-Missouria, Omaha, Dakota, Lakota, Kaw,
Cheyenne, and Arapaho Peoples, as well as those of the
relocated Ho-Chunk, Sac and Fox, and Iowa Peoples.

Library of Congress Cataloging-in-Publication Data
Names: Cherry, Jessica, editor. | Soos, Frank, editor.
Title: Wheels on ice: stories of cycling in Alaska
/ edited by Jessica Cherry and Frank Soos.
Description: Lincoln: University of Nebraska Press, [2022]
Identifiers: LCCN 2022007195
ISBN 9781496232472 (Paperback: acid-free paper)
ISBN 9781496233899 (ePub)
ISBN 9781496233905 (PDF)
Subjects: LCSH: Cycling—Alaska—History. | BISAC: SPORTS
& RECREATION / Cycling | HISTORY / United States / State
& Local / West (AK, CA, CO, HI, ID, MT, NV, UT, WY)
Classification: LCC GV1045.5.A4 W487 2022 |
DDC 796.609798—dc23/eng/20220321
LC record available at https://lccn.loc.gov/2022007195

Designed and set in Adobe Text Pro by L. Auten.

For Terrence Cole (1953–2020) and
Frank Soos (1950–2021), who left too soon.

For my uncles Dan O'Rourke (1945–2014), Tim Ernst, and Joel Ernst,
who showed me that life on the bike is better.

—Jessica Cherry

Contents

List of Illustrations   xi

Preface   xiii
JESSICA CHERRY

Introduction   xv
FRANK SOOS

Part 1. Bicycling in Alaska, 1898–1908

Introduction   3
TERRENCE COLE

From Dawson to Nome on a Bicycle   6
EDWARD R. JESSON

A Broken Chain and a Busted Pedal:
Max Hirschberg's 1900 Bicycle Ride to Nome   24
MAX HIRSCHBERG

Cycling the Arctic: Levie's Bicycle Ride
from Point Barrow to Nome   29
H. B. LEVIE

Part 2. New Wheels, 1980s–2000

Introduction   35
JESSICA CHERRY AND FRANK SOOS

Iditabike, 1987   38
CHARLIE KELLY

Iditasport Extreme: 350 Miles   45
ROCKY REIFENSTUHL

Iditasport, 1991   51
GAIL KOEPF

Hellbikes on Ice   54
ROMAN DIAL

Biking the Haul Road, 1986   63
DAN BUETTNER

Pribilofs by Bike, 1994   70
BILL SHERWONIT

Rough-Terrain Unicycling, 1997   75
MICHAEL FINKEL

Part 3. Wheels Now, 2001–2021

Introduction   83
JESSICA CHERRY

The Wind Grooms Our Trails   86
DANIEL SMITH

Skagway to Nome   92
JEFF OATLEY

The Government Sign   112
CORINNA COOK

Last Ride of the Season   115
DAVID A. JAMES

A Winter Bike Commute   130
MARTHA AMORE

The Bike Thief   136
DON REARDEN

The Killer Hill   140
ANDROMEDA ROMANO-LAX

Cryo-Cave! An Ode to Indoor
Training in Alaska   148
ERIC FLANDERS

The Iditarod Trail and Me   156
CLINTON HODGES III

That One Magnetek Time
I Jumped Over Five Cars   168
    M. C. MOHAGANI MAGNETEK

When There's No One Left to Fight   174
    RACHAEL KVAPIL

The Books I Carried   179
    ALYS CULHANE

Going Long, Going Solo   195
    CORRINE LEISTIKOW

Physical Education   203
    JESSICA CHERRY

There Is No Tomorrow   215
    BJØRN OLSON

A Positively Memorable
Mountain Bike Ride(ish)   222
    ERIC TROYER

Back in Alaska to Share the
Story of the Roads   230
    LAEL WILCOX

Nulato Hills: Biking Musk Ox Trails
in Western Alaska   233
    LUC MEHL

Growing Old with My Bicycle   240
    KATHLEEN MCCOY

The Magic Bus on the Stampede   244
    TOM MORAN

Tell 'Em about It: An Alaska Cyclist at Large   251
    EARL PETERSON

Acknowledgments   265
Source Acknowledgments   267
Contributors   269

Illustrations

Photographs

Following page 32

1. Four wheelmen riding from Valdez to Fairbanks
2. A 110-pound automobile, or a five-wheeled cycle
3. Children in Wales, Alaska, riding a wooden tricycle

Following page 80

4. Children with bicycles in Kotzebue, Alaska
5. Bill Fuller, near Fairbanks, pulling firewood
6. George Peck on mountain unicycle overlooking Resurrection Bay
7. Gail Koepf being passed by a Junior Iditarod dog team

Following page 264

8. Ridgetop tundra in the Nulato Hills
9. Trekking through downfall from forest fire in the Nulato Hills
10. Route finding through an old burn scar
11. Lael Wilcox and friend riding in Denali National Park
12. Bikes at a cabin near Willow, Alaska
13. Lael Wilcox on the Tony Knowles Coastal Trail in Anchorage
14. Lael Wilcox and family bike camping at the beach
15. Lael Wilcox at Hatcher Pass, Alaska
16. Clint Hodges III on the Iditarod Trail Invitational

17. Clint Hodges III riding single-track in Anchorage

18. Clint Hodges III riding on fresh snow

19. M. C. MoHagani Magnetek employs a beach cruiser in music video

20. Heather Best at Cooper Pass

21. Self-portrait on the trail

22. Paddling on the Chukchi Sea with bike in tow

23. Hunter and bike

24. Kids riding our bikes

25. Cycling through arctic fog

26. Pausing on the tundra

Maps

1. Place names described in the gold rush–era stories   2

2. Place names described in the stories for the period
   1980–2000   34

3. Place names described in the contemporary stories   82

Preface   JESSICA CHERRY

The idea for this book came together when Frank and I learned of our friend and colleague Terrence Cole's cancer diagnosis. We both had the idea that Terrence's 1985 edited volume, *Wheels on Ice: Bicycling in Alaska, 1898–1908*, ought to be reprinted. This book, nearly unobtainable, holds something of a cult status in Alaska. Also published as "Wheels on Ice: A Collection of Gold Rush Tales by Men Who Mushed with Bicycles Instead of Dogs" as an insert in the *Alaska Journal: History and Arts of the North*, the original included five stories. Frank and I also agreed that expanding this book to include more recent stories of cycling in Alaska would make for a more compelling and relevant collection.

We worked on the project together from late 2019 through the start of the COVID-19 pandemic; the murder of George Floyd in Minneapolis; the death of Terrence in Fairbanks; the election of Joe Biden and Kamala Harris; the January 6 riot at the U.S. Capitol; the fall of Kabul, Afghanistan, to the Taliban; the rollout of vaccines; the subsequent vaccine resistance; and the death from COVID of nearly seven million people at the time of this writing. Throughout Alaska and everywhere, Frank and I, and everyone else, cherished our biking time as an escape from all of these painful events. Cycling has a way of reducing us back to our childhood innocence, our troubles blown back by the apparent wind of moving forward. Just after the last of our author edits trickled in during August 2021, I received the message that no one ever wants to hear: my friend, mentor, and coeditor Frank had died in a cycling accident.

This wasn't Frank's first one-person cycling accident. In fact, in 2015, the night after winter solstice in Interior Alaska, a time when a spooky blue-and-pink veil covers the few short hours that the sun hovers near the horizon, Frank wrote an essay about his mortality in which he recounts a cycling accident from the preceding summer, very similar to the one in which he died. This essay appeared as a blog post for the 49 Writers organization during the period that Frank served as the Alaska State Writer Laureate. About the slow lengthening of the days after solstice, Frank wrote, "'More light': those were said to be Goethe's last words. They needn't be a valediction, though. Instead, let's think of them as a wish for everything that can happen in the coming light."

The first part of this book reproduces three stories from the original volume edited by Terrence Cole. We know from the pictures of Native Alaskans as well as non-Native women and children with bicycles in that era that these stories are not inclusive, but they are what we have right now. There are also language and viewpoints in these stories that modern readers may find offensive. Because this portion of the book is a partial reprint, we are reproducing the stories as they were written by their authors and assembled by Cole.

In the second part of the book, we pick the cycling story back up in the 1980s, as a whole new wave of settlers have come to Alaska, seeking either jobs in the new pipeline economy or to make a life "away from it all." Like the culture and landscape of Alaska at that time, cycling also underwent a rapid transformation with the advent of new technology. Most of these pieces are reprints from magazines or newspapers from the 1980s and 1990s.

In the third and final section of the book, we have contemporary essays and stories written by people riding and writing now. These pieces were solicited from cycling interest groups on social media and with old-fashioned posters and by word of mouth. We found pieces in various blogs and online publications and contacted the authors. If we missed someone's voice here, we apologize. We encourage everyone who is riding out there today to tell their cycling story.

Introduction

FRANK SOOS

Among the many mixed gifts given us by the Industrial Revolution, unquestionably the best was the bicycle. The bicycle. Affordable. Compact. Lightweight. Capable of traveling great and small distances with relative ease. Durable and easily fixable with a few tools.

It took us a while to get here with the bicycle. Apocryphal stories would have Leonardo da Vinci coming up with a design, and it makes sense. He thought of so many ideas, it would take centuries to catch up with and actually execute. But some say the sketch of the bicycle in one of the codices was probably a doodle by a bored monk made centuries later. It wasn't until the early nineteenth century that the velocipede, the running bike or hobby horse—no pedals, no sprocket chain, simply two wheels with a saddle between for the rider-runner—came along. It took a German inventor in the 1850s to come up with a bicycle with pedals. But this bike and its immediate descendants all had direct drive, culminating with the penny-farthing design. The penny-farthing was a challenge to ride and a dangerous design—at best it would remain a novelty and not a serious way to travel.

Beginning in the 1890s, people came up with a variety of "safety bicycles"—two wheels, usually of similar size, pedals and sprocket chain drive from crank arms to the rear wheel. The diamond frame design (two triangles back to back: seat tube, top tube, down tube, and seat tube, seat stays, chain stays) came along shortly thereafter. The vast majority of bicycles in the world today are diamond frame bikes. Finally, the pneumatic tire offered a more comfortable ride, a tire that could easily be removed, patched, and replaced. The modern bicycle had arrived.

These new safety bicycles triggered a bike boom around the world.

Here in Alaska and the Yukon Territory, another boom was well under-
way, the gold rush. Did bicycles make sense in a place with few roads,
none of them paved, harsh weather, and great distances between roadhouses and towns? Why not give them a try?

We have these early stories of bold cyclists making trips that are a
challenge even to contemporary cyclists with the latest gear and a wealth
of electronic assistance. We have Jesson's account of cycling the frozen
Yukon River, following the gold rush from Dawson, Yukon Territory,
where all the claims were staked to the next new thing in Nome, Alaska.
And we have distance cyclist Jeff Oatley's account of covering some of
the same ground 117 years later.

In the late nineteenth century the League of American Wheelmen
(now the League of American Cyclists) began to advocate for more
paved roads. Its call was soon taken up by the automobile industry.
And the car quickly began to push the bicycle aside. Why pedal when
a person could simply step on the accelerator? The bicycle became a
child's toy, set aside in the corner of the garage as soon as a kid could
get his learner's permit.

Bicycles had great days in Europe, where, after World War II especially, people found cycling to be a way to get out into the country, to
find joy in travel in a damaged continent.

Then, suddenly, surprisingly, cycling was back in the United States in
the early 1970s. People began to travel by bike. The 1976 Bike Centen-
nial began an era of cycle touring that has continued to this day, even
though cyclists had to push to make a place for themselves on the road,
to move bicycles back from toy to a useful mode of travel. Along the
way bicycles changed.

There's a world of difference between the bicycle Jeff Oatley rides
today and those cycles from the nineteenth-century boom. Bicycles
evolved, and as they evolved, they branched in many different directions. Multiple-speed bicycles with internal geared hubs and external
derailleurs came along, and the number of possible gears available
grew and grew. Brakes came along: coaster brakes and varieties of rim
brakes and finally disk brakes.

People began to design bikes for different applications, some never
imagined before. Road bikes became lighter; tires became skinnier.

My pride was an English-made Hercules, a "racing bike" with a three-speed Sturmey-Archer hub and caliper brakes. I rode it through my college years.

Experimenters in California began riding off-road—the advent of mountain bikes—beginning with old repurposed balloon tire bikes from the 1940s and '50s. This writer's first big-kid bike was a Schwinn Excelsior, a hand-me-down from my cousin that seemed to weigh as much as I did. The Excelsior became one of the go-to bikes for modification to early mountain bikes. Knobby tires and indexed shifting quickly came along because the terrain required them.

Soon enough, in Alaska fatter tires requiring fatter rims would come along because people wanted to ride on snowy trails. Alaskan cycle innovator Simon Rakower designed the SnowCat rim, a wide rim that would accommodate a wide tire at low pressure, a tire that would keep a bike riding on top of the snowpack rather than sinking in. Finding frames to fit such rim-tire combinations led to fat bikes, bikes specifically designed to be ridden on soft surfaces.

Evidence of the advent of off-road cycling can be seen in the Iditabike race. This spinoff of the Iditarod Trail Sled Dog Race was started in 1987, four years after the Iditaski began and twenty years after the dog race was first organized by Joe Redington Sr. and Dorothy Page to help revitalize the culture of mushing. Later known as the Iditasport and then the Iditarod Trail Invitational, early races featured standard mountain bikes, alongside skiers and snowshoers. In subsequent years, as technology improved, cyclists came to dominate the winner's circle in both the 350- and 1,000-mile winter races.

Now we have gravel bikes, designed for exactly what the name implies, bikes for gravel and dirt roads with their own wider tires. And a whole variety of utility bikes, the kinds of bikes often used in developing countries: bicycles that function as small trucks, carrying all sorts of loads.

In Alaska we have all the above, even bicycle rickshaws in Fairbanks and Anchorage. Beginning with the gold rush, people in the North made use of bicycles in this unlikely environment. As bicycles changed, Alaskans were among the first to try new innovations, to be the innovators themselves to meet the needs—and desires—of a variety of riders with a variety of styles.

In this volume readers will encounter those gold rush adventurers and more contemporary adventurers. From riders whose principal use of a bike is for a routine commute to riders seeking adventures, Alaskans on bicycles every day, in every kind of weather, on any kind of surface. Read all about us.

Wheels on Ice

PART 1

Bicycling in Alaska, 1898–1908

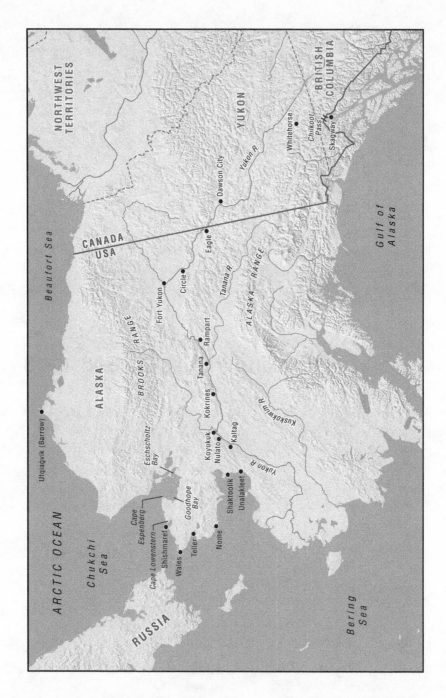

Map 1. Place names described in the gold rush–era stories. Map by Erin Greb.

Introduction

TERRENCE COLE

This is a collection of stories by men who drove bicycles, instead of dog teams, across the Alaskan frontier. In their own words, these early "wheelmen" tell about some of the most rugged rides ever taken on two wheels.

The Alaska gold rush era came soon after the height of the worldwide bicycle craze of the 1890s, when millions took to riding "wheels" for the first time. Like television in the 1950s and the home computer in the 1980s, the bicycle was the fad of the future in the 1890s.

The wheel craze started after the development in the 1880s of the so-called safety bicycle, the modern-looking chain-driven bike with the same size wheels in the front and back. Another vital improvement was the adoption of pneumatic tires, which made for a much smoother ride than had been possible on solid rubber. For good reason, early bicycles had been called "boneshakers." The "safety" and air-filled tires made cycling far more comfortable and less risky than it had been on the old "ordinary" bicycles, on which daredevil riders had to sit atop a huge front wheel, high off the ground. Women as well as men could ride "safeties" in comfort, and the bicycle soon became practical for commuting workers as well as fashionable for the well-to-do.

The Klondike Gold Rush of 1897–98 coincided with the bicycle craze in the United States. One eastern outfitter, eager to cash in on the bicycle's popularity, decided that a truly up-to-date prospector would want to pedal his way to the goldfields. According to an 1897 Klondike guidebook, *A. C. Harris's Alaska and the Klondike Gold Fields*, a New York company tried to produce a special "Klondike Bicycle" that would enable a modern prospector to easily ride a wheel across Chilkoot Pass and down the Yukon River to Dawson City.

"The Klondike Bicycle is specially designed to carry freight," the inventor declared, "and is in reality a four-wheeled vehicle and bicycle combined." The bike weighed fifty pounds and had solid rubber tires an inch and a half thick and a steel frame "wound with rawhide, shrunk on, to enable the miner to handle it with comfort in low temperatures." The Klondike bike also had two outrigger wheels that could be unfolded when the rider wished to carry a load of supplies. It was claimed that up to a quarter ton of freight could be stacked on the machine when the wheels were extended, though the rider would then have to dismount and pull his four-wheeled vehicle along the trail. When not carrying supplies, the outrigger wheels were folded up inside the frame, and the wheelman could get back in the bicycle saddle and continue his journey.

Though the Klondike Bicycle was probably never built, there were numerous gold seekers at the turn of the century who brought their wheels with them to Alaska. "Scarcely a steamer leaves for the North that does not carry bicycles," one Seattle newspaper stated in March 1900. The bicycle was of little use in the roadless northern wilderness during the summertime, when the trails that did exist became rivers of mud. But during the winter, on ice and frozen ground, a wheelman could pedal with relative ease, even without chains or snow tires. To some hardy travelers at the turn of the century, long before the invention of a practical snowmachine, or snowmobile, the bicycle appeared to be the ideal vehicle for covering long distances in Alaska cheaply during the wintertime.

Bicycles were relatively inexpensive and easy to repair. The early models were strong and simple, with no gears and few complicated parts. One Seattle bicycle dealer claimed that the brand it sold—the Rambler Road Wheel—was the best bicycle for Alaskan riders; it was equipped with a "G. and J. Clincher Heavy Tread tire, a detachable tire that can be repaired by man, woman or child." San Francisco dealer C. E. Baker, who sold the Baker "Special" bicycle, said his wheel was "well adapted for Alaska or any rough riding."

An Alaskan bicycle ride could be a rugged trip, but frozen rivers and dog team trails actually made quite good—though rough and narrow—

bicycle paths. By following the tracks left by the runners of a dogsled, it was possible for a cyclist to cruise right along through the snow. Even a novice wheelman in Alaska could travel faster than anyone else on the trail; dog teams and horses were both slower and far more costly than bicycles. Feeding and caring for weary animals in the Arctic winter was a constant challenge, but a man with an "iron steed" had no such problems.

The most heavily traveled route for bicycles in the North was the approximately four-hundred-mile-long winter trail from Dawson to Whitehorse. Roadhouses were evenly spaced about every twenty miles along the trail, and the wheel was excellent, as one hardware man who sold bicycles in Dawson said, for "anyone wishing to make a quick trip without freight or much baggage." In 1901 the *Skagway Daily Alaskan* estimated that there must have been at least 250 bicyclists on the trail to Dawson that spring, and the paper predicted that the day of the dog team would soon be over.

Despite such enthusiasm, the bicycle never did become accepted as a reliable means of transportation in Alaska. Severe cases of frostbite and snow blindness were common among wheelmen, who had to strain their eyes trying to follow a narrow trail through the snow. The bikes often broke down in the worst weather, far from town and the nearest supply of spare parts. In the low temperatures, bearings would freeze and the tires got stiff. A fall on the ice when the temperature was far below zero could easily shatter a pedal or a handlebar—or a knee or an elbow. For good reason, most of these early riders were thought to be a little mentally deranged.

Ed Jesson, whose story is the first in this collection, said that in 1900, when he decided to ride his bicycle more than one thousand miles, from Dawson City to Nome, no one believed he would make it. He described his brother's reaction: "What the hell are you going to do with the wheel he asked. Going to Nome, I said. He called Harry Smith and John Nelson, proprietors of the hotel, and some other old-timers. He said this brother of mine is going to try to go to Nome on a bicycle. He's crazy, they all said."

Read Jesson's firsthand account of his nearly unbelievable bicycle ride—and the other stories in this book—and decide for yourself.

—Fairbanks, 1985

From Dawson to Nome on a Bicycle

EDWARD R. JESSON

Ed Jesson first went to Alaska in 1896 to prospect for gold in Cook Inlet. He moved to the Yukon after the Klondike strike and was running a small trading post at Star City, about 120 miles downriver from Dawson, when the stampede to Nome began in 1899.

Jesson had seen many worn-out men and dogs on the trail to Nome, and he thought that bicycling might be an easier way to make a thousand-mile trek across the frozen wilderness.

Reprinted here is the story, told in Jesson's own words, of his ride from Dawson to Nome in February–March 1900. Jesson's amazing tale was preserved for history by Ruth Reat, a woman who worked for Jesson in San Francisco in the 1930s. She extracted the story from Jesson's diary of the trip and typed it up "with spelling and all just 'as was.'" Apparently, Jesson's original diaries, which filled ten books, were subsequently lost. Brackets indicate where Reat added material from Jesson's letters. [Readers should be aware that the following story, a historic reprint, contains derogatory language.—Ed.]

—Terrence Cole

The Nome stampeed had been on all winter. Many had started in boats in the fall of 1899 too late to reach Nome and by February 1900 the Yukon river trail was alive with dogteams and stampeeders with and without dogs. Any old way to get or part way. They bought any old dog or pup and stole what they couldn't buy and were on their way.

I had been hunting caribou at the head of Floom creek 75 miles up the 70-Mile river all winter and hauling them into Eagle City, about a 100 mile haul with my dogteam. Every trip I made into Eagle I heard more about Nome and the rich beach digings and saw more stampeders on their way.

At the mouth of 70-Mile river where it empties into the Yukon I had a store, postoffice and wood-camp. This was 120 miles below Dawson. By the time these stampeeders reached my place they were all worn out, dogs and all having left Dawson overloaded. They had sprained ankles, sprained knees and all stove up. They began to unload tents, stoves, picks, shovels, whipsaws and many other articles; they had too much flour, too much dogfeed, and they began to dump it all and lighten up to make better time. I had been getting the stampeed fever and by the time I had hauled in the 43 caribou and 2 bear that I had killed I'm telling you that my fever was up to the breaking point.

I had 2 nice buildings on Bonanza between Eldorado and Skoogum Gulch so I wanted to go to Dawson and sell them. This was about Feb. 10, 1900. I took 4 of my best dogs and headed up the Yukon for Dawson, meeting many stampeeders and they would ask, how is the trail. I said Fine and away we went. I was in a hurry to get to Dawson and they were raceing to Nome. Roadhouses were all making money but were intending to go to Nome when the river opened. Many of the wood-chopper camps were turned into roadhouses as it was quick money and they did not want to wait for the steamboats next summer to sell their wood. There were usually 2 to 4 or more men at these camps and as soon as they had enough cash they would send one or 2 of their men on the way to Nome to send them back the real news.

It was a clowdy day about 4 PM as I reached the river bank going up into Dawson. A young fellow at a waterhole near the trail yelled at me and said, the war is all over, United States win. Where did you get the news, I asked. He said that a young fellow just got in on a bicycle with a lot of the latest San Francisco and Seattle papers with big red boxcar letter headings all about the finnish of the Spanish Phillopean war.

I asked him, where is the bicycle, and he said right up here in the A.C. store for $150. My dogs were headed that way and in less than three minutes I had it. As the dogs reached the front of the store, I threw the sled on its side so they could not run away and as I entered the store I saw the wheel in the corner with a big tag on it: For Sale

$150.00. I looked the wheel over quickly and jurked the tag off and went over to the goldscales and told Al Wissel who was weigher that I wanted the wheel and handed him my poke. He weighed out the gold and I told him that I would get the wheel in the morning. With the tag in my pocket, I got the dogs straightened out and headed for the Klondyke Hotel. There I showed my half-brother Billie Zeilor the tag when he began to tell me all about our battleship Oregon busting the Spanish Col one at 4 miles away. Yes, I know all about it. Where are the papers, I asked him. What the h— are you going to do with the wheel he asked. Going to Nome, I said. He called Harry Smith and John Nelson proprietors of the hotel and some other old-timers. He said this brother of mine is going to try to go to Nome on a bicycle. He's crazy, they all said. We will have him put on the wood-pile until he comes out of it. Any way I got 7 of the latest papers with the big red headlines and next morning I went down to the A.C. store and got the wheel. I could not ride it and I began to think perhaps I was a little off mopping up the streets of Dawson trying to learn to ride it. They sure guyed me a plenty and enough and I never have been able to figure out which is the most. Enough or plenty? Anyway, I had to stay in Dawson 8 days to learn that wheel to stay inside of an 18 inch sledtrack. In the meantime I sold the buildings at the Grand Forks. Ben Downing was keeping my dogs and they were rested up and feeling fine and wanted to go. I had met a little fellow by name of Williams who wanted to go down and cut wood for me. He had done nothing all winter and was very soft. I told him to throw his blankets in the sled, grab the handlebars and we were off. I went ahead on the wheel and the dogs tryed to keep up with me and they did. I took about 25 headers into the snow and the dogs would jump on top of me and almost smothered me. I could not break the dogs from piling on top of me without whipping them unmercifully which would break their spirit and this was the only fun they had had all winter so I played the rabit and tryed to keep ahead of them. We passed everything on the trail and made the roadhouse half way between 40-Mile and Dawson for lunch but throughly tired. After lunch we lay on the bunks for a short nap and started on to 40-Mile. Williams wanted to wait until morning as he was all in but I got him started and we made 40-Mile in time for supper. The news of the war had already reached 40-Mile. The weather was getting very cold and not much doing at 40-Mile that evening and we were ready to hit the hay early.

Next morning, I believe it was 23 of February and the thermometer down to 48 below zero. It was almost impossible to get Williams started. The rubber tires on my wheel were frozen hard and stiff as gass pipe. The oil in the bearings was frozen and I could scarcely ride it and my nose was freezing and I had to hold the handlebars with both hands not being able to ride yet with one hand and rub my nose with the other. I threw the wheel in the sled and told Williams to get in also and we were all willing to stop at 27-Mile roadhouse when we got there. I had tryed several times to ride the wheel after I had got warmed up but the wheel would not limber up. Williams was very sore and stiffened up and happy to ride and make the short run that day. So were the dogs as the sled pulled hard in the cold weather. We had a good rest and it was still cold next morning but we had a short run in to Eagle Feb. 25. Everyone trys to take it easy during the cold spells and avoid long hard runs, it very seldome pays and is quite a hardship. At Eagle everyone that could get away was getting ready to head out for Nome. Woodchopers trying to sell their wood at any price to get enough money for roadhouse expenses. It moderated a little as we pulled into Eagle and I had not been able to ride the wheel much and it looked like a white elephant on my hands but one good thing it didn't eat anything and I didn't have to cook dogfeed for it. The heartbreaking job of cooking dogfeed after a hard days run and waiting for it to cool and then watching them eat and see that the big bullies don't take everything from the timmid ones is what made Scotty Allen's hair white. Then the dog mushers work is about through for the day whenever that is.

On Feb. 26 we left Eagle early and it was warmer and I could ride the wheel and we made Star at the mouth of 70-Mile long before lunchtime 18 miles below Eagle. The woodchopers there thought I was crazy to try such a thing as riding a bike to Nome when I had a good dogteam. I had the Star postoffice store and wood-camp there and J. D. Mathews for a partner. He was practically an invilad and his wife did most everything. We took inventory, straightened up the books and with all the dogs I went back to Eagle for a few things that we were short on.

In Eagle I met Walter King, Mahoney & Hayes headed for Nome. We left Eagle March 1st, 1900 at 7:30 AM arriving at Star 11 AM. We had a big caribou dinner and I loaded them up with all the caribou meat they cared to haul and loaned them my wolf robe and 2 of my best dogs with the agreement that if I broke down with the wheel I should continue thru with them if they overtook me on the trail. I cleaned the oil of the bearings of my wheel and graphited it and bid everyone goodbye and left at 3 PM Mar. 1st and stoped at the road house 20 miles below at 6 PM, the Montuck roadhouse. A friend of mine by the name of Peterson was runing this roadhouse and he was making arrangements to leave in a few days for Nome. I payed my bill of $3 which was the regular price, $1 per meal and $1 per bedbunk. I hit the trail feeling fine and made 35 miles for lunch. I was intending to take it easy as I was sure I had plenty of time. I arrived at Charley river roadhouse 4:45 PM. There I met more friends on their way to Nome. They were much surprised that anyone could make such good time or any time on a wheel. They were all anxious to read the papers and to see how many Chechacos were going to leave S.F. and Seattle for Nome by boat. Most every boat on the Pacific coast was getting fitted for a run to Nome. Some of these fellows were up all night reading the papers.

I was up early next morning March 2 for I was informed by the mail-carrier that it was the worst part of the road on the Yukon. Rough sideling and full of cracks and that I would have to carry my wheel most of the way to Circle City. The roadhouse boys would accept no pay and were out to see me off. The weather was better and I left at 7:15 and soon met a lot of indians hauling in caribou from Charley river to sell to the roadhouse and the Nome stampeeders. They had never seen a bicycle. Some of them could speak enough english to get by fairly well and had to interprit for the others and explain something of the wheel to them. After looking it over carifuly they wanted to see it again. The trail was good there so I got on and thought I made a pretty good showing as they kept yelling mush, mush, mush to see me speed up. They had asked how far I could go in one sleep. Meaning one day. I told them that I could make 60 or 100 miles on good trail which they could not believe. One fellow said, me guess 35 maby 40 miles thats all. I told him to come on run and follow me see how fast I go but he soon quit as I kept picking up a little speed.

After about a mile of good trail I got to the sideling trail caused by the great icejam which occures at many places on the Yukon in the freezeup. Water had backed up on the river bank and froze then the jam settled with a sloping icey bank and the river ice too rough and jumbled up for a trail. A little snow on this slopeing icey bank had covered the ice cracks which were dangerous for a wheel and bad for the toe-nails of the dogs. The sleds all slid down to the low side into the rough ice upsetting sleds and making very tiresome traveling. The sleds had scraped most of the snow off all of this sideling trail and left it in fine condition for the wheel as the rubber tire stuck to this trail very well and all I had to do was to look out for the ice cracks which were very numerous. I made the We[b]ber roadhouse by 11 AM. Had lunch and lye on a bunk an hour then started on.

I was anxious to reach Circle City as the mailcarrier told me that there were many there laying over from being stove up and repairing sleds and dog harness after getting through the rough ice ahead. I wanted to be up with the big crowd in case of a wind or snowstorm so that they could break trail ahead for me.

About 5 miles below Webbers the mountainous icejams began to block the way and all of the Nome stampeders will never forget that stretch of 12 or 15 miles of icejam. Over most of it I could only ride a few yards of the best of it and carried my wheel the rest of the way thru it. I was all tired out and hungry when at the end of the jam I saw a sign with Roadhouse on it. There was a little 10 x 10 durty half dugout shack. I went in and asked the fellow there if he had anything to eat. He said he had nothing but a little caribou stew, bread and butter, pie and coffee. I said, give it to me, I'm good and hungry. He put a 2-gallon granit bucket in front of me and a soup dish with the usual tools to work with and the rest of the stuff coming up. Help yourself to the mulligan he said and I sure did. I don't believe there was enough of it left to warm up again. I thought some of the bones in the stew quite small for caribou but payed little attention to it as he was telling me that it was such a fine trail and only 8 miles in to Circle City.

I left at 4:40 PM and was in Circle at 5:40 PM. The trail was fine and on the bank at Circle there was many watching me come in. A government hospital stewart insisted on me to stay with him as he had only one patient and said that the hotels and roadhouses were all full. I was glad to accept his hospitality and when I went in I found the patient to be a friend of mine from Juneau by the name of Oneal who had his feet frozen. I unloaded my papers [*Dawson Daily News, Dawson Nugget, San Francisco Examiner, Seattle Post-Intelligencer*] and they were up most all night reading the war news and the great preparations that was being made to send boats to Nome in the spring. I went down town and found a few friends of Oneal and brought them back to cheer him up. I was now past what the mail carriers called the worst of the trail and the wheel in perfect condition but I was badly bruised from many falls and bumps in the ice that a good rider would have avoided. The hospital stewart I forget his name fixed me up some liniment and after rubing my bruises with it I washed and supper was ready in the hospital. I enjoyed the fourth meal that day just as well as the first. At the supper table the boys asked me if I had stoped at the muskrat house. I looked up with surprise thinking that I had missed something on the trail and asked where it was? They said 8 miles up the river and asked if I ate there and what I had? I told them caribou mulligan. They laughed and said it was muskrat and I am sure it was after remembering the small bones in the stew and he had the house covered with muskrat skins. That was 75 miles for March 3rd over the roughest part of the trail from Dawson to Nome.

I left Circle City March 4th Sunday morning 11 AM and arrived at halfway island roadhouse 4:20 PM a distance of 50 miles. I went into the roadhouse and asked if they had anything to eat. The man said it was too early to eat and asked, where is your dogteam. I'm on a bicycle I said. He asked how can you ride a bicycle on the snow and ice? That's easy I said and that I had left Circle at 11 AM and here it was only 4:20. He gave me a cup of coffee and a piece of apple pie and he and Johnie McLoud went out to look the bike over. Johnie was born on the McKenzie river and had never seen a bicycle before and when he came back into the roadhouse he asked to ride it down to the indian camp. A large bunch of indians were camped in the woods a quarter of a mile below the roadhouse in tents. Johny wanted to see me ride it. After the pie and coffee I went out and got on the wheel. There was a long heavy grade off the river bank down onto the river and Johny tryed to keep up with me but he began to laugh and soon was left behind. I roade up to the tents and most all of the indians were inside. A couple that was outside began to talk pretty loud and soon they were all sticking their heads out then Johny came up and began telling them all about the wheel in their own language. They all looked the wheel over then wanted to see it go. The trail around the tents was good so I took a circle around and came back and there was more talk and a lot of laughing. One young fellow that spoke pretty good english said Geasus Crist. What you call em. White man he set down walk like hell.

Next morning Mar 5 I began to enter the great Yukon flats. Left the roadhouse 7:30 AM and arrived at Fort Yukon at 12 noon. This is a great indian camp and trading post. The indians swarmed around me trying to see what kind of a chechaco outfit I was driving. Archie Burns had been there a few days ahead of me driving a little white mare. That was the first horse the indians had seen and the camp was all excited over this (big white man dog). Arch[i]e said that she was about dead as he could get no feed for her. The indians ran to their cashes and brot smoked salmon for her. They all began to ask whats matter white dog no eat um salmon. No got foot like dog, no got foot like moose, no got foot like caribou. Archie got her about a mile below Fort Yukon and she staggered to one side and there she died. I was told that the only place I could get anything to eat was at Mrs. Captain Hills where she served wonderful meals. I took the wheel in with me fearing that the indians would stick something in the tires or do something else that would do the wheel no good. The indians flocked in and crowded in until Mrs[.] Hill had to run them out the third time for they would not leave standing room or room to move about.

I left at 1:30 PM with a crowd of about 200 on the heigh bank watching me go down the river. I arrived at a mail cabin 4:20 PM and slept on the floor with 8 others as the bunks were all full. 66 miles for Mar 5th. Next morning I left this mail cabin 7:15 with a wind in my back and made the [next] mail cabin 33 miles for lunch at 11 AM. I stoped only a short time for lunch fearing the trail would drift full and made the next mail cabin 30 miles at 2 PM 63 miles for March 6th.

Not sleeping much last night I had lunch and took a nap, had supper and went to bed had breakfast and felt fine and in good trim for the next run but it was very cold, the thermometer standing at 38 below. I left at 7 AM making the first mail cabin at 11 AM 32 miles, had a little lunch and made the next cabin 33 miles 4 PM 65 miles for that day and the weather growing colder.

I had been passing many teams on the trail and I passed a big Norwegan who had been doing 40 miles a day on skates but he broke in on an ice crack then he had hard going. A big crowd was in the cabin but they always found room for one more and among them were several old Dawson friends of mine. We had a lot of fun telling our experiences on the trail that evening of March 7th. Next morning Mar 8th it was very cold. The only thermometer that they had there was a little bottle of quicksilver which was frozen solid. They claimed it was 45 below and when the quicksilver freezes the old timers claimed that it was too cold to work and that your ax would break if you choped wood.

The dog teams all pulled out early but I waited until 9:30. The sun shone bright and it looked warm but you couldn't fool my wheel. It was frozen like gasspipe and with a fine trail I could only make about 100 yards at a time and it was much easier to carry it than to try to push it beside me. At last we got going and made fort Hamlin about 12:30 a distance of 25 miles. Lunch and off again and this is where the great Yukon flats end and the river is confined to heigh cut banks. About 10 miles below Ft[.] Hamlin I saw a comical sight. It was a red short haired dog frozen as hard as stone and someone had stood him on his nose on a little snow mound near the trail his tail strait up and feet in a trotting position. He looked like a circus clown doing his trick.

I arrived at a roadhouse [at 3:00 p.m.] on the North bank of the river with a steap trail to climb about 200 feet above the river trail. This was one of the best eating places on the line, only 40 miles run. They had a real baker here with everything from cookies, doughnuts, pies, cakes and all kinds of good bread. After supper the long table was cleared off and moved to one side of the room and a lot of nice hay stacked along the other side for the bed. A long piece of canvass over the hay, then blankets. Every one 18 of us slept with our clothes on and did not need-much over us as the house was nice and warm.

Big Murphy the mule pack train man from Dawson slept next to me and we all decided he was a sawmill man before morning. I left here 7 AM and the thermometer was 38 below zero. I reached the next roadhouse run by a one-armed man. Arriving here 34 miles at 11 AM and after having a good lunch reached Rampart City 35 miles at 4 PM a total of 69 miles for Mar 9th.

I took in the sights at Rampart and found that the Pelly Kid had all the squaws[1] drunk and fighting and the lonely marshal was busy trying to find out who caused the trouble. I left Rampart March 10th at 9:30 AM in a strong wind down stream. It grew stronger and drifted the trail full and some places the ice was slick and clean. I was backpedling to keep from going too fast and at times the wind picked me up and landed me where it pleased, into a snowbank or an icejam upside down. I soon came to the Rampart canion, the narrowest and swiftest part of the Yukon. The wind was howling down thru these narrows and a gust caught me on a smothe stretch here and whirled me into a rough patch of ice almost busting my knee, skining my hands and elbows and broke one of my handlebars. The wind pulled us out of the rough ice and was kiding [kiting?] us down over the glare ice at good speed. I began to grab the different pieces of the handlebar and stick them in my pockets as I had on a duck hunters coat with full sleeves and pockets all around. At last we landed in another ice jam and hung up. I was quite a while rubing my left knee so I could use it and by pushing the wheel along and leaning on it I found that I could hobble along on it.

Down river 3 or 4 miles on the North bank I could see a long row of steamboat wood and thinking I would have to siwash[2] it that night this wood looked good to me if I could only get to it. I was soon out of the narrows and my knee was beginning to limber up and with my eye on that wood pile I could see a small lean-to cabin back of it. It looked cold with no stovepipe or smoke. Soon I saw a stovepipe sticking above the snow covered roof. I thought it was queer for I was sure that no stovepipe was there a little while ago. I was traveling under a slow bell and then I saw smoke curling up from the pipe and believe me, that did look good. At last I got around the woodpile out of the wind and here were 3 friends of mine that had just got in and put up the stove and I could not see them until I got behind the woodpile. They were broke and had nothing but a tent, stove, 2 or 3 blankets and 3 very poor dogs and were happier than many millionaires as they were on their way to Nome.

What have you to eat I asked. Not much, tea, beans, hotcakes & mush they said and what do you do in a case like this. Here is a pound of butter, 2 cans of milk, a piece of bacon, some crackers and a little eggfrypan. That is what helps me land so hard in the icejams when I take a header off the wheel. Ah! we will live heigh tonight with butter on the hotcakes and milk on the mush in the morning. How are you fixed for blankets, I asked. Not much but we can make out as long as the woodpile holds out they said. They got in some good spruce boughs for the bed and everything was fine. I split up a nice strait grained piece of spruce and with my knife made 2 nice pieces to tape on each front fork of the wheel letting them extend heigh enough to fasten a cross stick to them to act as a handlebar. I made a real good job of it. They claimed this was 40 miles from Rampart. Next morning March 11th I started out with my repair job and was very careful with it. The wind was still strong and I was very careful with the wheel on bad trail and walked quite a bit until the trail got better. I had started at 7:30 AM and arrived at the A. C. Co Tanana station 1:30 PM. Mr. Egan had me stay with him at the A. C. Co. Messhouse and he showed me the government blacksmith shop where they had a good mechanic who fixed my wheel in fine shape for the rest of the trip. As usual many sat up all night reading the papers. The government was doing considerable work here at that time.

March 12th at 8:30 I got my papers and hit the trail to try and pass a preacher and a man with 2 horses pulling double enders and cuting the trail all to pieces. This was worse than the rough ice. The horses broke thru every step and it was the hardest riding I have ever seen. I had to get ahead of these horses. The horses feet were bleading and every little ways the sleds would slide off the heigh trail that was packed by dog teams and the wind had blowed most of the snow away on the sides. In trying to get back up the trail they would twist 8 foot sections right out of the trail. Most of the dogs had broken many of their tonails off having caught them on the edges of these horse tracks or holes. The trail was bloody for miles from the bleeding and limping dogs. What those dog men said and thought about the 2 men and horses would burn up a ton of asbestos fireproof paper. It was heart-breaking to see those poor pitiful dogs looking up at you as you had to harness them up for another days hard work. Many men had sprained their ankles and were limping. I was never more pleased with my wheel than when I passed them about 3:40 that afternoon and the wheel still in good condition and at 4:45 stoped at a wood camp 55 miles below Tanana. On the 13th of March my birthday at 7:30 AM I left this camp and about 10 AM it began to warm up and snow. At 12:30 PM I arrived at Cochrans trading post and store. It was snowing so hard that I could not see the trail so I had to lay over here and as usual the natives had a time looking at the wheel. This was 40 miles from the wood camp. Every few miles there was some one camped in their tent along the trail so that there was someone out breaking trail early and late and the days were long.

I left Cochran at 8 AM of March 14th with a bad trail and a bright sunshine. I traveled slowly to let the dogs break trail. About 3 PM it began to rain and I could not ride the trail being too slick and sloppy. At 6:30 I sloped at a deserted wood camp with some other stampeeders 38 miles below Cochrans. This was the only place on the trail where I had no blanket but it was warm and we kept the door open all night. I slept on a sprucebough bed with a coat under me and a parka over me. I used all of the lunch I had here so it was a case of make the next roadhouse for lunch.

We left here on 15th at 6:15 in a snowstorm packing my wheel in snow knee deep leading the poor dogteams and no sign of a trail for about 7 miles when I found the old trail. It was drifted and hard to follow but at 12:45 I found the roadhouse and I was about tired out. Here I had a good lunch and a rest and about 6 PM the dog teams began to get in after a hard days pull. The snow storm had cleared up about 10 AM. Here we had good meals and the dog teams pulled out at 6 AM and I left at 8 AM, with a good trail ahead on the 16th and made 55 miles to the Koyukuk station in a light rain 6:30 PM. I believe Charley Grim was runing the place for the A. C. Co. I bought a pair of mucklucks as it was too wet for moccasins.

That night several of them sat up most of the night reading the papers. It froze a little that night and we had the slickest trail I ever saw. March 17th left Koyukuk at 8 AM arriving after many slick falls at Neulato [at 11:45 a.m.] only 18 miles. I was not feeling so well so layed over until the 19th. This was headquarters for a lot of indians and of course they all had to inspect the wheel. Some of the indians took me back of a house to show me the hide of a very bad bear they had killed. It was nailed on the back of a house and so full of holes that it was worthies. It was a brownie and tryed to fight until shot to pieces.

Leaving here on the 19th at 4 AM for the Coltag portage with 25 lbs of provisions on my back to last me to Una[la]kleet on the Behring sea. The trail was badly cut up with a lot of water on it between Neulato and Coltag. The weather was very warm and I arrived at 12 noon 40 miles. Here I had to sleep in an indians bed. I sprinkled it well with ground sapidella seeds and hung all of my clothes outdoors then sprinkled them good inside before puling them on in the morning. Sapidella seed powdered will sure keep the seam squirrels on the run.

I left Coltag at 4 AM to cross the portage of 85 miles. I met a little man with 5 nice birddogs in his team and he was traveling light. He said that we cant make it across in one day and if you will take this little camp ax and go about 40 miles and have wood and boughs cut ready for camp you can stay with me tonight. Leaving my pack with him I took the ax and found a wonderful camp where several had left that morning. Lots of wood cut and 4 beds of boughs. I made one good double bed, cut a lot of shavings and had everything in fine shape when he arrived. We put up the tent over the bough bed between 2 trees and while he got supper I had the dogfeed cooked. We made about 35 miles as the snow was mostly gone and it was hard pulling for the dogs and bad wheeling. We went to bed about 3 PM intending to travel by moonlight and got up 11 PM but it was too dowdy and dark and we sat by the campfire until 4 AM before we could see to travel. Then I lead the dogs until it was light enough to see to ride the wheel over the moss and niggerheads.[3] The niggerheads would catch the pedals and often throw me causing me to go slow. As I got near the coast it grew cooler and the trail better until I struck the Una[la]kleet river which had 2 to 4 inches of water running over the ice and here I had to walk or ride about 6 miles down this little river. My mucklucks came in handy here but they were so slick on the bottoms that I could scarcely stand on them. I found it easier and safer to ride the wheel but could go only a little faster than a walk as the hind wheel would throw water all over my back when I tryed to speed up.

Arriving at Una[la]kleet at 4 PM making about 55 miles. I got a good room here from a halfbreed native who had a store and trading post and he surved good meals. In the room next to me they had an organ and were playing and singing church songs. I layed over here on the 22 to rest up and feed up and oil the wheel. The natives as usual crowded into my room to see the wheel and ask questions. They spoke good english and had lots of money as they caught lots of fur seal and otter. There was several pictures on the wall in my room and among them was a picture of a man on a bicycle all decorated for a 4th of July. 2 of the young fellows were looking at the picture and then at the wheel and one of them said to me, I see um on paper lots of time, I don't know. I see um now, its allright. I had to ride it around for them and they wanted to buy it. How much it cost? I said $150. Allright me buy um. They wanted to buy it right there and then.

The little old gentleman that I stopped with on the cutoff got in early the 22nd and told me that we would have a bad camp ahead and that I had better figure on stoping with him again 40 miles up and across a port to the Behring sea. He gave me his little ax and I left at 4 AM in the morning against a strong head wind and a lot of natives to see the wheel mush out. Arrived at Skaktolik [40 miles], the lowsiest looking layout I ever saw. The North wind howling and the cabin more than full as the wind had been too strong and drifted trail for them to pull out. It was 4 PM and I found some driftwood, had it ready and kicked around in the snow and got a lot of hay for a bed. Made arrangements to sleep in an old leanto where a very old couple were living. When my trail friend got in and sized up the durty layout he said this is pritty tough. I told him to go up and look at the other place. He came back and we made the best of the place we had as the other place was crowded with stampeeders that could not buck the storm the last few days besides the esquemaux that lived there.

Next morning the wind was howling and I went up to see if anyone was going to pull out. A young fellow was outside coughing up his breakfast. Inside the boys were all laughing siting at the table eating with the esquemaux all around them watching them eat. I asked what they were laughing about. They said that the fellow outside was not fit for the country with his weak stomache. That the young squaw standing there had been licking off her babys face just like an old bitch would her pups and he lost his breakfast just for that.

I said that I was going to pull out for the Denby city roadhouse if anyone started and a big husky said follow me I'm going. The trail was drifted and I had to pack my wheel across the cutoff 18 miles and the wind still howling. There was only one big cabin roadhouse there, crowded full and 15 or 20 tents in the brush of stampeeders that had been hung up for several days waiting to cross Norton sound. There was also a stampeed up a creek near there that was causing some excitement and some were going up there as soon as the storm was over. The friend I had camped with went up on this stampeed and I never saw him again. Stampeeders from Nome were also going up. On the 25th the wind was still howling and snow flying and I stayed in the crowded roadhouse. On the 26th the wind had died out entirely and we had a nice suny morning. I left at 7:30 AM and crossed Norton sound and up the coast a ways making 60 miles and stoped in a tent that night with a stampeeder at 6 PM.

Next morning it was cold and I started about 8 AM and traveled about an hour when I thought one wheel was a little soft. Seeing an Egalo with a dog and man on top of it some distance up the beach I rode over to get in a warm place to pump up the tire. Here I found a Chelilian an old forty niner and a marine engineer who left Nome early in the fall and came down here to put in the winter as wood and cabins were so scarce at Nome. They had a good outfit and here they had grouse, ptarmagan and fish also to help their variety. They were off the trail in a little cove and wanted the news saying they had met no one all winter. Come on in. The only entrance was a square 18 inch hole in the center of the top with a sliding fraim covered with transperant fishbladders for a window. Here was a fine 18 foot circular room, fireplace in the middle and nice clean hay around the sides for their beding. I could not get away from them until 10 AM the next day. The engineer began to read aloud while the fortynine miner began picking grouse and the Chelalian got his fire ready to cook and they wanted me to stay 2 or 3 days. This Egalo was built with logs stood up endwise with tundra cut and banked all around the outside about 3 ft thick and grown togather, covered with a roof and tundra on top. There was something in the pots and frypan cooking all the time. They said that there is nothing at Nome now, stay here a while.

Next day 28th of March about 9 AM I got away crossing a narrow steep portage accross to Gullivan bay and [8 miles] up the bay to Dexter trading post. Here I had a fine lunch at 12:30 AM then crossed Gullivan bay and another portage over to Tewak [at 3:00 p.m.] making 45 miles. I was intending to make Topcock but got 5 or 6 miles up the coast and a head wind was so strong I could not ride against it so turned around and let the wind blow me back to Tewak. There were several native houses here none of which looked good or clean however. I had to stay and at one there was an extra bed and the woman with a little boy and her brother lived there and she said, me Toms wife to introduce herself. Her brother and another young fellow had brought in a hair seal the first one shot that season. When I saw the way she cooked that stuff I had no apetite for it so got out my little frypan and fried some of my bacon and made myself a hardtack sandwich for supper. 3 or 4 of the boys here had a lot of fun trying to ride the wheel until I was afraid they may break it and took it in the house.

It was an easy day into Nome from here if the trail was good. Next morning an old native tryed hard to give me some good fatherly advice about the trail but I could not understand him. He made a powerful effort but I could not get it until about an hour and a half later. The trail was fine and I was making good time when all of a sudden I saw no sign of the many sled tracks I had been following but very blue ice under me and the sled tracks began over a hundred yards ahead of me. I was going fast and began to pedal lightly as I had speed enough to carry me to the old tracks ahead. I drew a long breath when I got on old ice again and got off the wheel. Looking the situation over I could see where a large section of ice had gone out to sea and steping to the edge of the old ice I gave this blue ice a kick with my moccasine heal and up came the blue sea water. I am sure I could not have walked across it.

I had wanted to stop at Topcock the rich beach diging but being so far from the beach did not see anyone in my excitement and they most likely were at lunch then and my eyes were very sore from sun and glare ice. About 1:00 I reached Port Safety. There I heard about the dirty dozen of 13 men at Topcock that would let no one else get in on their rich diging. At Port Safety I had a good lunch rested and then bowed my neck for a run into Nome and arrived there at 4 PM March 29th. A big crowd was on the beach looking for dogteams and the latest news. With field glasses they could see dogteams as soon as they came around the point of Cape Nome. When I came around the news went around that a dog team was coming. Someone said that it was a fast team then someone with better glasses saw it was someone on a bicycle and by the time I arrived a big crowd was there to get the war news. I told them that the war was all over United States wone and got out my papers with the big headlines. They had been paying $5.00 for the latest papers and here was Major Strong of the Nome News and the man from the Nome Nugget wanting the papers. A fellow back in the crowd said is that you Ed Jesson. Yes, I said who are you? My eyes were so sore I could not reconize him and here was Chriss Hammersmith an old friend from Cook inlet and we had sawed the lumber for boats togather at Lake Bennet. He asked me to go down to his cabin and my eyes would be OK in a few days. Fine. Who had I better let have these papers until my eyes get so I can hunt up my friend.

Give them to Major Strong he said so I handed them to the fine old gentleman and said use them as you please but try and save them so I can give them to my friends in a few days. He said give me their names. I will hunt them up and send them down to see you.

The musitions in the big dance hall had a rest that night. Some one read the San Francisco Examiner from the musicians platform until he got thirsty then another would read while the crowd cheered and drank toasts to the Battleship Oregon and the gunner on the Oregon that shot the Spanish Battleship Colon 4 miles away and busted her from stem to stern. Hats and caps in the air and toasts to the comander of the Oregon and Hurray for Admiral Dewie. It was a wild night and later they read the Seattle P.I. telling of all the boats being fitted for the trip to Nome in the spring as soon as they could get thru the Behring sea ice. Major Strong came out with morning and evening specials until he and his little paper staff were exhausted. It was cold and windy at Nome. One morning Chriss and I got up and we were snowed in and we could not get out of the house. Chriss was used to it and said we will have breakfast first then we can shovel out. He kept a shovel in the house for that purpose. After breakfast he shoveled the house almost full of snow before he could get out. The snow was even with the top of the house and the stovepipe just reached above it. Chriss went over to a neighbor and got another shovel and we worked until after one PM geting the snow away from the door and window.

There was more about doings at Nome but that is another story. The stealing of tents and moving houses while the owners were out prospecting. Fighting shooting and the town was put under marshal law with Captain French in charge with Judge Rowson and Waterfront Brown and the deputies could not handle the job with their little lousy jail chucked full.

The wheel stood the trip in splendid shape and to my great surprise I never had a puncture or broke a spoke the entire trip.

Notes

1. A term for an Indigenous woman that is now considered derogatory.—Ed.
2. A term for a North American Indian of the northern Pacific coast that is now considered derogatory. Also used to mean to camp without a tent (*Oxford Languages*, s.v. "Siwash [n.]," accessed April 18, 2022, https://www.lexico.com/en/definition/siwash).—Ed.
3. A former name for several things thought to resemble the head of a Black person. Now taboo in normal usage (Harold Koch and Luise Hercus, *Aboriginal Placenames: Naming and Re-Naming the Australian Landscape* [Canberra: Australian National University Press, 2009], 200). In Alaska this term was used to refer to the thick grass hummocks of the tussock tundra, which can be nearly impassable on a bicycle.—Ed.

A Broken Chain
and a Busted Pedal

MAX HIRSCHBERG

Max Hirschberg's 1900 Bicycle Ride to Nome

Unlike Ed Jesson, Max Hirschberg knew how to operate a bicycle before he rode his "wheel" from Dawson to Nome in 1900. Hirschberg was born in Ohio in about 1880 and went north at the time of the Klondike Gold Rush "to see what he could do." He ran a roadhouse in the Dawson district but sold out in 1900 to join the stampede to Nome.

Hirschberg followed a "2-inch trail" with his bicycle much of the way to Nome. It was a rough trip. The journey took him about two and a half months, during which time he suffered from snow blindness, exhaustion, and exposure. Crossing the Shaktoolik River, he nearly drowned. He was in the water for almost two hours, and during that time he lost his watch and his poke with $1,500 in gold dust. He saved his bicycle, however. Just east of Nome, on the ice of Norton Sound, his bicycle chain broke. A strong wind was blowing, and he made a sail with his coat that he rigged on the bike. Hirschberg then sailed across the ice the rest of the way into Nome.

At the request of his wife, Max wrote the story of his bicycle ride to Nome in the 1950s, so that his children and grandchildren would know the true story. He died in 1964. Hirschberg's granddaughter, Penni Busse, submitted his account of the ride to Nome to *Alaska* magazine, which published the story in February 1978.

–Terrence Cole

In January 1900, I secured a dog team and an outfit to go over the ice, down the Yukon from Dawson to Nome. I sold my share in a roadhouse and my mining claims in Dawson. My partner, Hank West, however, did not believe the reports about the gold strike in Nome were authentic. I did, so we parted.

In Dawson I got my outfit and dog team, and I stayed at the Green

Tree Hotel. About midnight, I was awakened by the smell of smoke—the hotel was on fire. I jumped into my clothes and rushed outside. Hundreds of people had formed a bucket line from the Yukon River to the hotel. I joined the line, and we passed buckets of water to quench the fire and to wet blankets on adjoining buildings. The fire department was helpless because the fire hose froze in the extreme cold. Every available man joined the bucket line, but the building burned to the ground.

Broken boards were scattered over the snow. It was pitch dark and I stumbled on a board that contained a rusty nail. I went to the hospital with blood poisoning. It was March before I was up and around again, too late to get to Nome by dog team. With the spring thaw under way, the Yukon would be unfit for travel on the ice. I knew the news of the gold strike at Nome would bring thousands of people from the States to Nome by boat, so I had to get there quickly. I decided to travel by bicycle. I had been an expert bicycle rider for years, and I figured I could reach Nome before the Yukon became unfit for travel.

Many dog teams, driven in single file, had preceded me down the river, and had made a hard trail about two inches wide where the sled runners cut deep troughs in the snow. I rode this narrow road, stopping at Indian villages or roadhouses.

The day I left Dawson, March 2, 1900, was clear and crisp, 30° below zero. I was dressed in a flannel shirt, heavy fleece lined overalls, a heavy mackinaw coat, a drill parka, two pairs of heavy woolen socks and felt high-top shoes, a fur cap that I pulled down over my ears, a fur nose-piece, plus fur gauntlet gloves.

On the handlebars of the bicycle I strapped a large fur robe. Fastened to the springs, back of the seat, was a canvas sack containing a heavy shirt, socks, underwear, a diary in waterproof covering, pencils and several blocks of sulfur matches.

In my pockets I carried a penknife and a watch. My poke held gold dust worth $1,500 and my purse contained silver and gold coins. Next to my skin around my waist I carried a belt with $20 gold pieces that had been stitched into it by my aunt in Youngstown, Ohio, before I had left to go to the Klondike.

A number of friends, including my old partner, Hank West, waved good-by.

The road out of Dawson was broad and well packed, the air was cold and exhilarating, and the sky was clear and calm. There were numerous dog teams headed for Forty Mile, Circle City and points farther down the Yukon. Whenever I approached a dog team, the driver would accommodatingly pull off the trail and restrain his howling, snapping dogs from nipping me. I passed many dog teams before reaching Forty Mile. At the combination bar, gambling room and roadhouse, I thawed out before a roaring wood fire in an oil-tank stove. Eight or ten whiskered men were sitting and smoking, talking about the rumor of a nearby gold strike.

The Yukon River at Dawson, was about 1,500 feet wide. When the river froze, huge cakes of ice, some standing on edge, others slanting, formed a barrier to the opposite shore. As the final freeze occurred, cakes of ice from the lowered river caused the trail to resemble a sidehill slope. There were overflows covering the ice in places, some frozen over with newly formed ice, which broke when stepped on, leaving a few inches of water over the solid ice beneath.

The trail led along this slanting ice, then along the bank of the river, across frozen cracks winding in and out from the tundra, and back to the sloping ice along the riverbank. Creek overflows were numerous, and by the time I reached Forty Mile, my socks were wet and ice covered my felt shoes. It took me quite a while to orient myself to my two-inch trail, and I had many spills on this early part of my journey.

A few miles below Forty Mile I crossed the boundary line between Canada and the United States. A thrill shot through me as I caught sight of Old Glory waving on U.S. soil.

Eagle City was my next stop, about a hundred miles from Dawson. Calico Bluff was about ten miles farther and at the mouth of Seventymile River was the mushroom town of Star City. Bold, rugged mountains, conspicuous by their height, were visible for a considerable distance. About 180 miles from Eagle City is Circle City. There were many log cabins, saloons, a hospital and an Episcopal church. Adjoining Circle City was an Indian village.

Here the river widened into the Yukon Flats for about 250 miles down the river. Not even a hill was in sight, just scrubby, stunted spruce along the shore.

Twenty miles or so below Circle City was Charley Creek, where I came to a Native village and a little farther on was a roadhouse. Some ten miles farther was Charley River, where I saw hundreds of caribou.

The most dangerous and difficult parts of the flats were between Circle City and Fort Yukon. Save for a portage land trail of eighteen or twenty miles out of Circle City, the trail was on the river, which split into many channels without landmarks. The current was so swift that I encountered stretches of open water and blow holes. Snow storms completely obliterated the trail.

At last I made Fort Yukon, the most northerly point reached by the Yukon River, and about a mile north of the Arctic Circle. There were several saloons, Native cabins, a church and stores displaying marten, fox, wolf and bear skins. It is a site of the oldest English-speaking settlement on the Yukon River. The oldest white man's graves in Alaska, with the exception of Nulato, are those in the little Hudson's Bay cemetery near Fort Yukon; the headboards were dated 1850 and 1860. In 1862 the Church of England had a clergyman here, a Mr. McDonald, who married a Native girl and translated the Bible and prayer book into the Native tongue.

Next, I reached Birch Creek, and the end of all mountains for the first time. Down the Yukon some seventy-five miles, I came to the upper Ramparts, where there was a trading post. Then I came to Rampart City and another Native village. Rampart City consisted of stores, log cabins and saloons. It furnished supplies for the placer gold mines on adjacent creeks. About forty miles farther I came to the rapids, where the ice was free of snow, and for twenty miles my bicycle skidded on the slippery ice, causing me numerous falls.

I arrived at the mouth of the Tanana River, where there was a trading post. I saw Mount McKinley far to the south, as the day was clear.

About five miles out of Tanana I skidded on the glare ice. When I picked myself up, I found I had broken a pedal. I returned to Tanana, and, with the help of the storekeeper, cut out wooden pedals and drilled a hole through the center of each. I also bought bolts, nuts and washers. The pedals wore out about every seventy-five miles.

Two hundred and fifty miles farther on, I came to the Koyukuk River, and twenty miles beyond that I arrived at Nulato, where a Russian trading post had been established in 1822.

As I wheeled into Nulato, a Jesuit priest met me outside of his home and invited me to stay with him overnight. Next day he took me to his workshop and fashioned a new pedal for my bicycle out of galvanized sheet metal and riveted it together with copper rivets. Luckily, I had the extra bolts I had bought at Tanana, for he had none. This pedal lasted until I reached Nome.

About fifty miles out of Nulato, I reached the Kaltag cutoff and headed overland to the Bering Sea, away from the Yukon, which wound its course to St. Michael. The days were warmer and the trail had begun to thaw and at times became indistinct. Water was flowing in the creeks and rivers. As I crossed the Shaktoolik River, I broke through the ice. Water was running under the surface ice, although there was still ice on the bottom of the river. I succeeded in breaking the surface ice and, hanging on to my bicycle, reached the opposite shore.

As I neared the Bering Sea, I saw what appeared to be glare ice off the shore. I headed for this and before I could stop, I found I was in calm, open water. I succeeded in wading back to shore and, although wet, continued on toward Nome.

Near Norton Bay was a roadhouse, where I dried off and had lunch before continuing. The boys at the roadhouse warned me that the ice would shift in Norton Sound but I started across it anyway. Just as I was nearing the opposite shore, the ice shifted, leaving about eight to ten feet of open water between the ice and the shore. I took a chance and leaped to the shore, where I picked up a piece of driftwood, jumped back on the ice floe and poled myself and my bicycle back to the shore, and went on my way. Just east of Nome, I skidded on glare ice. When I picked up my bicycle, I discovered the chain had snapped and broken.

There was a fair wind blowing toward Nome, so I picked up a stick, put it on my back inside my mackinaw coat, and began sailing for Nome. At times the wind was so strong that I was forced to drive into some soft snow to stop my wild flight. Without my chain I could not control the speed of my bicycle. However, I finally arrived at Nome, May 19, 1900, without further incident. I had had my twentieth birthday on the trip.

Cycling the Arctic
H. B. LEVIE

Levie's Bicycle Ride from Point Barrow to Nome

In addition to Ed Jesson and Max Hirschberg, at least two other men—John Sutherland and H. B. Levie—rode bicycles from Dawson to Nome in 1900. "I rode my bicycle night and day . . . well sometimes it rode me," Sutherland said thirty-five years later. It took him sixty-two days to make the grueling trip. The ice in Norton Sound had gone out by the time he reached the coast, and he had to walk all the way around. When he didn't show up at first, in Nome, Sutherland was presumed dead. "When I got to Nome I let everyone know the report had been greatly exaggerated," Sutherland said. "I had lost twenty pounds, but I still tipped the scales at two hundred thirty."

H. B. Levie also had some hair-raising adventures on his bicycle ride to Nome in 1900. "H. B. Levie started this morning for Nome on a bicycle," the *Dawson Daily News* reported on February 9, 1900. "He has a small knapsack strapped to his back to carry a few articles of clothing, the sum total of his baggage." He wore three pairs of gloves for protection, but by the time he reached Nome in late March, his skin was badly cut and burned, and he was almost totally snow-blind.

"His actual travel time was twenty-two days and would have been less," the *Nome News* stated after his arrival, "had he not been poisoned eating oysters."

Levie was an old vaudeville man. He at one time owned the largest theater in Cripple Creek and had hired a troupe of performers to work in Dawson City. Yet his best performance was probably his bicycle ride from Point Barrow to Nome in the winter of 1901. The story of Levie's ride along the coasts of the Arctic Ocean and the Bering Sea—"probably the most unique trip ever taken by any cyclist in the World"—was recorded on the front page of *Nome Gold Digger* on January 16, 1901.

—Terrence Cole

Thrilling Trip from Point Barrow to Nome of Levie, the Famous Yukon Wheelman

On the Fifteenth Day Out he Reaches Town, Having Traveled over Nearly a Thousand Miles of Ice and Snow. Hospitably Received by Indians. Gambling for Enormous Stakes is Being Practised at Point Barrow.

From Point Barrow to Nome is the remarkable trip just finished by H. B. Levie, the well known Yukon cyclist on his wheel. Although but once in danger of his life it is probably the most unique trip ever taken by any cyclist in the world. Leaving Point Barrow, December 26 [1900], his only hard experience was on the Good Hope Bay, January 3, where he became bewildered in a snow storm and was all night on the ice, having nothing to eat but some raw tom cod. But fortunately [he] had a sleeping bag which saved him from freezing to death.

In the long trip only three white men were met between Cape Prince of Wales and Point Barrow, named Joe Galvin, George Libby and Jim Ryan, at Cape Lowenstern.

Mr. Levie left here October 18 on the ill fated *Rubin Richardson*. After a stormy trip, he arrived at Teller and there engaged two Indians with their boat to take him up the coast. All went well until Shishmaref Inlet was reached where they encountered ice and could go no further with the boat. Leaving the Indians to return he carried his wheel to the shore ice and started on his trip to Point Barrow where he arrived on December 20.

At Point Barrow he found about sixty souls, made up of natives and white men from the whalers, these whalers being in the harbor. One store is at the Point, owned by Cal Brower. He also found . . . Herron, Grant Crumbley and Jim Marshal, three well known Colorado gamblers, who mysteriously disappeared from Nome early in the season and was [*sic*] thought to have been lost at sea.

Levie states that the principal business of the camp is gambling and that some of the whalers would make the games at Nome look like a deuce shot. Twenty checks represent one barrel of whale oil, valued at $400. He saw pots with eighty checks in, representing $1,600. Gambling is also carried on with ivory, whalebone and furs.

Levie left Point Barrow, December 26 on his return trip. Crossing the Arkron Divide to the Arkron Indian village, arriving there December 28, having covered a distance of 92 miles. He left Point Arkron on the 29th, after a day's rest and reached Eschscholtz Bay. Crossing the bay on December 31, he rested there with some Indians until January 2, reaching Good Hope Bay the next day. Levie made Cape Espenberg the day following and on the 5th inst. Cape Lowenstern, a distance of 114 miles from Cape Espenberg. From there to Shishmaref Inlet [is] a distance of 125 miles. He struck across the Inlet for Cape Prince of Wales, which he reached on January 7, where he met the first white men on his trip down excepting three prospectors at the Good Hope Bay. He arrived in Teller on the night of the 8th, 42 miles from Cape Prince of Wales and rode into Nome the next day, making the entire trip from Barrow to Nome, a distance of nearly 1,000 miles in fifteen days.

Mr. Levie is reticent as to his business at Point Barrow, but it is understood that he went up there on official business for the government. He left here today for the outside by way of Dawson, on Government and Company business, expecting to make the distance from here to Skagway in twenty-one days.

1. Four wheelmen riding from Valdez to Fairbanks
by bicycle, ca. 1896–1913. They stopped in
Tiekel Canyon, where photographer P. S. Hunt
took this picture. Crary-Henderson Collection,
Anchorage Museum at Rasmuson Center.

2. A 110-pound automobile, or a five-wheeled cycle,
powered by a Smith Motor Wheel, ca. 1916–17. Photo
by A. J. Painter. Buzby and Metcalf Photograph
Album, Archives, University of Alaska Fairbanks.

3. Children in Wales, Alaska, riding a wooden tricycle,
ca. 1913–39. Gonda Winkler Collection, Anchorage
Museum at Rasmuson Center.

PART 2

New Wheels, 1980s–2000

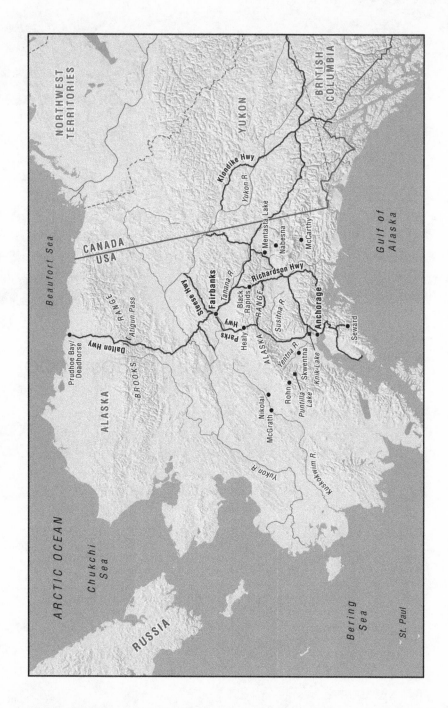

Map 2. Place names described in the stories for the period 1980–2000.
Map by Erin Greb.

Introduction

JESSICA CHERRY AND FRANK SOOS

Since the start of the gold rush era, many people have come to Alaska for its combination of mythological romance and economic opportunity. Whether it's the get-rich-quick hopes of the gold rush Sourdoughs, farmer colonists of the New Deal, GIs of World War II, oil pipeline workers, back-to-the-landers, or contemporary adventurers, Alaska has long held a special allure. One side of that allure is the grim and grueling struggle: the proverbial man against nature. The other side may be writing about it. Of course, Jack London was the most famous such writer of the gold rush period, and in his stories, survival alone is a victory. Some succeed; some don't. Long before the dawn of reality TV shows about gold mining or crab fishing, something about Alaska encouraged people to do something extreme for the sake of telling a good story.

We got a taste of that performance in Levie's theatrical telling of his athletic feat in part 1. Now, in this section of the book, we hear several stories about the race first known as the Iditabike. The first author, Charlie Kelly, is not only one of the founding fathers of modern mountain biking but also a gifted writer and journalist who understands the storytelling potential of this type of race in Alaska. However, the push and pull between authenticity and performance in the so-called Last Frontier existed long before the advent of social media. Performance in its purest form, be it athletic or artistic, can elevate not only the actor but also the audience. Part 2 is where we see extreme recreation and its reportage gain new momentum as a subculture in Alaska.

When postwar settlers Joe Redington Sr. and Dorothy Page teamed up to organize the Iditarod dogsled race in 1967, just eight years after

Alaskan statehood, the goal was to revitalize the culture of mushing. Less than one month after the race, oil was discovered at Prudhoe Bay. To build a pipeline, Indigenous land claims had to be negotiated, and the unique legal and governance structures that are Native corporations first came into being. Alaska went through a period of rapid change in which its urban areas grew exponentially. Modern housing was constructed in many Native villages. Parks and recreational opportunities on rivers and trails became increasingly accessible. John McPhee's book *Coming into the Country* describes this sort of teenage period in Alaska's history. After initially struggling to sustain the dog race, Redington promoted a ski race along the revamped Iditarod Trail and eventually the Iditabike, now part of the multisport race known as the Iditarod Invitational.

Apart from a brief history of the Unangan presence on the Pribilofs, we don't see Native Alaska called out explicitly in part 2 of the book. We have only one story by a woman (though other women participated in the early Iditabike races). What we have are really stories about how new technologies in cycling (two wheels and one) and new infrastructure (the Dalton Highway and Iditarod Trail improvements) make Alaska's lands accessible to a new generation of settlers and visitors, hungry for either adventure or escape.

Venturing farther into "the country" in the 1980s, the Iditabike helped drive the development of what we now call fat bikes. A film about the early race by Mark L. Foreman, *Bicycles on Snow: Iditabike 1988*, is a good window into the technology at the time. Racers ride rigid forked mountain bikes with twenty-six-inch wheels and pack their gear in touring-style panniers. The results are what a knowledgeable snow cyclist might assume. The mountain bike tires often sliced into the softer snow when temperatures warmed; Alys Culhane described her race as "the Iditapush."

The first Alaskan to win the Iditabike was Dave Ford, who welded two rims together, fitted them with two tires, and found more floatation over the snow. Subsequently, Fairbanksan bike tinkerer Simon Rakower developed a commercially available extra-wide rim called the SnowCat. Since only very wide forks and stays could accommodate such rims, the changes that led to fat bikes were soon to follow.

About the same time, people began to cycle the Dalton Highway, also known as the Haul Road, designed to carry supplies to the North Slope oil fields. Then the road was very rough: all coarse gravel and riprap. Still, it was done, and the initial Haul Road riders set an example that many cyclists have followed to Prudhoe Bay and to destinations in the Bush. We see people like Roman Dial start to combine cycling and packrafting, after having read the gold rush accounts. To round out the roster of extreme and quirky Alaskans, we have an unforgettable portrait of a unicycling judge in Seward. The subjects of these pieces are all in pursuit of a perfect machine, a harrowing adventure, and a good story.

—Anchorage (JC) and Fairbanks (FS), 2021

Iditabike, 1987

CHARLIE KELLY

As the editor of the *Fat Tire Flyer*, I received an announcement of the formation of a club called Mountain Bikers of Alaska. A note at the end mentioned that the club planned to put together a mountain bike race on the Iditarod Trail.

I included that news in the magazine, which inspired several of my readers to fly to Anchorage to join the Alaskans for the first event in 1987. The club had never dreamed of the event going national, but with out-of-state riders and coverage in bicycle magazines, it did.

The captain's voice came smoothly over the loudspeaker. "Ladies and gentlemen, as some of you may be aware, we've had a little problem, but it's under control now."

I looked out the window to see which wing had fallen off or which engine was on fire. But all it turned out to be was an attempted hijack, the old finger-in-the-pocket, would-you-believe-I-have-a-gun? routine that went out with *Get Smart*. Talk about clichés—the guy wanted to go to Cuba, but the plane was going to Alaska. Now he's going to jail, but his baggage probably went to Argentina.

But the hijack attempt and the ensuing SWAT, FBI, and National Guard invasion of the plane when it landed in Anchorage faded into soft focus next to the more clearly etched events that took place over the next few days on the Iditarod Trail. The hijack turned out to be just the icing on the wing.

At the airport I got quite a reception, although the hijacker got a bigger one. Laurel Bull and Janet Niichel picked me up and whisked me to the local REI, where I spent a bundle making sure I would stay warm.

It turned out that I was a modest celebrity among the Iditabikers. All right, maybe I wasn't so modest, but I was still a minor celebrity. The reason for this was that the only notice outside Alaska of the race had appeared in the *Fat Tire Flyer*, and those few paragraphs had resulted in riders from five other states showing up, turning the race from local challenge to a nationally covered event.

From REI we went back to Laurel and Dan Bull's house, the unofficial HQ for the Iditabike, where the floor of the spare bedroom was littered with gear belonging to the other Californians, Howard Drew and Janet Niichel.

How cold was it? It was so cold . . . it was so cold . . . well, it wasn't that cold, down to about zero Fahrenheit, T-shirt weather in Alaska. But it must get pretty cold because the ice on the lakes is a couple of feet thick.

We got moving long before dawn on race day; the first item on the agenda was the pancake breakfast at the VFW hall. As the riders chowed down, they offered pessimistic predictions as to what might happen out on the trail, such as a foot of new snow or temperatures of forty below zero. The general consensus was that the tougher it was, the better, and one rider even insisted that the six-hour mandatory rest stop was for wimps only. He had reason to eat these words later, when the course turned out to be tougher than even he was ready for.

Everyone had a secret weapon, ranging from the chemical heaters that permitted riders to travel with lighter camping gear up to sled systems that allowed the rider to tote a huge pile of supplies sufficient for forty-below nights and sixty-knot winds. Mandatory equipment for riders included a sleeping bag, tent or bivy sac, stove, and flares. You can't just go out and buy a sled for a bicycle; they aren't made commercially. So each sled-toting rider dreamed up his or her own, attaching at either the chainstay or seat cluster or to a touring rack. Because the pannier loads were lighter and also because the trail conditions never got extreme, the traditional touring setup turned out to be faster, although it provided less margin for extra equipment. For future races, organizers planned to examine each rider's equipment carefully to make sure no one cut the safety margin by traveling too light.

The starting line was on a frozen lake at Knik, a one-saloon town known as one of the hotbeds (coldbeds?) of sled dog racing; that should give you some idea of the climate. The majority of the people at the starting line were in the race, and the rest were either related to someone in the race, officiating, or exploiting the event journalistically. There was a rumor that a spectator was going to show up, but he must have gotten lost.

Enough preamble. After a couple of aborted countdowns, someone finally said "go," and with the traditional whooping in unison from the riders and the others gathered at the line, the pack shoved off. The front end of the race immediately turned into a duel between two "Lower 48ers," Dave Zink of Minnesota and Mike Kloser of Colorado, while the sled toters moved to the far back of the rapidly stretching pack. The dynamic duo cranked through the forty-one-mile Big Su checkpoint together a little over three hours into the race, and Mark Frise of Wisconsin pulled in twenty minutes later, followed closely by Alaskans Les Matz and Mark Corson. From here the going got tougher as the riders hit deep snow on the trail, churned up by the thousand dogs and sixty-plus dogsleds that had preceded them and kept soft by relatively warm temperatures around the freezing mark. The next thirty miles took them over six hours, and the two leaders pulled into Rabbit Lake a minute apart before leaving together.

The trudging on the trail took more of a toll on Frise, who was by himself, having left Big Su about twenty minutes before Matz and Corson, and when he reached Rabbit Lake, he trailed the leaders by over two hours.

Meanwhile, back at the starting line, I was getting all this news over the shortwave because the plane that was supposed to fly me to Rabbit Lake broke part of its ski landing gear and couldn't set down on the frozen lake. Because the dogsled race was going on at the same time, the planes in the area that might have been available for charter were already in use, and the airspace over the Iditarod Trail was so crowded with small planes that most of the pilots not already out there didn't want to go.

Finally, the race organizers found a Cessna 180 four-seater for me and two other journalists, but we could only go to the halfway point at Skwentna because this plane didn't have skis and needed a real runway, if the snow-surfaced strip at Skwentna qualifies anywhere but Alaska as a runway.

In the Lower 48, when you get in a small plane, the pilot goes through a checklist of about thirty items to make sure the plane is going to work when he turns the key. In Alaska, where every fourth adult has a pilot's license, he gets in, turns the key, and asks you where you want to go as you taxi down the runway. If you give the pilot a compass heading, he says: "Don't give me that crap. Just point." Flight plan? Surely you jest.

We didn't know which way to point, so we just told the guy to fly us over the Iditarod trail to Skwentna. In return, he asked whether any of us had problems with airsickness. I don't, but I was a minority among the three passengers. The other two guys confessed to having a touch of the green face, and the pilot got a big grin.

Even following the trail visually from the start, we had a hard time keeping track of it in the maze of snowmobile trails. Finally, we spotted a biker, obviously Nels Johnson of La Crosse, Wisconsin, from his distinctive yellow North Face outfit. Having identified the proper trail, each of us kept one eye on the ground and the other on the sky for other planes in the immediate vicinity, which came along every couple of minutes.

At one point we spotted a biker and asked the pilot if he could come around so we could shoot a few photos. "No problem," and the next thing we knew, he stood it on one wing and turned it around in the same radius in which a Volkswagen turns. The stall warning buzzer went off, which didn't bother me until I asked later what it meant, and the other two guys turned green. They don't have a ride like that at Disneyland.

Skwentna is a town of 150, but on this day, since it was the first major stop for the sledders, it was the most crowded it ever gets, with people checking out the Iditarod. There were about two dozen planes parked next to the snow runway and a bunch of ski-equipped planes on the frozen Yentna River close by, where several of the dog teams were resting.

As we got out of the plane, a teenager on a snowmobile offered to run us around the area for a few dollars, and since we were far ahead of the bikers at this point, we took a ride to the river and spent the afternoon hanging around the mushers.

Concerning the bikers, there was no news except for a shortwave report of the first three to drop out. After exhausting the possibilities of beer drinking and storytelling, we crashed on the floor of the one-room schoolhouse.

Middle of the night. "Wake up. They're here."

"What the hell time is it?"

"Quarter to four."

We rolled out of the sack and stumbled into the kitchen, where Kloser and Zink were chowing down on moose stew. "I can't believe I just pushed my bike seventy miles," Kloser said. It had taken them nearly fourteen hours to cover the sixty-six miles from Big Su, and then they had wasted another hour by getting lost within a mile of the checkpoint and wandering around on snowmobile trails in the dark.

There was another guy at the checkpoint with a bicycle, a hardcore type named Roman Dial, who did a good job of embodying the Alaska spirit. Not having the money to enter the race, he had started with the racers but turned off the trail and, by taking an easier route, had beaten them to Skwentna by four hours.

Zink and Kloser were hating life. Kloser took off his shoes and inspected a bandaged toe. "I froze this one skiing once, so it's real sensitive. Looks like I'm going to lose the nail. I'll live."

The prospect of returning through the miles of mush was depressing for them, so we held a hasty strategy session between the four journalists, the race official, and Roman Dial. Dial offered to lead them back on the Yentna River route he had taken, and both riders embraced the suggestion.

A little more than an hour after Kloser and Zink showed up, three Alaskans cruised in—Les Matz, Carl Tobin, and Mark Corson. Mark Frise had wrestled with indecision about continuing, quitting the race for a while, then deciding to go on. In doing so, he had dropped hours behind, taking an entire day to cover the sixty-six miles from Big Su to Skwentna. In addition to the news of trail conditions we were getting from the riders, the radio and phone reports were that half the entrants had already dropped out. The race was rapidly turning into an all-time classic, if that is spelled o-r-d-e-a-l.

A little over five hours behind the leaders, Martha Kennedy pulled into Skwentna, after riding alone through the night. Of all the remarkable stories of endurance that came from the event, hers was the most impressive, since she had none of the emotional support of those traveling in groups.

After resting and eating, and with the news that the return route was much faster, a much-refreshed pair of leaders pulled out into the bright morning sun along with guide Roman Dial. From this point on they had smooth sailing and made excellent time. But now a new problem arose. Kloser and Zink had become close buddies, as they had endured hardship together, and in some respects were not really racing against each other since when one stopped to adjust clothing or even admire the scenery, the other waited. But someone had to win this thing, and both felt an agreed-upon tie wouldn't be appropriate. They decided to sprint the last hundred yards or so across Knik Lake to the finish.

By the time they reached the finish, they were ahead of even the more optimistic estimates of their arrival, and it was almost a surprise for those waiting when the two appeared on the far side of the lake in the long northern twilight. Both came out of the saddle to the sound of excited cheering from a dozen people at the finish line, and as they crossed, Zink was the winner by about two bike lengths.

Relaxing afterward over beers and mooseburgers in the Knik Bar, both riders allowed that for most of the distance, it had been a team effort more than a competition between them, and although Zink was willing to call it a draw, Kloser wouldn't let him. "No way. You won."

The next rider, Carl Tobin, finished nearly three hours later, having moved up a couple of places when Matz and Corson, who were ahead of him, went off the trail by mistakenly following the tracks of some of the riders who had quit the race. First woman Martha Kennedy, like Zink a resident of St. Paul, Minnesota (the two had trained together for the race), took an astonishing sixth place overall, arriving at 4:30 a.m., having once again pushed through the night alone.

Nels Johnson was the only real casualty. Although he is an experienced cold-weather rider, Nels checked the condition of his feet only because the checkpoint official suggested it. He was shocked to find one of them blackened and frostbitten, the result of wearing too many pairs of socks, which cut off the circulation. Nels was flown to an Anchorage hospital for treatment, where prompt attention saved his toes; Nels said he would be back next year.

In all, thirteen riders finished, the last taking over two days to cover the distance. Using the lessons learned, the Mountain Bikers of Alaska planned to make next year's race even better, and actually started the planning as soon as the last rider (organizer Dan Bull) finished.

There was no doubt in my mind that though the inaugural event had a few rough edges, the Iditabike would in future years become a classic event of the sort that defines the human and mechanical possibilities of mountain biking far better than any number of lap races around parking lots for points. It may not be the national championship, but winning the Iditabike takes more strength, heart, and soul on the part of the rider than any other fat tire event. And aside from winning, just finishing is a victory.

Iditasport Extreme

ROCKY REIFENSTUHL

350 Miles

The human-powered Iditarod Trail race, where humans become the dogs. There's more than one way to test yourself against the snowy trails of Alaska's winter—try leaving the dogs at home and walking 350 miles... in six days!

[Although this piece describes Reifenstuhl's 2000 footrace in the Iditasport, it is included because of the author's standing as a legend in Alaska's extreme cycling community at that time.—Ed.]

Of Dogs and Men

The Iditasport Extreme is a winter race, for runners, bicyclists, and skiers, along a 350-mile segment of the Iditarod Trail. In February 2000 fifty-five competitors lined up to experience this wilderness adventure in this millennial year, to taste Alaska's backcountry like few in the world have or could. I've spent my share of time racing on the trail during each of the last twenty years. In 1999 I placed third in the Iditasport Extreme's bike category. Last year, however, I entered in the foot division with my brother Steve, one week after winning the 100-mile race on the Iditarod Trail.

Rules, We Don't Need No Stinkin' Rules

The race has almost no regulations except for a required campout the first night, signing in at the six checkpoints, and the rule that warns "no outside support." Each racer is allowed two twenty-pound, airdropped resupply bags: one at Skwentna (100 miles) and one at Puntilla Lake (170 miles). Other than that, you're on your own. As one reporter wrote, "Forget the Eco Challenge, the Raid, and the Beast, those races are merely dangerous, Iditasport Extreme is potentially deadly."

Steve and I set off from the start at Knik Lake at 3:00 p.m., heading for the required campout twenty-five miles down the trail. Pulling our homemade sleds that contain food and survival gear, we're stoked with optimism but tempered by a very healthy respect for the power of the Alaska winter wilderness, which tolerates no weakness. The gear we carry is standard outdoor equipment of the highest quality. Our shoes, however, are half to one full size larger than normal to accommodate liner socks, GORE-TEX socks, and outer socks and to allow room for the expected foot swelling, which, along with assorted blisters and lost toenails, is unavoidable in this race.

Trippin' on the Trail

After the first night, we fall into a pattern: traveling twenty to twenty-two hours per day, dozing less than two hours per night. Sleep deprivation brings on hallucinations, especially in the dark. Steve and I know, on some level, that the things we're seeing can't be real, but images created by a mind with none of the normal filters become that mind's reality. These visions become part of a hazy fog we travel through.

Into the Heart of Darkness

We leave Skwentna (mile 100) at 4:30 a.m. and trek to Finger Lake (mile 130). This is the third checkpoint, and we spend thirty minutes in the luxurious warmth and comfort of a beautiful lodge. Sleep and rest beckon us, but the snow is falling, building up. We break free of the lodge's grip and dive into thick darkness speckled with a swirl of fat flakes. It's going to be a psychedelic night, no doubt. After hours of climbing, sometimes hand over hand up dangerous snow chutes, we decide we must bivy despite the storm.

I feel like I could easily perish here. Thank God for my brother's skills and our confidence in each other. Cold, wet, tired, no . . . exhausted, we methodically setup a double bivy bag, put in two pads, two individual bags, and then another open bag over those. I suck down some chocolate for fuel, pull my poor feet out of wet shoes, place everything where I hope it won't freeze solid, and hunker down into full mummage. It's 3:30 am; we've been on the trail for twenty-two and a half hours. I'm asleep in less than sixty seconds.

Alaska Range Pass, Day Three

Six o'clock comes early. Now for the tough part: pack up wet gear while snow continues to fall; put on cold, dry socks, shoes, gaiters; and go. After three miles we come upon a biker huddled in a bivy bag beside the trail. It's Pierre, a naturalized Frenchman who last year was circled by a snowmachine, then deliberately hit from behind while he was riding to the finish on wide-open Big Lake. Here he is, back for more abuse. But pushing a loaded bike through this deep snow is too much. Soon after we leave, Pierre catches us. He has only a hydration pack and some food. "I leave the damn bike behind. I've had enough pushing. I'm going home."

The next checkpoint, Puntilla Lake, is on a five-mile-long glacial lake above tree line. We arrive at 3:00 p.m. and leave at 4:00. That time is spent in a flurry of activity. We gather and pack airdropped gear we'll need for the next 170 miles; change socks, mend feet, layer clothes for the inevitably colder temperatures on the north side of the Alaska Range; and, finally, shove as much warm food into our faces as possible.

The new snow is only several inches deep here, and in many places the winds have removed it, leaving a crust, which we inevitably break through just often enough to destroy our rhythm. For the next fifteen miles, we pick our way through a barren, desolate country of snow, ice, rock, and wind. The 3,700-foot elevation of this pass might seem minor, but try it in February after three nights on the trail, at 1:00 a.m., with the thermometer plunging past zero. I'm now limping on a twisted ankle. Not good. I keep a careful eye on Steve, figuring that he's silently considering whether or not he'll have to shoot me.

Trail conditions become rougher as we descend the Dalzell Gorge. Many Iditarod dogsled teams damage sleds, dogs, or drivers on this section of the trail to Rohn. Finally, the gorge opens up to reveal a series of frozen lakes. Dawn chases the hallucinations away just as they threaten to become overpowering. It's well below zero when we pull into the checkpoint (one very small cabin and a two-holer outhouse) at 9:00 a.m. Jasper, Rohn's official Iditarod Sled Dog Race checker, has some extra pancakes. We gobble them along with anything else not nailed down. We fall all over ourselves thanking our generous proprietor and plan to include him in our wills.

Into the Interior: Buffalo Country

Nikolai, eight-five miles distant, is our next objective, with a midpoint way station at forty miles called Buffalo Camp, a Native encampment used when hunting bison. We slide across a vast river valley punctuated with tree carcasses and other river flotsam. Crossing frozen water with no help within fifty miles or more makes us discuss our vulnerability, our insignificance, our fear. Soon we're in the "rain shadow" of the Alaska Range. Incredibly, we find ourselves pulling our sleds across grassy tundra tussocks, like naked sentinels awaiting their white blanket. This is buffalo country; there are telltale scat piles everywhere; we keep our eyes open for these large beasts.

Nightfall finds us in the Farewell Burn, a vast area consumed by fire in the late 1970s. I can't help thinking of Jack London's line: "In the winter the land is locked tight as a drum." It is tight, rigid, absolutely unyielding. It's now the middle of the night, five below, and the hallucination monster is pretty much in control. We've "seen" the Native camp at least fifty times. Finally, the real thing appears, complete with barking dogs! But alas, we're too late, there's no room, and the residents are probably too unhappy at being awakened to let these foolish pilgrims in for a rest. Another camp, another fire; it's bivy time again. We've been moving for sixteen hours and savor our two hours of blissful sleep.

At 6:30 a.m. we head north for Nikolai, only forty miles distant. Mount McKinley dominates horizons across much of southern Alaska. Here it's no different. There is a twist though. The last time we saw it, McKinley was directly in front of us. Now it's behind our right shoulders. As always, the journey to the next official checkpoint takes us through an infinite number of mental checkpoints, each marked with a small indulgence. Guess I'll have another smushed almond butter sandwich now, or would I rather have a cheese tortilla? I already ate all my butter. Damn good it was too!

Bingo Anyone?

Finally, we cross the southern branch of the Kuskokwim River and make out Nikolai's onion-domed, Russian-influenced church. We check in at the Teen Center, where Native townspeople are playing bingo as we begin our business of drying clothes, doctoring feet, sucking soda, and eating food. The normal heat inside the building feels shocking, oppressive. I actually wash my face and feet and a few other selected areas. After the bingo game is over, we are treated with a mixture of curiosity and disbelief. "You really just walked three hundred miles?" Yep. "In those sneakers?" Yep. "You really like those sodas, don't you?" "Yep, love 'em."

McGrath is our last leg, so to speak. And I don't have much in the way of legs left. Most of this stretch follows the Kuskokwim, which forces us to follow its frightfully lengthy meanders. Some are as long as six miles, but cutting across them without a trail is nearly impossible. Before 1:00 a.m. two snowmachiners, traveling from the wet town of McGrath to dry Nikolai, stop to chat. They pull out some bottles of beer, offering us a different kind of hydration than we've been using. Sure, give me a couple!

The walking is good on the river, but Old Man Sleep is overpowering and forces us to lie down on our sleds and catch a ten-minute nap. We've been on the trail without sleep for twenty hours now. This is hard. This is very hard. We are forced down twice more. Willpower is something we discuss for a while. I walk arm in arm with Steve, partly for my own support, partly for the closeness that I feel for him. It has gone back and forth during the days on the trail, but right now it is I who receives his strength.

We make our way toward McGrath in the swelling light of dawn, and it becomes crystal clear why the ancients worshipped the sun. We decide that the luxury of a thirty-five-minute bivy on the brightly lit trail will aid our overall progress. Yes!

Angels and Heaven

Rejuvenated by the rest, Steve and I press on at four to four and a half miles per hour for quite a while. But some sad soul has moved a couple of the official Iditarod Sled Dog Race markers, causing us to follow a wrong trail for half an hour. We must be careful here. Frustration, in our condition, could be deadly. Night is approaching, and our feet are pretty shot. Suddenly an angel appears in the form of a Cessna 172. The pilot circles, flies fifty feet over our heads, and drops us a note: "You're three river bends from McGrath." This guy is in our wills also! There's still another ten miles to go, but the news is a tremendous psychological boost. The temperature drops to five below, then ten. No matter, the lights of McGrath suddenly loom ahead.

We cross the finish line after six days, ten hours, and fifty minutes on the Iditarod Trial, taking first place in the foot division, tenth overall, and finishing ahead of all the skiers and a slew of bikers. Steve and I have shared six and a half days of soul-rattling intensity that reaffirms our unshakable love for each other. Upon reflection we hope we captured a small kernel of what Alaska Native elders have passed down for thousands of years: "Wisdom is derived from direct experience with the natural world." Steve and I live for these times: to become one, to see what the other sees, think what the other thinks. We have melded during this epic, building on the bonds formed during childhood days of tree houses, forts, and explorations into our local "wilderness." The blisters and sore muscles and tendons will fade, but the hauntingly intense experiences are etched in our memories forever. Sharing this journey is a gift, one that deepens our respect for untamed places and our understanding of each other. Nothing in the future will seem difficult or undoable. This is a uniquely powerful event, in a spellbinding country. It leaves no one unchanged.

Iditasport, 1991

A dim ribbon of light from my headlamp bobs on the frozen river ahead, searching desperately for the next trail marker. The river is a quarter mile wide, affording ample room for error in this arena of darkness. I stop peddling, switch off my lamp, and see the sky alight with pinpoint stars: their beauty startle me for a moment. With no moon and little light, I can barely see the riverbank to my right, aware that soon I must turn from the Yenta River onto the Susitna River. I continue tentatively until another marker dimly reveals itself. My uneven pace and search go on.

The annual Iditabike race is, by nature and due to nature, unpredictable. In its fifth year this two-hundred-mile race through Alaskan wilderness has become even more unpredictable since changing its name to Iditasport and including ski, snowshoe, and triathlon divisions. The allure of the race is the same as that of the Arctic: the unknown; the challenge. No one really knows his or her capabilities until tested, and each year the entrants find new obstacles to overcome and new dimensions to their character.

The course is steeped in Alaskan history. During a diphtheria scare in 1925, the Iditarod Trail and dogsled was the only way to deliver medicine from Anchorage to Nome. The annual Iditarod Dog Sled Race still commemorates that thousand-mile journey. Iditasport is shorter in distance but shares many of the challenges and is fully human powered. As an aside, I wonder how many know that around the turn of the century miners used bicycles on Alaskan winter trails to reach the goldfields?

It is February 17, my second night on the trail. Darkness still fills more than half the day. The first forty hours I traveled alone, but tonight I've buddied up with Sergei, a competitor from the USSR. We share no language but communicate through vocal expression and hand signals flashed in a beam of light. I am awed by his having undertaken this adventure . . . in a foreign land where people and signs are unintelligible to him. The darkness and loneliness are deeper for him. Through an interpreter, later, I am told that he is in awe of my strength as a woman and mother. I smile and hope he means strength of mind, for that is what the race takes.

The Iditasport is a perfect event for women, an endurance event in which mental stamina is as important as physical strength, in which small size and lightness can be an advantage in floating those fat knobby tires over a snowy trail. I slow when Sergei's front tire occasionally breaks through. A few extra percentage points of body fat are valued as insulation and storage of water and energy. Sergei is out of water, and I empty my CamelBak into his water bottle. A woman may never come across the line first, but a higher percentage of female entrants finish the race each year. In this race a finisher is indeed a winner. They have endured the same physical trail as the leaders and were victorious for a longer time over the real challenge of the race: the Alaskan winter.

In 1990 subzero temperatures and fear of frostbite and hypothermia were my concern. This year it is the dark hours and isolation that challenge me. I slept for two of the forty-eight hours it takes me to finish. The human body is a marvel of adaptation.

Sergei and I cross the finish line together. He slowed some for me the last couple miles across the hardpack lake. Sergei is the fourth-place male cyclist. I finished tenth overall and was the first woman. Only three bikers cross the line before me. Five skiers and one triathlete completed the top ten on the two-hundred-mile course, and four snowshoers finished their one-hundred-mile race. A nice mix. Although gold is the purse, the real prize is the camaraderie of like-minded people representing diverse backgrounds and places. The curious press asks about next year. Others ask "WHY?"

As a forty-year-old mother of two strong-willed daughters, who are only beginning to face the challenges of life, I believe in role models.

The reason I ride through the winter in Fairbanks, Alaska, would require pages and still only touch on the quiet beauty and mystery of the snowbound land stretching as far as the imagination. The harsh environment strips away layer upon layer of domestication and security and forces one to face the spirit of the land. A bike does not violate that spirit.

Hellbikes on Ice

ROMAN DIAL

Like the isolated Galapagos, Fairbanks in the 1980s was a veritable hotbed of thriving mutants who evolved a suite of novel outdoor skills built on the experience and wisdom of the climbers, canoeists, backpackers, skiers, snowshoers, hunters, and homesteaders who came before them. But by adapting an explosion of new gear to novel techniques, Fairbanks adventurers marked the beginning of outdoor pursuits that would spread across the world over the coming decades. One of those would later be called "bikepacking," but in the 1980s three of us called it "hellbiking," and this story, written in 1989, was a nod to Terrence Cole's 1985 collection, *Wheels on Ice*.

The soggy clouds of August wrapped around black peaks like washrags around bad plumbing, the leaks oozing, dripping, spilling down as big puddles of glacial ice across the valley floor. Jon Underwood, a six-inch crescent wrench in hand, squatted on the aquamarine "sliprock" (hellbiking lingo for a glacier's naked surface) and eyeballed the situation. At his feet a mountain bike lay crippled, the right pedal snapped off its crank.

"How far to the Denali Highway?" he asked.

Carl Tobin squinted into the distance. "Forty-five, fifty miles. Twenty miles of ice, then thirty miles of river."

This was a guess. Aside from a shortage of spare pedals, we also lacked a map. Jon set the wrench down, picked up the pedal, turned it in his palm.

"Guess I should have switched both pedals back at Black Rapids."

Three days earlier he'd replaced the wobbly-feeling left pedal at our resupply point, the Black Rapids Lodge on the Richardson Highway.

"How far back to the lodge?"

Again, we estimated. "Thirty-five, forty miles?"

Thirty-five miles that reached back over a glacier pass, through shin-deep snow, past crevasses, over unstable moraines, through bad brush, and across a river demanding multiple ferries of bikes, men, and gear in our single four-pound, five-foot packraft. This onerous list filled us with a fear of the known. The unknown via the Susitna Glacier didn't seem so bad. The route was downhill, for example, always a bike tour bonus.

Bike tour? How about mountaineering expedition? Scrambling over the thirty-mile Black Rapids Glacier, we had jumped a moulin stream—a vertical shaft in a glacier kept open by pouring water. Then at the pass, portaging bikes like pillories, we had roped-up and trudged five miles through a crevassed snowfield, always wondering: "Clip-in to the bike? Unclip from the bike? Which way to best survive a crevasse fall?" Which way to rationalize an absurdity?

Over the years we've developed a taxonomy for crevasses. *Guppies* are the smallest. A glacier traveler can bridge these tiny cracks with a size 9 boot. *Sharks* bite extremities, usually a leg (or legs) to the waist. Injury may result but rarely death. *Whales* can swallow the unfortunate, possibly killing and consuming the body. *Rippers* are cavernous. A roped climber falling into one of these plunges downward, then pendulums into a distant wall as the rope rips through the ceiling.

How to rationalize an absurdity . . . Walking past whales' tails and swarms of sharks, loaded bikes cinched tightly around our necks, the snow-slogging portage over the pass had dragged on like a waking nightmare. Yet one day before, on a highway of sunny sliprock stretching from the terminal moraine (the accumulation of stones and debris deposited by the glacier at its toe) to the firn line (where previous years' snow has been consolidated by thawing and refreezing but not yet been converted to ice), we had rolled—as in a dream—effortless and exhilarated.

Earlier signs had suggested retreat. Jon's rear rack fell off the first day out of Mentasta at the eastern end of the Alaska Range. Carl inadvertently swam the glacial Chistochina River with his bike on the second day. And on the third day I realized I'd forgotten the map. By the fifth day we all saw that we had carried too little food: the leg of our journey that we'd hoped to pedal in six days might take twelve. And there, high on the Susitna Glacier, we realized that we had carried too few tools, not enough parts, and no spare pedal.

We discussed abandoning our 250-mile, two-week mountain bike expedition through the glacial gut of the Alaska Range following the Denali Fault. Why had we pushed on this far anyway? Stubbornness? Stupidity?

Part of the "why" concerned bettering our previous 150-mile hellbike trip through the Wrangell–St. Elias from Nabesna to McCarthy. Some of it had to do with my own plans for an even bigger, full-length traverse of the Alaska Range. I would start with this 250 miles of mountain biking through the Hayes Range, then follow that with 450 miles of walking across the Denali and Lake Clark National Parks. For Jon the trip simply answered the query "What's next?" after Nabesna to McCarthy. As for Carl, a two-thousand-foot avalanche ride down a north face had permanently subtracted nearly ninety degrees of motion from his knee. The accident had occurred in this very mountain range at the height of his climbing career. Hellbiking offered him a new medium to paint bold, defiant strokes across wild landscapes, to flip the finger at conventional wisdom's button-down view of the possible.

Conventional wisdom viewed mountain bikes as alien to the Alaska Range, a view concerned less about the impact of rubber knobs on the environment than with the damned hard impact of the environment on riders, their bicycles, and alas, their pedals. Conventionally wise people claimed bikes can't be ridden on glacier ice, crevasses are treacherous, big wilderness is too big for bikes. These people said, "Bicycles should stay on the road."

We responded that creativity is the bastard child of the conventional: the art of adventure is what we do, and the science of adventure is what we prove.

Back at the broken pedal, I posed a hypothesis. "How 'bout Jon takes the raft and the paddle and goes out the Susitna alone and we take the rest and head over to the Gillam?" The Gillam was the next glacier leg on our tour, several miles away over a seven-thousand-foot pass.

Jon, here on his first-ever glacier trip, second-ever wilderness trip, looking at fifty miles of raw wilderness over glaciers, rivers, and brush, with no map, no partner, and no right pedal, answered simply, "What's the river like?"

"As I recall, it's big, slow, and full of quicksand," volunteered Carl, who'd floated it twice after climbing Mounts Deborah, Hess, and Hayes.

A swarm of crevasses, like sharks schooling from the depths, creased the snow up-glacier.

"Let's get down to the moraine and talk about this," I suggested.

In blowing rain we mounted our bikes and began coasting down the glacier.

Sunny sliprock bears the same resemblance to icy winter roads of civilization that granite cliffs bear to concrete slabs: superficially similar but aesthetically distinct. Peppered in pebbles or dusted in loess, the ice often lays naked, its blue-, green-, or white-hued flesh pockmarked and rough skinned. Sunshine reveals compressed ice as a wonderland of traction, an alpine version of Moab's celebrated sandstone, with rolling basins, steep headwalls, and tight narrow ridges. Like its Utah namesake, sliprock as a medium inspires the rider. The surface, anchored beneath spectacular mountain scenery, creates an extraordinary experience as cycling adventure.

Extraordinarily miserable, that is, in the rain, going downhill in gusty high winds, bikes laden with Patagonia pile, ice ax, packraft, and more food than we wanted to carry but less than we needed to eat. As usual, we had eschewed panniers, instead strapping loads onto a rear rack and half-filling our rucksacks with gear. This way we could shift the load depending on the balance of riding versus carrying that each day offered. Unfortunately, as the corrugated ice dropped at three hundred feet a mile, any load at all—backpack or bikepack—was unwelcome.

Soon we'd each spilled and bumped our butts sufficiently hard that slipping on foot instead of on studless tires seemed safer. Five tight-jawed miles later, chanting the Talking Heads' "Psycho Killer," "I'm tense and nervous / And I can't relax," we embraced the medial moraine as an old friend, a friend that we'd normally avoid.

Cold, wet, and miserable, we pitched camp in the lee of a Subaru-sized boulder, paving the floor and lower walls of our floorless, nylon pyramid tent—held up by our packraft paddle—with flagstones. Inside the airy blue tent, warmed by the cookstove's heat, we kept the outer bleakness at bay and talked cold turkey.

Carl is a Himalayan veteran with radical first ascents in Alaska and Canada. Recently, he'd been kicking ass as a mountain bike racer. Together we'd shared a rope on rock, ice, and snow for more than a decade. Indeed, I had apprenticed much of my mountain wilderness experience under his tutelage. Consequently, when Carl spoke, Jon and I listened to our elder.

"I predict, if tomorrow's like today, we're not going up to Icy Pass and over to the Gillam. We're all going down with you, Jon, out to the Denali Highway."

I'd risked my life with, and even for, Carl. This provided me some veto power in response to proclamations like "We're all going down" and other statements of retreat.

My dreams of a full-range traverse were at risk here. Hundreds of miles of Alaska's wildest terrain to fumble and fondle were slipping from my grasp. I wasn't ready for this expedition to dissolve just yet.

"Hold on a minute," I stammered. "Why not wait out the weather, like we would on an alpine climb? We know the ice is out of condition now, but with some sunshine—"

"It'll shape up into something rideable?" Jon laughed and clapped his hands together.

"Like on the Black Rapids? Best riding of the trip. But we only have one day. We don't have enough food to wait out more."

The next day the peaks were engulfed in storm. Jon puttered about the tent. I greased my WTB hubs, bottom bracket, and headset. Carl took a break from the 'mid and searched for food he and a climbing partner, David Cheesmond, had stashed after the first ascent of Mount Deborah's east ridge six years earlier. Finding that food cache would've encouraged us with needed rations and a good omen.

But instead of clearing, the clouds slipped off the mountains and slid down to envelop us, aborting Carl's search and soaking our already soggy spirits. We could stretch our food four more days, enough to finish the remaining one hundred miles of our planned route, but only if the weather cleared.

The second night passed at our boulder-strewn camp, but the weather remained. Drizzle dripped from peak-clogging fog. We all knew what this meant: a Susitna bailout.

Nobody spoke. Victims of the conventional, we loaded gear into stuff sacks and backpacks and prepared for retreat.

"So, bikes don't belong in the gut of the Alaska range after all," I mused to myself, disappointed that my Alaska Range traverse would have a hundred-mile gap in it.

Stuffing the 'mid, my disappointment erupted like a festering boil.

"Listen: I'm taking the rope, the axe, crampons, megamid, and stove and going over the pass anyway!"

Carl answered in a heartbeat, "Not without me, you're not."

Jon's face twisted wryly into a grin. "Guess that means I'm going too."

Unanimously, we asserted ourselves, full of empowered self-determination to prove again that in the science of adventure egos outsize brains. We headed off up-glacier.

While the west-facing Susitna had offered all the traction of an inclined hockey rink, the south-facing glacier leading to Icy Pass surprised us with its traction. Equally remarkable, Carl discovered the Tobin-Cheesmond cache of peanuts and kippers. God does indeed smile on us mortals of simple mind.

Encouraged, we pedaled higher. Bare ice and rain gave way to névé and sleet, the wind increasing with altitude. At seven thousand feet we dropped our bikes, punched into a whiteout, and followed our compass north to the col, scouting the route over the divide.

This was full-on stupid. I wore every stitch of clothing I'd brought, from pile pajamas to Capilene balaclava, all worn as armor against the cross fire in a battle of the air masses. There along the crest of the Alaska Range, a coastal low-pressure system struggled with an interior high for supremacy. Caught between combatants, we stumbled upward, three fools linked by 120 feet of five-millimeter Kevlar cord and the same mentality that sends dogs after porcupines again and again.

We reached the col, anchored our packs in the lee, then returned for our bikes. The wind twisted and jerked the bicycles on our backs as we stepped over the divide. An icy ramp led left, merging with a glacial bulge split by crevasses. We crept along, winding our way through a

59

historical impasse recorded in David Roberts's 1970 expedition classic, *Deborah: A Wilderness Narrative*.

Nearly thirty years earlier, a whale had swallowed Don Jensen, roped to Roberts for safety, then chewed him up and spit him out at Roberts's urging. Two decades later these crevasses again enforced retreat when a pair of experienced Fairbanks ski mountaineers balked at the maze.

Icy Pass had turned back both groups. We felt honored: the col let the bicycles pass.

Safe on the snow flats below, we looked back. The science of adventure had proven itself irrational: during a blizzard, sixty miles from any road or man-made trail, over a pass that repulsed experienced mountaineers, we'd crossed the glacial spine of the Alaska Range with mountain bikes. The idea of it made me sick.

We pedaled down-glacier, bunny hopped a few guppies, but mostly bike hiked through ankle-deep slush. Near midnight we anchored the 'mid to a rocky moraine. The shelter barely survived a thrashing storm. With great relief we exited the glacial system the next day. As Jon's first experience with glaciers had stretched rather uncomfortably over a hundred miles and a week, he swore them off, if not forever, at least for a day.

Two days later we nearly lost ourselves again high on ice in swirling clouds. Like the proverbial three blind men feeling an elephant, each of us massaged his memory of the map, and each arrived at different conclusions. Until this point we'd followed glaciers and river valleys familiar from a dozen years of hiking, skiing, climbing, and floating. Now we stumbled around nearly lost on a question mark–shaped glacier, wondering not only where we were but where the hell we should go.

Finally, Carl said: "Let's go back. We can head for Healy the way I walked out twelve years ago after Clif and I left the Gillam."

"Can you remember the route, Carl?"

"Yeah, I think so. We go down the Little Delta, turn left to climb over a tundra plateau, then drop down to a small creek. I think it's Buchanan Creek. We follow that upstream, climb the pass at its head, and drop down again. That should put us close to the Wood River."

Down the Little Delta we went, turning left at Carl's signal, humping our bikes over a tundra plateau, coasting down to the creek bottom below by milking all the elevation we could, gently bumping along the tundra. Then Carl indicated that we climb up to the pass above. We pushed, then portaged to the top, arriving in cloud. So far, so good.

Carl waited as peaks tore a hole in the weather. He took in what the view revealed, turned around, looked from whence we'd come, and looked ahead again. With a perfectly straight face, he announced: "Nope, this isn't it. I've never been here before in my life."

This was funny, hilarious even—an excellent joke.

"No really, Clif and I must have gone farther north before climbing up. It *was* twelve years ago."

Off memory's map we pulled out the compass and aimed it over the pass: west. Thank God. Salvation. At least we weren't lost. Sure, we didn't know where we were, but that's only half of being lost. The other half is not knowing where to proceed.

We knew where to proceed. We climbed into our saddles, pushed off, and pedaled into the fog, heading west.

Okay, so usually we carry maps. And we think about the maps we carry. We prefer the 1:250,000 scale USGS Alaska topos. These sheets show the big picture, the prominent landmarks needed in regions where no marked routes exist at all. Useful landmarks show up more clearly on the four-miles-to-the-inch quads than they do on the one-mile-to-the-inch maps, where the important contours sometimes get diluted in detail. Besides that, a two-hundred-mile trip fits conveniently on two big maps, a lighter and more manageable load than fifteen or twenty of the 1:63,360 scale.

The cabins shown on Alaskan topos, most mapped before I was born, usually no longer exist. Rarely does anyone own or permanently occupy those that do. Hunters and trappers maintain them for temporary use.

I confess that we sometimes find shelter in these crude cabins. We look for cabins on the map, and if we are near, we visit, sometimes meeting extraordinary people. But wandering around half-lost on the north side of the Alaska Range, my mind grappled with the irony of looking for a cabin to find a map.

Of course, we did find a cabin with a map inside it and then located the cabin on the map in a weird sort of wilderness recursion. We were right where we wanted to be. Carl couldn't have done better if his memory had been cartographic.

We even found a lodge where the master hunting guide within, Lynn Castle, insisted we lay down our bikes and explain how in the hell we'd made it two hundred miles through the Alaskan bush on bicycles. "Those things got motors?" he asked. Then we feasted with him, bathed in a sauna, slept in beds, feasted again, and in the morning rode on.

Lynn promised the final thirty miles would pass in six hours. It took twelve, much of it in a dry creek bed with pool drop architecture. The creek bed exhilarated me but depressed poor, pedal-stub Jon. Until then, where stand-up balance was crucial, Jon had kept up admirably, toeing the pedal's inch-long axle stub the hundred-mile distance since breaking it. The inconvenience—compounded by a blown transmission in the Wood River valley when a stick in the spokes snapped a derailleur—slowed Jon little on our route of gravel river bars, wild animal trails, and firm downhill tundra. But the look on his face said it was getting old, and the hole wearing at the toe of his shoe said likewise.

We arrived in Healy at a Parks Highway roadhouse, just north of Denali National Park, late in the evening of our fourteenth day. Stinky, beat, and happy, we gulped two full meals apiece in an hour.

Sitting there with a belly full of greasy goodness, I appraised the value of persistence. We'd endured daily rain, skimpy rations, broken bikes, self-doubts. We'd crossed big rivers, bigger glaciers, the biggest mountain range in Alaska. Our mechanisms for success? Jon's enthusiasm and Carl's wisdom keeping us rolling confidently on wheels well lubed with humor.

By trip's end we claimed again: "Our mission? To boldly bike where none have biked before!"

Or likely, would ever again.

Biking the Haul Road, 1986   DAN BUETTNER

ON THE HAUL ROAD—The six of us sat huddled 'round a table at the Hilltop Truckstop. A small, simple café just north of Fairbanks, it's where Prudhoe Bay–bound truck drivers meet and eat before the 519-mile haul to the Arctic Ocean. We needed to hitch a ride, but we weren't sure how to go about it.

A waitress, busily smacking gum, arrived to take our order. Maybe she knew a driver who'd take us? We made the mistake of asking.

"Hey, you guys!" she yelled, her voice high and shrill to attract the twenty or so truckers seated in the tiny dining room. "These guys are looking for a ride up to Prudhoe. Any of you guys wanna give 'em a lift?"

The room fell silent for a moment as twenty pairs of unkind eyes turned from their food to the six of us, dressed in shiny black cycling tights. I felt like I'd just taken a bone away from twenty Siberian huskies.

"The last guy looking for a ride to Prudhoe waited for three days," our waitress observed, breaking the silence. The men turned their attention back to their food.

"If you think you're going to make it alive, you better have heavy winter clothes, a serious firearm, and something to protect you from flying rocks," shouted one of the men from the other side of the room.

"What do we need all that stuff for?" I asked.

"Truckers barrel down the middle of that highway at up to eighty miles an hour. If they don't run you over, their tires spit gravel at you just like a shotgun. If the trucks don't get you, you'll be going through some of the worst grizzly territory in the world—and they got no fear of humans."

"We're going to be on bicycles. We can just get off the road when trucks come, and we'll take our chances with the bears," I countered. "Plus, we'll be back by mid-August; what do we need winter clothes for?"

At this, about half the dining room broke out in laughter. Another driver turned to us and said casually, "It's already snowed up there twice—you guys are going to get yourselves killed."

Definitely not encouraging. But nine people had spent a year planning and preparing for this trek. We had enlisted more than thirty sponsors and had just finished a nonstop, seven-day-and-night marathon drive in our cramped van from Minnesota. We weren't about to get scared off by a few truckers—even if they did know every inch of the Dalton Highway.

We six had set out to break the world record for bicycling from Alaska to Argentina, a distance of eighteen thousand miles. By the time you read this, we'll be somewhere in the Lower 48, headed south on a trip we've dubbed the "World Record Bike Trek across the Americas." We believe we'll be the first in history to completely traverse North, Central, and South America by bicycle. Our goal is to begin our journey with our rear tires in the Arctic Ocean and end it with our front tires in the Strait of Magellan at the tip of Argentina.

Bret Andersen, Martin Engel, Ann Knabe, and I will be in the saddle. Steve Buettner and Rafaela Salido will back us as support crew. Along the way we hope to fulfill our theme of friendship among nations.

But right now the problem is that the only road running to Prudhoe Bay, the Dalton Highway, is off-limits to the public. We appealed, unsuccessfully, to the State of Alaska for a permit to use the highway. When a simple request failed, we applied for a study permit and contacted both Minnesota's U.S. senators, who contacted an Alaska senator and the governor's office.

Nothing doing.

We finally spent two days in Fairbanks staking a claim to prospect gold north of the haul road's checkpoint. With this gold claim permit in hand, we were issued a road-use permit—at least for part of the road.

Now, however, we'd run into more problems. The truck drivers outside the Hilltop Café told us that our support vehicle, a Dodge van, had neither the gas capacity nor suspension necessary to make the 1,038-mile round trip. "Just imagine making a thousand-mile trip on the face of the moon," one experienced driver said.

We finished our last real meal and headed out to the parking lot. We strategically positioned ourselves to snag a ride. Bret and Martin hung out by the door, Ann stood on the side of the road with her thumb out, and I sat in the parking lot with a walkie-talkie tuned to channel 19 and broadcasted our plea: "Breaker one-nine for you northbound truckers."

It took four hours before the walkie-talkie hooked us a ride; a semi with a sleeping compartment pulled over. "Glad you stopped me," said the middle-aged trucker, stepping out of the cab. "I'll help you get your bikes loaded up."

"See you in a few," we four bikers yelled back to Steve and Rafaela, who were staying with the van.

As we started off, the trucker, Jim Davenport, said, "Nice to have company—driving this road alone for ten years gets pretty boring."

Eighteen hours of nonstop conversation later, we pulled into Prudhoe Bay.

It's not hard to see that most of the settlement came up on the back of semitrailers. The town's hotel looked like a series of huge mobile homes. A thirty-eight-degree wind blew off the bay at about thirty miles per hour. "A warm summer breeze up here," remarked Jim, seeing us hop about trying to shrug off the cold.

In front of us spread ugly industrial buildings, oil wells, and the white-capped Arctic

Ocean. Behind us, as far as we could see, stretched the vast green-brown tundra.

ARCO Alaska Inc., one of the oil companies whose property runs to the edge of the water, had given us special permission to cross its encampment to the Arctic Ocean. We met its security guards at the front gate. After taking our photographs and having us sign disclaimers, they loaded us in an ARCO truck and drove us the last six miles to the beach.

With our back tires wet with sea seawater and dressed in every piece of warm clothing we had, we started off with our security escort. Before we even made the six miles back to the front gate, one pack rack had fallen off and two tires had gone flat. "And you guys think you're going to make it to Argentina?" laughed our escort.

At 6:00 p.m. we left Prudhoe Bay behind. The Dalton Highway shot out in front of us and disappeared on the horizon in a tiny point. We strapped ourselves into the toe clips and began pedaling over a gravel surface much like a bed of oblong golf balls.

Martin and I, thinking that we'd start right in with a twenty-mile-per-hour clip, spun out, slipped, and landed on the ground with the bikes on top of us, our feet still strapped in the pedals.

A very official sign beside the road again reminded us that we were entering a restricted highway—permits absolutely required. Bret read the sign, then yelled into the wind, most of his words lost: "What if . . . some Alaskan Big Brother . . . watching?" We were a good bit north of our gold claim.

"Bret, this is 1986, not 1984. Besides, we're at the end of the earth. Nobody's interested," I said with false confidence.

Cold and exhausted at 11:00 p.m., we started looking for shelter to make camp for the night. Although the sun was now near setting, gloomy clouds hung in the sky. The frigid wind, now out of the east, had intensified. Strong gusts literally blew us across lanes and off our bikes.

We bucked the wind another hour, searching for shelter: a tree, a rock, a parked car, anything. Well after midnight, we found a small mound of gravel beside the road.

Our $500 tents blew away twice before we figured out that the only way to anchor them was to strap them to the bicycles. The wind also blew out our "wind-proof" camp stove three times, so we settled for a supper of crackers and gorp, then crawled into our wind-whipped tents.

A warm sun awoke us the following afternoon. Our tents were standing straight in the very still air.

"Hey, are you guys up yet?"

"Yes. It seems like we're in a different place," Bret answered from our tent.

"I guess the tundra is more benign than we thought." Ann sounded relieved.

We crawled outside, and before the tent fly was zipped, thick clouds of mosquitoes attacked. Waving her arms wildly, Ann slapped at the ruthless creatures.

"A benign place, Ann?"

In thirty minutes we were on the road, skidding, sliding, and crunching gravel. Without the wind we reached breakneck speeds up to ten miles per hour, but a new malady plagued us: mosquitoes found a comfortable draft in the airspace directly behind us and fed on our helpless backsides.

Forty miles, seven hours, and about one hundred bites later, the golf ball gravel ended and dirt began. Relieved, we shifted gears and reached new speeds of thirteen miles per hour. The tundra began to roll by. We saw grazing caribou, the mosquitoes relented, and the midnight sun spread an orange glow over the tundra.

This night no one dared call the tundra benign. Within ten miles the gently rolling hills turned into steep climbs and bumpy drops. At the end of a particularly arduous climb, a truck driver with a six-pack of soda waited for us next to his rig. "I heard about you guys on the CB. I thought you could use these."

Panting, pooped, and parched, we thanked the man and guzzled the pop.

"You guys goin' all the way to Argentina?"

"We're going to try."

We chatted for almost an hour as the friendly driver produced a seemingly endless supply of cookies, candles, and other goodies from his truck. "Yeah, you guys are doin' the right thing, taking advantage of your youth, but I think you're nuts goin' down to Nicaragua and El Salvador with all those terrorists and wars and everything."

"Well, we think people who package up to twenty or thirty years of their lives, label it a career, and sell it for a few hundred thousand dollars whether they like it or not are the crazy ones," I offered. "You end up dead for sure taking the career route. If we get killed, at least we lived first. Anyway, we have escorts through the dangerous countries. We'll make it."

"I can't shake a stick at that," he said.

Obnoxious headwinds marked day three. And on day four the hills turned into the Brooks Range, which crested near the seven-thousand-foot Atigun Pass. It took three hours of continuous climbing up the steep, treeless mountain to get to the top. The mountains erupted from the tundra, gray and brown and jagged. The somber colors were enlivened only by the green tundra and fiery wildflowers.

With one final grunting thrust, we topped Atigun Pass and began a twenty-minute rock 'n' roll descent. We dropped onto a long, high plateau and into a herd of caribou grazing near the road. We also descended into the grizzly zone our friends at the Hilltop Café had warned us about.

We soon came to a small shack with a huge stop sign.

"Oh-oh, there it is," I thought, the checkpoint to catch outlaws on the road without a permit. I imagined a 250-pound Yukon Jack character with a 45 mm carbine slung over his shoulder marching out of the shed to arrest me.

But it seemed to be vacant. I was just past the shed, about to make a clean getaway, when the door swung open and my heart skipped a beat. Out shuffled an old man wearing an overcoat a couple of sizes too big.

"Hey, you! Come back!"

I squeezed my brakes lightly and debated making a run for it but turned around, remembering the friendship theme of our bike trek.

"I heard about you guys on the CB. I made some fresh coffee and got a plate of cookies all ready."

Ten minutes later we were all sitting around the shed sipping coffee and nibbling cookies with the checkpoint supervisor.

"I don't try to stop anyone from running the checkpoint," he said congenially. "I write their license plate down in my log, and the trooper stops by once in a while to get the plate numbers without permits." The old man got up to adjust the flame on the coffee.

"And what happens to the people without a permit?"

"They get fined. I think it's $50. No, wait, I think they changed it to $25."

And to think of all those days we spent trying to be legal.

Just down the hill from his checkpoint, we hit the tree line—a welcome sight after four days of tundra. That night, after we ate our last package of noodles and a can of "meat product," the support vehicle met us coming north.

The van meant fresh food, light loads, and a good night's sleep in our foldout camper. We almost felt like we'd reached Argentina.

The reality that our bike trek record was still eight months away hit hard the next day, when we mounted our bikes in a rainstorm. The nice thing about the Dalton Highway in the rain was that there wasn't dust when a semi passed—just a wall of mud. By the time we finished the first ten miles, bikes and bodies bad a thick coating of liquid Dalton Highway.

We left Prudhoe Bay at 6:00 p.m., Friday, August 8. On Friday, August 15, we approached the Hilltop Café. We'd averaged seventy miles a day over a road that truckers claim is the toughest in the world.

Exhausted, smelly, mud caked, we four cyclists hobbled into the Hilltop. I don't know if it was the smell of us or the sight of us, but the roomful of truckers fell dead silent and watched us take our seats around the same table we'd had the week before. The same waitress hurried over to our table, looked kindly at us, and said in an almost motherly voice, "Did you guys make it all the way?"

"Well, it must surely smell like we made it, no?"

"Hey, you guys!" she announces to the dining room. "These kids made it all the way from Prudhoe . . . on their bikes."

Some of the truckers who'd laughed at us came up and shook our hands. The waitress even gave us extra french fries with our burgers.

We ate our meals with complete confidence that the next 17,500 miles would be no problem. No problem at all.

Pribilofs by Bike, 1994 BILL SHERWONIT

We came prepared for the worst: fog, chilling gales, nonstop drizzle. Because that's what you get on St. Paul Island in summer: windy, gray days and constant dampness.

Here in the middle of the Bering Sea, about three hundred miles from mainland Alaska, the summer sun normally shows up every couple of weeks or so. And a heat wave translates into temperatures in the fifties. Wonderful weather for northern fur seals, not so pleasant for humans—or at least visitors who haven't grown up on the island.

Those drizzle- and fog-loving seals, including the largest northern fur seal colony in the world, are a major reason that hundreds of tourists each year endure St. Paul's dreary and sometimes nasty summer weather. Birds are another.

The largest of Alaska's five Pribilof Islands, St. Paul, is by all accounts a birder's paradise, inclement weather or not. The island is seasonally inhabited by legions of nesting seabirds that travel here from wintering grounds scattered throughout the Western Hemisphere. It is also the accidental landing spot for Asian "vagrants"—birds seen only rarely in North America—occasionally blown to the Pribilofs by strong westerly winds.

Our group of two Alaskans and two Californians had come to see both seals and birds and also to learn more about the island's Native culture, St. Paul being home to the world's largest Unangan (Aleut) community.

The island's Unangan people and fur seals have been inextricably linked since at least the late 1780s, though there's evidence the relationship extends much farther back in time. Russian commander Gerassim Pribylov reportedly "discovered" St. Paul in 1787 while seeking a new source of pelts for his country's fur trading industry, though Unangan oral history indicates the uninhabited island was already well known to the region's Native residents.

A couple of years later, the Russian American Company forcibly relocated Unangan hunters and their families to St. Paul. Their descendants have continued to live here for more than two centuries, but only in recent years had the local Indigenous culture been featured in the island's tours.

Our interests were similar in many respects to those of other St. Paul tourists. But our approach was rather unusual: we would tour the island on mountain bikes.

Bicycling, we'd been told, was an excellent low-budget alternative to the island's package tours, which in 1993 ranged from $800 for a two-night hotel and transportation package to $1,600 for a one-week stay and tour, meals not included. It seemed an attractive alternative—as long as we didn't mind the possibility of miserable biking conditions, with lots of wet and windy weather.

Fine, we decided. We'll take our chances.

So, that June we boarded a jet bound for St. Paul, with baggage that included bikes, heavy-duty rain gear, and lots of warm clothes. After all, the island's average June temperature is forty-one degrees, with nighttime lows that routinely fall into the high thirties. National Weather Service records show the temperature once dipped to sixteen degrees in June and that early-summer snowfalls sometimes blanket the island.

Given all that chilling data, imagine our surprise, even delight, when we touched down on St. Paul and found the Pribilofs to be baking in a Bering Sea heat wave, with clear skies, bright sunshine, and temperatures reaching into the upper fifties. It had been like that for at least a few days, we learned. Very strange weather, the locals told us.

Given our biking plans, we expected the island's weather to quickly revert to its usual form. But sunny weather blessed us for most of the next six days, with only brief spells of clouds, fog, drizzle, and once, a downpour. It's true the wind hardly ever let up, but with the sun blazing overhead and the unusually warm air (by local standards), the breezes proved more refreshing than chilling.

So, for most of a week, we explored St. Paul Island by bike and foot, in the most pleasant Bering Sea weather imaginable, at least for tourists.

While bikes solved most of our needs, lodging offered its own challenge. St. Paul's only hotel was reserved for package tour customers, and no camping was allowed, which quickly eliminated our most obvious options. Through persistent research we discovered an unofficial (and somewhat unusual) B & B, run by a woman named Lillian Capener. A transplanted Montanan, she had moved to St. Paul in the late 1960s to perform missionary work with her husband, Alvin. A widow since the mid-1980s, Lillian operated her B & B during the summer tour season, but first and foremost, she told us, "I remain a missionary." And that is a story in itself.

Not everyone in our group was a gung ho biker, so we probably didn't take full advantage of our personal wheels. And to be honest, we didn't have to. We'd primarily come for St. Paul's famed wildlife, and we found some excellent bird- and seal-viewing spots near the village, so naturally we spent most of our time there.

We saw all of the major seabird attractions—puffins, murres, auklets, kittiwakes, and cormorants—and other birds as well, though none of the Asian vagrants that really serious birders come hoping to see. That was no big deal to us, thanks to the seals. My favorite times on St. Paul were spent watching the island's northern fur seals.

In the early 1990s the Pribilof archipelago was summer home to about a million northern fur seals, more than two-thirds of the world's population. Some 80 percent of the Pribilof's seals congregate at St. Paul's fourteen rookeries and nonbreeding haul-out sites. (The remainder, we learned, gather at St. George, the only other Pribilof island inhabited by humans, forty-seven miles to the south.)

The fur seals spend their winters at sea, then begin arriving at the Pribilofs in May. Large male breeders known as "beachmasters" show up first and quickly establish territories, which they aggressively defend while building harems of up to one hundred females. Pregnant females don't arrive until June. They usually give birth to a single pup within forty-eight hours of arrival, then mate again within a week, while still nursing their newborn.

Once they've established a territory, breeding bulls usually don't leave their kingdom for several weeks. They may lose up to 25 percent of their body weight during this fasting period, during which they neither eat nor drink but spend plenty of time in battle.

The baking effect of June's prolonged heat wave only served to aggravate an already tense situation, and competing bulls would occasionally explode into vicious fights. Heads bobbing and weaving like two heavyweight boxers, the seals feinted, ducked, and jabbed. But instead of throwing punches, they came at each other with wide-open mouths filled with sharp, flesh-tearing teeth. Showing incredibly quick reflexes, they snapped and counter-snapped, pulling out clumps of hair and tearing gashes in each other's hides. Witnessing the fights, I came to better understand the phrase "the fur is flying."

Though fascinating to watch, the fights (fortunately) were few and far between. Mostly, the seal bulls napped or watched over their harems, warning off challengers with a variety of groans, grunts, and growls.

While we frequently biked or even walked to seal rookeries along St. Paul's southern shores, only once did we travel to one at its far northwestern corner, about thirteen road miles from the village. And then we took the easy way. We joined one of the daily bus tours, which were open to independent travelers as well as the package people—for a fee, of course, but a reasonable one.

Joining the tour proved a wise decision. While being guided to some of the island's better viewing spots for both birds and seals, we learned about St. Paul's Unangan history and culture. (That, too, is another story.)

Only on our last full day did a low-pressure system arrive to push out the sun, replacing it with a steady, daylong downpour. Spoiled by our previous good fortune, we chose to rent a van rather than pedal through wind and rain—another wise decision.

Aside from its usually foul weather, St. Paul is in many respects ideal for biking. Fourteen miles long and eight miles across at its widest point, the island has forty-five miles of coastline and more than fifty miles of volcanic cinder roads.

Several of the best wildlife-viewing sites are within easy biking (or even walking) distance of the village. And the island's subdued volcanic terrain makes for mostly easy pedaling. There were times we got on our bikes, no particular destination in mind, to simply explore St. Paul in a relaxed manner, without having to stick to any kind of schedule. A number of times we combined bike rides with off-road hikes across open meadows, to savor both the weather and the landscape. During our short stay, certainly, we'd discovered nothing less than an island paradise, even without those Asian birds.

Rough-Terrain Unicycling, 1997   MICHAEL FINKEL

Riding a unicycle up and down mountains requires the balance of a gymnast and the temperament of a teenager.

Why the red unicycle was left in the Seward, Alaska, dump and what inspired George Peck's wife, Carol, to bring it home are both unclear. "I'm a salvager and recycler" is all she will say. "She's a dump rat," Peck says. Carol put the unicycle in the garage, and Peck found it there. This was almost fourteen years ago. His life hasn't been the same since.

"I glom on to things," Peck says. "He gets obsessed," Carol says. Peck taught himself to ride the red unicycle—no books, no instructors. He practiced daily for more than a month before he could wobble up and down his driveway. Then he attempted to take the unicycle onto the roads. Riding a unicycle is as precarious as it looks—the "cone of balance," as Peck calls it, is extraordinarily precise. A pebble can be enough to put you on your back. So can a patch of sand or a gust of wind or a crack in the pavement. This may be why the red cycle was tossed into the dump: Seward is possibly the worst spot on the planet in which to ride a unicycle. The place is all sand and gusts and cracks, not to mention ice and snow and logs and boulders and mountains.

Peck learned to ride his unicycle under all conditions. He discovered how to make the cycle hop, and he honed the skill until he could pop over logs two feet in diameter. He figured out how to power through boulder fields, how to jump up and over picnic tables, how to turn in ankle-deep mud. He became skilled at riding in dried-out riverbeds, across frozen lakes, up mountain trails, and through wind-crusted snow. This is clearly not what unicycles were designed to do. When the red unicycle fell apart, Peck drove to Anchorage and bought a new one. When that broke, he ordered another. After a dozen more were destroyed, he began designing his own.

For almost a decade and a half, no matter the weather, Peck has gone mountain unicycling nearly every day—twice a day most weekends—in and around Seward.

People in town are used to seeing him. He has ridden the shoreline so many times that he notices if a rock has been moved. Seward sits on Resurrection Bay, on the eastern edge of the Kenai Peninsula. It is separated from Anchorage by 125 miles of glaciated mountains and sprawling ice fields. The town is so remote—a Galápagos island of sorts—that something odd or fantastic can develop there and never be discovered by anyone beyond the city limits.

Until three years ago, when he attended the International Unicycle Convention in Minneapolis, Peck was completely unknown in the unicycling community. At the meet he learned of a handful of other mountain unicyclists. He found out that his sport had not only other participants but also a name—"muni," short for "mountain unicycling" (a name, Peck feels, that is a little too cute; he prefers "rough-terrain cycling"). Later, through a unicycling newsletter, he read of plans for an inaugural muni convention. Last October he flew to Sacramento for the first annual California Mountain Unicycle Weekend. Thirty-five of the best rough-terrain unicyclists in North America came to show off their skills. No one was half as good as Peck. He is now widely viewed as the best mountain unicyclist in the world. He is credited with helping to invent the sport, and the cycles he has designed are probably the sturdiest and lightest unicycles ever built. He is riding rougher terrain every month. And he is almost certainly the world's oldest mountain unicyclist: Peck is fifty-six.

Carol and George Peck and their two children, Kristopher, twelve, and Katy, seven, live in a small brown house two blocks from the center of town. Attracted to Alaska's frontier image, Peck moved to the state in 1974, after a stint in Nepal with the Peace Corps and almost ten years in the University of Idaho's graduate schools, where he earned degrees in physics, law, and teaching. He came to Seward

to take the job of magistrate, a position he still holds. He met Carol
Griswold in 1981.

The inside of their house, especially during the long Alaska winter,
is a scene of unmitigated chaos. Peaches and Boomer, a pair of para-
keets, like to dive-bomb visitors' heads. Berry and Jessie, two Labrador
retrievers, wrestle in the kitchen. Katy prefers roller skates to sneakers,
and Kristopher wouldn't be caught dead without his skateboard. The
living room contains three unicycles, a small trampoline, a basketball
net, an electronic keyboard, two acoustic guitars, two fiddles (Carol
and George play in a local folk band), an indoor garden, an eclectic
library (one shelf devoted to entomology, another to dog training), a
general scattering of children's toys, several of Carol's junkyard furniture
discoveries, a hamster cage, a fish tank, and a midden of unicycle parts.

"George has been a teenager for forty years," Carol says. This is only
partly true.

When Peck is in his courtroom, facing the daily litany of drunk driving
and domestic violence cases, he is fifty-six years old. When he is awake
at two in the morning, mulling over the physics of wheel diameter and
axle size, he is fifty-six. When he is riding, he is seventeen—though he
doesn't use swear words. When he falls, he says things like "Gargle!"
and "Yug!" and "These shoes are explosively decoupling with the pedals,
and that's disconcerting."

Peck is a little over six feet tall and about as thin as a fence post. He
has the air of a mad scientist. His hair appears to be an assemblage of
cowlicks. He is profoundly nearsighted and wears round gold-framed
glasses. A house-wide search for his car keys is an almost daily event.
He eats dinner as if a cash prize were to be awarded to the first finisher.
His unicycle is built of top-quality titanium and tempered aluminum
parts, special-ordered from a custom manufacturer, but Peck often rides
wearing faded jeans, a stained sweatshirt, and leather work boots. On
the front of the family's washing machine, using word magnets, Katy
has assembled a succinct ode to her father: DAD IS FUNNY.

On weekend days Peck takes his first ride soon after sunrise, usually
with the dogs. He rides along Resurrection Bay, the sharp summits of
the Chugach Mountains forming a backdrop. He pedals in fits and starts:
a powerful flurry to ascend a flat-topped rock, an immediate ninety-

degree turn on the top, a momentary pause to consider the drop-off, and a careful hop down to the sand. His arms provide counterbalance, waving in controlled, tai chi–style movements. The tip of his tongue flits in and out. In rough-terrain cycling, top speed, even going downhill, is about six miles an hour. "It's not exhilarating," Peck says, "but a series of little joys." He cuts through a puddle, cracking a thin film of ice, and chugs up a dirty snowbank. He falls twice, gracefully, and climbs back on.

A unicycle is both more and less than half a bicycle. It has a solid hub and lacks any gears, meaning that one rotation of the pedals produces one rotation of the wheel. This is called direct drive and is the reason a unicycle is limited to low speeds. You can't coast, but you can ride backward.

"Unicycling is intrinsically a slow-motion event," Peck says. "It is more about rhythm and mental dexterity than about strength—it has more in common, I feel, with a chess match or a Bach concerto than with any extreme sport. And it's actually very safe—far safer than bicycling. I've never had an injury so bad I couldn't ride the next day. Much of the thrill, really, is in pondering the ergonomical conundrums. Torque. Pedal separation. Crank-arm length. Spokes. You need the cycle to be sturdy, and you need it to be light and maneuverable. And everything has to be balanced on one tiny axle. It's nearly insolvable. The five best riders I met at the California weekend were a physicist, a mathematician, a neurophysiologist, a computer analyst, and an Intel executive."

He says this as he rides. If a visitor jogs alongside him (the pace is perfect), Peck will furnish an hour-long disquisition. He will expound on Alaskan geology. He will talk about unicycling up street curbs and about the appropriate pedal positions for optimum torque and about the time he beat a pair of bicyclists up the steep Crown Point Mine Trail. He will insist that it is possible to unicycle nearly any surface that can be walked, provided one has the right unicycle.

Peck estimates that he has spent $2,000 on his current unicycle—but he is still unsatisfied. About once a week, he visits Ron Henderlong, who helps to improve his unicycles. Henderlong Enterprises is a welding shop located in a garage not far from Peck's house. Henderlong is shorter than Peck but probably twice his weight. The lower half of Henderlong's face is devoted to a terrific beard and mustache, between which is inserted a steady stream of Marlboros. He wears a patch over his right eye. On the floor of his garage is a masking tape outline of a body, with a wrenchlike shape stenciled in the body's right hand. "That's the last guy who went into my toolbox without asking," he says. According to Peck, Henderlong is a genius with hot rod engines and cutting-edge unicycles. He customized Peck's shock-absorbing seat post. The two men can talk shop for hours; Peck always leaves with a new idea or two. "I'm tired of giving him six-packs of beer," Peck says, "but he won't take any money."

If you really want to make Peck mad, ask him if he is a clown. "That word makes my teeth set right at the top," he says. The image of unicycling, Peck fears, automatically brings clowns to mind. He has been asked more than once if he works for a circus. Some have wondered if he entertains at birthday parties. One person questioned whether riding a unicycle is an appropriate activity for a judge. "Unicycling is at the very bottom of the respectability curve," Peck says. "Nobody would accuse me of being irresponsible if I were a skier or a Rollerblader. I'm trying to get as far away from clowns as I possibly can." He tries not to use the term *unicycle* anymore: too circusy. He prefers to call what he rides a "cycle."

Sometimes Peck thinks that if he can only free his sport from the clown associations, nothing will stop rough-terrain cycling from becoming the next big thing. He likes to point out that unicycling has been around longer than bicycling: one of the original cycles, the "penny-farthing" with the giant front rim, was little more than a unicycle with a training wheel. Combine modern materials with the old idea, toss in a few log jumps, and rough-terrain cycling should be Olympics bound: "Bored teenagers in California will be hopping their cycles over their Volkswagens."

Then he thinks better of it. "Cycling is safe and slow," he says, "and safe and slow are unhip. People want sports that are like video games. Maybe that's why there are so few riders." Peck estimates that there are perhaps two hundred muni participants worldwide, including a club based in England and a Frenchman, Thierry Bouche, who has unicycled down a twenty-thousand-foot peak in South America. No company in the United States sells mountain unicycles (with so few riders, there's no incentive to manufacture them), and without good cycles available, there won't be many more converts.

The sport is nearly certain to stay tiny. And in Seward, at least, it is likely to remain a solitary pursuit. Peck hasn't let this discourage him. Recently, his cycling entered an entirely new phase. He acquired a contraption called an ultimate wheel, which is a unicycle without a seat—just a wheel and two pedals. It looks impossible to ride, even when Peck is riding it. It took a month of intense Ultimate Wheel training, combined with the skills of years of unicycling, for him to balance on the thing. He says he's glommed on to it. Carol says it's a new level of obsession. He and Henderlong are sure to re-equip it with sturdier parts. And Peck is already riding it up and down Alaska's mountains.

4. Children with bicycles in Kotzebue, Alaska, 1968.
Dove Kull Papers, Archives and Special Collections,
Consortium Library, University of Alaska Anchorage.

5. Bill Fuller, near Fairbanks, pulling firewood, ca. 1973–2001. Photo by John D. Lyle. John D. Lyle Papers, Archives, University of Alaska Fairbanks.

6. (*opposite top*) George Peck on mountain unicycle overlooking Resurrection Bay near Seward, Alaska, ca. 1990s. Courtesy of George Peck.

7. (*opposite bottom*) Gail Koepf being passed by a Junior Iditarod dog team near Skwentna, Alaska, in 2002. Photo by Rocky Reifenstuhl. Courtesy of Gail Koepf.

PART 3

Wheels Now, 2001–2021

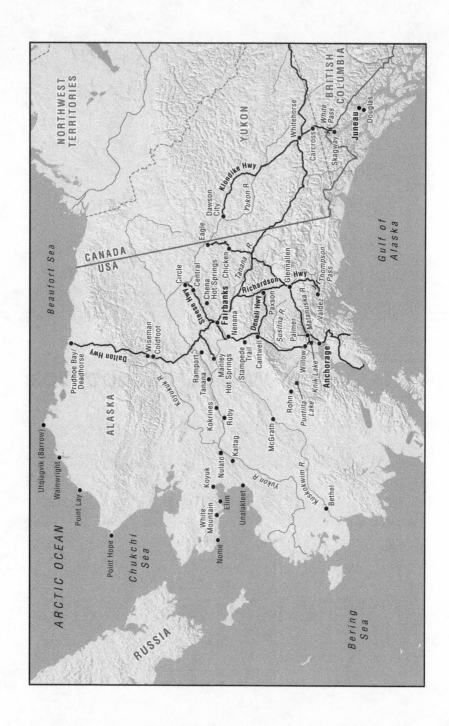

Map 3. Place names described in the contemporary stories. Map by Erin Greb.

Introduction

JESSICA CHERRY

The way he tells it, Nick Hanson launched his BMX bike off the highest coastal sand cliff in Unalakleet, Alaska, in the state of profound despair and grief of one who was done with living. By the time he landed, unharmed, he was in a completely different state of mind. "Man, I wish I'd filmed that jump!" This is precisely the kind of gift a bicycle can help provide: a lifeline back to safety on our darkest days. A place to spin our wheels can be a very good thing. Hanson would go from being a young competitor in the World Eskimo and Indian Olympics to become one of Alaska's most creative and courageous athletes of all time. When a kid in Unalakleet introduced him to the American Ninja competition, the two of them began constructing a training course on the beach in western Alaska. As I write this, Nick is on his way back to Los Angeles to film his seventh Ninja competition. Between competitions he serves as a motivational speaker and a mental health advocate for youth in rural Alaska.

In this final section of our book, nearly all of our authors call out the unique challenges of surviving and being healthy in Alaska, both the physical and mental challenges. Some of the pieces we have here touch gently (Amore) or more strongly (Reardon and Magnetek) on the economic and cultural disparities of our state, the experience of racism, and how the bicycle as a vehicle rides through that uncomfortable space. The narrator of one of the most amazing cycling stories I have ever heard is no longer with us. Philip Tattayuna Penatac grew up in Nome and was living outdoors, year round, in a tent in Fairbanks where one of our authors, Jeff Oatley, ran into him frequently. Philip was an enthusiastic cyclist who dreamed of competing in the Iditarod Trail Invitational and riding victoriously into his hometown under the ceremonial wooden arch of the famous trail. He also spoke of that community as a painful place to which he simply could not return. Instead, Philip managed to compete in the Tanana River Challenge in 2013, which is a winter race on the frozen Tanana River between Fairbanks and Nenana. Forty-five miles before the end of the race, Philip experienced a myocardial infarction, a heart attack. Somehow he still finished and was driven back to Fairbanks, to the hospital there, and treated. Two years later he'd go on to bike the Denali Highway. Despite his traumatic past, his battle with mental and physical health, and his life without a house in one of the world's harshest climates, Philip never lost the dream of cycling. I wish he was here to tell his own story, but he passed away in 2019.

There are other stories about contemporary Alaska that are missing here. We had hoped to have more pieces by veterans or active-duty members of the armed services. In the summer of 2020 a team of intrepid cyclists from the 354th Contracting Squadron at Eielson Air Force Base, near Fairbanks, were cycling the Steese Highway from Fairbanks up to Circle City, on the Yukon River near the Arctic Circle, when at 6:00 a.m. a tragic accident occurred just west of the community of Central. The young but decorated squadron commander, Maj. Michael "Cal" Gentry, was struck and killed by the support vehicle his friend was driving. What did it mean to Cal Gentry and his friends to ride the remote Steese Highway on a late-summer morning? How does the passion and commitment to cycling among these men compare to, or offer an escape from, their experiences in the unending wars of our present time? We won't know. We hope that in pulling together this collection, more of their stories will emerge.

Despite these particular omissions and many others unnamed, we have tried to find an assortment of contemporary personal essays and stories that describe a range of experiences by Alaskan cyclists who are able to put their stories on the page. Some of these authors, such as Clint Hodges, Luc Mehl, Bjørn Olson, and Lael Wilcox are serious, Alaska-born riders who also write prolifically for web-based outlets, their work accompanied by stunning visual media. For other elite riders, such as Jeff Oatley, this is the first time they have tried to write openly about their chosen pursuit. We have another group of authors who are professional writers, activists, lawyers, doctors, engineers, or teachers who are also cyclists.

Reading and writing a personal essay both require wandering down a proverbial trail, not unlike the riding of a bicycle. In the first part of this book, we got a glimpse into the lives of cyclists in the middle of a profound shift in Alaska's history: the gold rush. In the second part of this book, we jumped forward to another settlement boom driven by resource extraction—the oil pipeline—but also a generation of settlers who, conversely, wanted to live closer to nature. In the third and last part, the narratives unfold in the near present, when Alaska is confronting a very uncertain future. The frontier hasn't so much closed as it has disappeared as a figment of the colonial imagination. The choices in today's Alaska are playing out in stricter legal, economic, and cultural frameworks, as they must. If the world decides, in fact, that fossil fuels do more damage than good, where does that leave a largely resource-based economy? How much of the state will turn to ecotourism and recreation, as rising personal income in countries such as China and India encourage whole new waves of visitors? Transportation, trails, land use, and development are all part of this story that we are currently writing together. For many of us living here now, bicycling is not just our means for coping with modern life but our vision for a better, more inclusive, more sustainable future.

—Anchorage, 2021

The Wind Grooms Our Trails DANIEL SMITH

It seemed to me something like a vision quest. I was the hottest I'd ever been and slick with my own sweat. The barrel stove a few feet in front of me glowed red as if translucent, showing the fire roaring inside. I squirmed uncomfortably away, but there was no refuge in the squat little sauna, and in my nakedness I was defenseless against the searing heat. I splashed tepid water on my knees and shoulders, but it did little to soothe their burning. I felt light-headed, a little detached, vaguely wondering if this was even safe or if my skin might start bubbling.

"The wind's letting all the heat out of my sauna," the man next to me said. He leaned forward to adjust the blanket weatherproofing on the short, lopsided door, accentuating his own nakedness in the dim light. He said he'd been using this sauna for sixty-six years; he was used to the heat. I was not.

"I threw a hunk of seal meat in there. That stuff is pure BTUs, should get it going," he said, stretching himself out on the wood slat floor next to the stove. He rubbed his aching knees and grunted.

He never called it a vision quest; he called it a journey. I hadn't realized it was anything other than a sauna, but as soon as we got inside, the talk turned spiritual. He said that the sauna was a place to think and reflect, to talk or be silent, to find new ideas and solutions to problems.

"You might leave the sauna with something you didn't have before," he said.

Most of all he talked about *aŋaayun* (pronounced with a nasal -*ng* at the beginning). *Aŋaayun* didn't create the wind and the rain, he said; *aŋaayun is* the wind and the rain. He offered thanks, *quyaana aŋaayun*, as he threw four splashes of water on the stove, one for each cardinal direction, then threw some on the wall so it wouldn't catch on fire. The water cracked and hissed violently on the stove and steamed away.

It was his turn to speak, so he spoke of *aŋaayun*, and I was content to listen. His words seemed to echo out of the past and resonate in the humid air around us; they confused the flow of time, and I felt I might have been sitting in any of the sauna's sixty-six years or in some era much older. They lulled my mind away from the heat, allowing it to wander.

Aŋaayun *didn't create the wind and the rain;* aŋaayun is *the wind and the rain.* I listened to the wind howling outside, knocking on the door, plastering the sauna with wet snow. *If you're looking for* aŋaayun, *you've already found it.* The wind is always blowing here; it's hard to escape unless indoors, and then it rattles the walls around you. *Quyaana aŋaayun.*

My mind returned when he started talking about biking. He said he'd seen us riding our fat bikes around the village and our tracks out on the sea ice and embedded in snowmachine trails. He invited us over because he recognizes that we're outdoors people and outdoors people are usually of sound mind, so he was curious about us and wanted to get to know his neighbors.

As a newcomer to the village, this felt like validation from a respected hunter and dog musher who had spent his life in the wind and the rain. He had also acknowledged my source of pride: the five-inch-wide tire track my bike leaves like a ribbon laid across the land. The wind often blows away the uncompacted snow around the tracks, leaving long ridges like strange snakes slithering across tundra and sea ice alike—a curious sight among snowmachine tracks and the deep footprints of musk ox. My tracks serve as arguments for fat bikes as instruments of adventure, novel yet worthy of this landscape. They're a sign that reads "I was here too."

It was a couple weeks before the sauna that Teresa and I had run into him out on the ice. He and two other guys were collecting driftwood logs and caught up to us as we rode home beneath the cliffs west of town. The first one of them to reach us stopped and killed the engine of his snowmachine.

"I thought I was seeing things!" he exclaimed, surprised that the two small shapes on the ice in front of him had materialized into people on bicycles. The wind was cold and rising, but we stood and chatted on the ice, an encounter as old as the Iñupiat themselves. It wasn't long until our neighbor and his friend caught up and talked with Teresa while I waited ahead. I was happy to be seen outside, on the ice and in the weather. Increasing our association with the land increases our connection to the community; people know us from biking around town and from finding our tracks. They always ask where we went riding, then ask if we saw any animals. In this instance we were invited to a sauna.

We had started the ride by following a snowmachine trail out of town, climbing a series of long, gradual hills until we overlooked the ice to the west and the mountains to the south. The land here is rolling and smooth with snow like the sensuous curves of a body, coming together in drainages like pressing flesh, brown willows sprouting from the folds like hair. We followed one such drainage back down to the beach, flying down a gentle sidehill on wind-packed snow so hard we left no tracks. The willows rushed past. It's a rare and precious thing here to move without pedaling, and now we were soaring down the long drainage. My wide grin pulled at the frozen hairs of my beard.

We landed on a frozen lagoon behind the beach where the sun was shining blindingly but the wind was searing, burning the exposed skin around my eyes. We rode home under the tall, rocky cliffs that rise above the sea, clinging to them against the looming vastness to our left, where the sea ice stretched away to the horizon, giving the feeling we were biking along the edge of the earth. The snow was blown in awkward drifts that we stumbled over and threaded our way through, a stark contrast to the smooth descent down from the hills. We followed in the snowmachiners' tracks once they left us.

We either make our own trails or follow snowmachines, but the wind grooms our trails more than anything, deciding when and where we ride. Some days it feels like there's nowhere to go, when the wind piles up the snow in soft, impassible patterns and drifts that we churn through then turn for home. Some days the wind scours away the loose snow, leaving the snowmachine trails firm and the sea ice an endless canvas on which to paint our tracks. A well-balanced bike ride has some of both, the agony and the ecstasy all at once.

I used to snowshoe up and down the hill of a favorite route near town to pack the trail, but the relentless winter storms negated my work until I conceded and just rode on top of the wavelike drifts that curled and crashed against the hillside like a surreal single track. Snowdrifts are the technical terrain in this stretched-out landscape, offering the steepest angles and the quickest turns. They're extraordinary sculptures left in the wake of blizzards, more carved than compounded and baked hard in the kiln of the cold. They swell and ebb against buildings and spill across roads. But no matter how delicately formed or intricately patterned, I can't resist laying a five-inch-wide rut down any drift solid enough to hold me. Art destroys art.

I miss the labyrinthine trails of Anchorage, carved out of the woods by fat bikers like the patterns chewed into tree bark by beetles, but I feel like fat biking here is stripped down to its essence of using a bike to move over the land. It feels organic without groomed trails, bouncing over the postholes left by musk ox, but never the ruts of another biker. It feels timeless, a modern means of doing what people have always done here. And it feels holistic as I contend with the tough conditions and revel in the good. The frustrations and exhilarations are both amplified, but the satisfaction of the adventure tips the scales to being worth the effort.

We were home off the sea ice just four hours after leaving, having traversed a world-class route from our front door and satisfied to think that we were fat biking on new frontiers.

It was the part of the sauna when we acknowledge the uncountable things, he said. All the willows on the tundra, all the thoughts in people's minds—there's too many to know, so we acknowledge them all. He might have thrown more water against the snarling stove, but I was too overwhelmed with the relentless heat to notice. I squirmed and gulped for air like a salmon on the shore. I didn't want to appear weak, especially after he had just acknowledged a kinship between us, but better that than to pass out. So I excused myself and crawled out of the knee-high door, not bothering to grab my towel on my way out into the weather.

I leaned on an upturned icebox and breathed the cold air, thinking about how this "journey" had deteriorated to standing ass-out in the wind of a winter storm, getting pelted with wet, stinging snow from head to toe and all the sensitive bits in between. After I caught my breath, I looked up, squinting against the flying snow, and saw the entire dog lot staring back at me, sitting calmly, unperturbed by the weather.

Shame, their eyes said.

It occurred to me that human eyes might see me as well, and I hoped the ladies inside weren't looking out or that no one would drive by and see the *naluaŋmiu*'s pale butt reflecting the headlights of their snow-machine like the moon. I wondered if maybe I should have worn my bathing suit after all. I had debated whether or not it was sauna etiquette, but once inside, I'd realized just how ridiculous my tropical toucan swim trunks would have looked next to a naked Iñupiaq man in a sauna that's been slowly sinking into the permafrost for most of a century. They would have been anachronistic at best, tying me to the present instead of letting the journey take me where it would. At worst they would have been—

Embarrassing, the dogs said.

When I returned to the sauna, I felt refreshed, like I'd passed through the suffering and could enjoy the experience again. We talked about the weather, the village, and its people, but the conversation kept going back to the land and to biking.

He said we'd be real happy to have our bikes in the spring, describing how the snow melts and drains away, leaving the sea ice perfectly smooth. He said he likes to go out on a sled and just sit in the middle of the bay in a T-shirt.

"You don't need no acid or nothing—the mirages go up real crazy," he said.

I closed my eyes and tried to imagine such a day. After so many months of winter, it seemed almost fantastical, but in the radiating heat from the stove, it was easy to feel the sun's warmth on my arms. I heard the crunch of studded tires gripping the ice. I saw mountains floating over the horizon, disconnected from the earth like islands in the sky. I felt that I was floating, too, frictionless over the ice, and that I might go anywhere like a raven in the air. The wind and the rain were nowhere in sight. It was as surreal as he'd said.

The storm knocking on the wooden walls opened my eyes. The vision was gone, and *aŋaayun* was all around us. We were sheltered in a tiny sauna but still consumed by it. We sat and listened to it rage against the walls, and I thought about how he had said that I might leave the sauna with something I hadn't had before. True enough, I was developing splotches of heat rash on my shoulders and knees, dark red like the hunk of musk ox meat his wife had given us. She had been sitting on the floor when we arrived, slicing up the entire haunch, the hairy hoof detached and weighing down one corner of the cardboard cutting board.

I thought of all the musk ox out on the tundra, exposed to the storm as I had been. I could still feel the phantom sting of snow where it had pelted my skin and wondered if the musk ox felt it at all through their burly coats. They're much hardier than I am, but still the wind blows on us both. It forms a connection between us. I had just felt the wind blow over me the same as it does the musk ox and the mountains and was beginning to realize that the wind connects *everything* here.

Aŋaayun is the wind and the rain, he'd said, but I saw it now as more holistic, not just the elements but everything they touch as well. I imagined *aŋaayun* as the hub of a wheel from which everything radiates like spokes, each its own entity but all connected to the center they revolve around. Musk ox, snowdrifts, and sea ice are *aŋaayun*, and I am too. I wondered if this was the destination of the journey, if I had found what I hadn't had before.

I thought about how my fat bike serves as a conduit connecting me to *aŋaayun* and its wheel. My bike carries me up and down the dynamic drifts the wind deposits and destroys. It allows me to travel over the land the same as foxes and musk ox always have, leaving my tracks in the snow alongside theirs. Biking here revolves around the whims of the wind and the rain, so I do too. Maybe this is what our neighbor had seen in Teresa and I in the first place, what he meant by us being outdoors people: that we, too, are groomed by the wind and the rain the same as the trails we ride. *Quyaana aŋaayun.*

Skagway to Nome

JEFF OATLEY

On December 31, 2015, I decided to try to ride the Yukon Quest Trail. I didn't know if anybody had ridden the entire Yukon Quest Trail before. That wasn't part of my thought process. I knew my friend Andy Sterns and two others had ridden a chunk of it. I also knew that Mike Curiak and Pat Irwin, two legitimate winter biking legends, had ridden a section of it too. I'd always thought I'd ride it at some point. I needed to do something different. It seemed like that time had arrived.

The Yukon Quest is a thousand-mile sled dog race. I tend to think of the Quest as the "real" long-distance sled dog race, not the Iditarod. The Iditarod starts in March, with the return of the sun to the North country. The Quest races out of the darkness of January. The Iditarod gets the attention, but the Quest is tougher. The terrain is more challenging, with more climbing, four major summits, and the potential for *severe* winter weather on all of them. But it's where it falls on the calendar that sets it apart. It's the darkness and the cold of an interior subarctic winter.

Part of the challenge of riding the Quest Trail is that a large chunk of it only exists from the time the Quest trailbreakers put it in right before the race, until the first snow or windstorm after the last musher passes. Some years that's a short window. The other part of the challenge is that you've got to cover some long, lonely stretches of trail, during a reliably cold and dark part of the winter. It's intimidating.

I didn't put a lot of planning into it in January 2016. I managed to get food drops out to some of the more remote areas and planned to figure the rest of it out as I went. If I made it to Whitehorse . . . fine.

If not . . . fine too. I needed to do something different. I needed to get moving again. I liked the idea of spending some time alone on the trail.

A few weeks later, my wife, Heather Best, and I rode our bikes down our driveway and pointed them toward Whitehorse. She rode the first 220 miles to Circle with me . . . three beautiful days . . . great weather, great northern lights. From Circle she hitched a ride back to Fairbanks, and I headed up the Yukon River.

After she went home, I settled into the rhythm of being solo on the trail. Over the next twelve or thirteen days of solitude, I had an amazing trip across a beautiful, if sometimes a little harsh, Interior Alaska and Yukon landscape. I saw thousands of wolf tracks. I saw a few wolves. I saw caribou and moose. I saw the northern lights. I felt the sting of the wind as it rolled down the rivers feeding the Yukon, causing drifting and bike pushing at each of their mouths. I slept in trapper's cabins that seemed like they'd been there forever. It felt like I had traveled through time as much as through wilderness.

I'd left Fairbanks a week ahead of the mushers. I wanted to cover as much of the route as I could before the race caught and passed me. I figured that'd reduce my chances of getting stuck if a storm came through after they had passed me. But with no traffic, and some windy areas, leaving that far ahead meant I had to do a lot of trail breaking by myself. There weren't many easy days once I hit the Yukon River. Most of it was just slow riding. A little bit was tough pushing. Lots of windblown snow.

I went almost six hundred miles without seeing anybody else out on the trail. I went three straight days without talking to anybody, other than myself. It was incredible to be so far out in the country and not have another soul around. I probably should have felt pretty vulnerable, because I probably was. But I mostly felt . . . larger-than-life . . . like I just had the shot of tequila right before the one that was one too many.

The Canadian Rangers breaking the Yukon Quest Trail caught up to me about 30 miles outside of Braeburn, Yukon, only 120 miles from the finish in Whitehorse. I was in my sleeping bag just off the edge of the trail in a nice camp spot under some pine trees. Led by the legendary Ranger Bob Daffe, they said that they'd been following my tracks a long time and looked at me a little bewildered. I think they were having trouble believing that I was out there by myself . . . on a bicycle. I think they were also having a hard time believing that it had taken them four hundred miles to catch me. It was one of those rare times when I felt like what I was doing wasn't normal . . . or was maybe "Fairbanks normal."

I made it to Whitehorse two days later. I had mixed feelings at the finish line. I didn't want to stop. I've always had mixed feelings at the finish of a big race. But this was different. This ride (mostly) lacked the stress of sleep deprivation and consequently lacked the relief that comes when that stress ends. I loved being alone on the trail; riding, eating, sleeping; and doing each of those things whenever I wanted. I rode relatively fast and was efficient on and off the bike. Things that had served me well during many races. But I stayed well rested and mentally engaged the entire trip. My longest day was probably seventeen or nineteen hours. But most stayed close to twelve hours. That might sound like a long day on a bike. But it's not. Twelve hours is civilized. It's twelve hours off the bike too. Plenty of time to rest.

I'd gotten to Whitehorse without thinking much about how I'd get home. I had thoughts of turning around and riding back. The risk of the trail being gone and the lack of food drops made that too tall of a task. Plus, I hadn't accounted for being gone for a month. I booked a flight from Whitehorse to Fairbanks, via Vancouver and Seattle. The only route available and twenty hours of travel time. I could get to Miami faster.

Sitting in the Vancouver airport, having a pre-lunch beer, I remember thinking that if I did the Quest Trail the other direction, I could then take some trails from Fairbanks back up to the Yukon River at Tanana. From there I'd just have to travel a lightly used 120 miles of trail from Tanana to Ruby, where I could get back onto the Iditarod superhighway and take it the rest of the way to Nome. It would be a huge trip!

It was clearly a great idea! For the next ten months I mostly didn't think about it. Then in December I brought it up to Heather. Then I brought it up at work. They seemed okay with me being gone for thirty days, plus or minus. Heather immediately started planning the sections she wanted to ride with me, and the logistics of meeting me and extricating herself. I think I went from not really thinking or talking about the trip to being fully committed in about twenty-four hours.

The route has some historical context as the travel corridor of the gold rush era. Heather and I have traveled some of that country in the summer. We've hiked the Chilkoot Trail, floated the Fortymile River and sections of the Yukon River, and we've read books on the history of the gold rush.

Probably thirty thousand people made their way north during the gold rush from 1897 to 1904. Almost nobody made any money gold mining. Most of the money was made *off* gold miners. I can't help but think that as much as "gold fever" was a real thing, most of those people, if they weren't doing it simply as an adventure, were led to do it by their innate sense of adventure. They had hopes of striking it rich. But they knew they were in for an adventure. That's what I wanted. Why not retrace my own version of that route?

Then I decided that I should start in Skagway, where most of the gold rushers had entered the country. And I decided to arrive there by boat, like they did. And I decided I should travel over Chilkoot Pass, like they did. Then I realized that would likely result in me being killed in an avalanche 12 miles into a 1,900-mile trip . . . Like some of them did. I decided to take White Pass (like some of them!) and stay on the highway until Carcross. With intel from friends in Whitehorse, I knew from there I could tie trails together to get to Whitehorse. After Whitehorse I knew the rest of the route to Nome. If I could average sixty miles a day, I could do it in about thirty-two days.

In late January I flew to Juneau, to hang out with my friends Dea and Ben, drink some beer, and get on a ferry to Skagway.

As Ben drove me to the Juneau ferry terminal in the predawn darkness, we didn't really talk much. When we got there, unloaded my gear, and said goodbye, Ben had this "Are you sure about this? It's not too late" look. And I just tried to have this "I got this" look. He snapped a picture, and I got on the ferry and settled into my thoughts.

As the ferry made its way up Chilkoot Inlet, into Taiya Inlet, and finally, as Skagway came into view, I think I was feeling what the stampeders had felt one hundred–plus years earlier. Not the ones who had gold fever, which I very clearly do not have. But the ones who were looking for an adventure. Holy shit . . . this is gonna happen!

I was excited to panic levels. I got off the ferry, had somebody take a picture, and started riding. I wasn't in Skagway five minutes. It was thirty-five degrees Fahrenheit in Skagway and minus ten at White Pass, about twelve miles later. I was happy to be back in the cold. I get by okay in warm temperatures, but my gear, preparation, and mentality are biased toward the cold.

In the fifty or so miles between White Pass and Carcross, I was passed by one vehicle and had amazing northern lights. I was startled by the WELCOME TO BRITISH COLUMBIA sign. I hadn't thought about the little sliver of BC that I would cross through between Alaska and the Yukon. I stopped a couple times to snack and took a few extra minutes each time to turn my headlamp off and watch the light show. The next morning I left Carcross on trails. A few wrong turns and dead-end trails later, I made it to Whitehorse. The ride from Skagway had gone well. Two days . . . 125 miles. Right on schedule.

In Whitehorse I met up with the Wild & Free team . . . friends from Fairbanks. They were there to race the Yukon Quest. They'd taken me in the previous year when I arrived in Whitehorse without a plan. They did it again this time. After a "meet the mushers" event, we had some beers at the curling club. The next morning I hit the trail. I left Whitehorse two days ahead of the mushers. Much better timed than the previous year. No trail breaking to Fairbanks.

The ride from Whitehorse to Eagle was mostly fast and always cold. Temperatures hit minus fifty degrees Fahrenheit a few days. Luckily, it didn't get much colder than that—some of that country can. After leaving the Pelly River, the firm, fast trail and cold temperatures made it difficult to regulate my temperature and keep skin covered. It's an up-and-down section trail. I got too warm on a few climbs and then quickly got too cold on the descents. I frost-nipped my nose and cheeks a little bit. I flash-froze a few fingertips picking up a titanium pot at minus fifty-something.

The Quest leaders passed me at the Scroggy Creek cabin. It was deep in the Yukon gold country, near the Stewart River, on a negative-forty-five-degree night. I stayed up most of the night, watching the dog teams and frost-coated mushers going about their business, outside of an uninsulated plywood shack. It felt like I was *in* a Robert Service poem.

I climbed slowly for several hours, away from negative fifty on the

Indian River to minus twenty on the four-thousand-foot-high King Solomon's Dome, twenty miles outside of Dawson City. Traversing King Solomon's Dome was the most magical night I've ever experienced on a bike . . . or off one. Four thousand feet above sea level in the interior is essentially the stratosphere. It was so eerily calm and peaceful. The moon was bright enough that I didn't need a headlight to ride. The snow sparkled like millions of diamonds. The silence was overwhelming. I've marveled at nights like that hundreds of times on a trail, usually deep in the middle of nowhere. Everything about this felt different. Like those nights were somehow cheap imitations of this one. I don't know why, but this night felt singular. Palpably different, serene, and ethereal. Dreamlike.

I took a layover day in Dawson to hang out with friends. That hilly seventeen-hour day, in those temperatures, had taken a lot out of me. I had a goal of getting to Nome. But I make a pretty serious effort to tamp down the mentality that a bike ride is anything other than just that. It's not an "expedition." I can approach it seriously without giving it its own seriousness, I think. Keeping that mentality can be a struggle. When you're alone on the trail, battling everything from the weather to your own thoughts, it can feel dramatic at times, and it can feel like you really are doing *something*. I was determined to not lose sight of the fact that this was a fun trip . . . a bike ride. Just a bike ride. It would be long. At times it would be difficult. But it was my vacation. I was out there to have an adventure and to have fun. Hanging out with Wild & Free, drinking beers with Yukon Quest folks . . . that was going to be more fun than a night on the trail. If my trip had ended before I left Dawson the next day, I wouldn't have been disappointed. Well, I would have been. But I'd have been able to find solace in how much fun I'd had while it lasted. It would have been one of the most fun rides I'd ever done. I was doing it the way that I'd hoped, and I was only 650 miles into it.

A couple days later, descending from American Summit toward Eagle, Alaska, I met Heather on her bike riding toward me. She had flown into Eagle that day to join me for the ride to Fairbanks. I was giddy to see her. I'm occasionally torn between wanting to ride with her and wanting to spend some time riding by myself. Whenever I've done enough of one, I always want the other. By this point I'd had plenty of alone time.

The next morning we left Eagle and headed down the Yukon River. It was a bright sunny day, and temperatures bounced between minus twenty and minus forty for no obvious reason. The beautiful day and being with Heather boosted my already high spirits.

Riding with her is tangibly different than riding solo. She asked if I wanted to lead. I didn't. After ten days of being completely alone on the trail and making every decision, and finding and following every line, it felt good to follow, to put the micro-decisions in her hands and make a few other decisions by committee. It was immediate stress relief. Stress that I hadn't realized was there until it was gone.

After an only mildly eventful trip down the Yukon River—a normal amount of wind, filling my pants with water from my CamelBak, visiting friends along and on the trail, almost burning a dilapidated cabin down when my stove leaked fuel—we left the Yukon River at Circle. Two days later, on a sunny, calm, and warm afternoon, we pushed our bikes to the top of the absurdly steep Eagle Summit climb. While taking a break at the top, I told Heather that the next big climb, Rosebud Summit, would be a piece of cake . . . that I had "summit magic" on this trip. Five hours later we felt our way across the three-mile traverse of Rosebud in a howling, blinding blizzard. I did not learn a thing about opening my mouth from that.

Arriving in Fairbanks, we rode off the Chena River and straight to our house in the hills north of town. The next evening, a few more food drops in the mail and a little bike maintenance done by my buddy Jeff Gillmore, we rode out of town on the Dunbar Trail. We connected with the Old Manley Mail Trail and were headed back toward the Yukon River.

Heading into Manley, we ran into our friend Ed Plumb skiing toward us. Heather had talked Ed into driving the 150 miles to Manley to pick her up and take her back to Fairbanks. That allowed her to ride another two days with me instead of ending her trip at our home in Fairbanks. Things had gone well since she joined me in Eagle about a week earlier. She wanted a couple more days of riding. One of the first things Ed said was, "You'd better get going. There are going to be three snowstorms in a row coming up the Yukon River."

I didn't linger in Manley. I ate half a calzone and stuffed the rest in a pack and took off. Heather and Ed went and soaked in a hot spring before driving home. I knew what was coming. I had to choose between the unmarked river trail and the Tofty Road route, which is just a trail in the winter. The road would be higher and maybe windier but easier to navigate if it got really snowy and blowy. I usually prefer overland travel, so I took the Tofty route.

You can't expect to cross 1,900 miles of subarctic winter and have every day be blue skies and firm trails. It doesn't work like that. Truthfully, I want some of the days to be hard. I'm okay with a few of them being very hard. I want to be pushed to my limits occasionally. Snow biking is good for that. When it's good, it's kind of incredible. But when it gets bad, it can get so ridiculously, stupidly difficult. On some level I'm sure that is part of the attraction to me.

As I pedaled toward Tanana and the Yukon River, the wind increased but wasn't much of a problem. A little minor drifting. Some short hikes. When I arrived at Tanana about 10:00 p.m., the first snowstorm was cranking up. Good timing. I'd ridden ninety miles that day. Somebody let me into the school; I found my food drop and settled in for some sleep. I knew there wouldn't be much trail left by morning, but there was no point worrying about that.

By morning the snow had stopped, and the temperature had dropped quite a bit. I knew the 120 miles to Ruby was going to be a tough slog. I slipped out of town quietly. There're always a handful of trails leaving a village. Some go to cabins; some go to traplines, hunting or fishing grounds, woodcutting areas; some connect to other villages. It's not always obvious which one you want. When lacking better intel, my rule of thumb is always "take the best trail."

None of the trail choices I could find were good. They were all blown in. I left Tanana on a trail that immediately went out toward the middle of the Yukon River. It wasn't close to rideable. It felt wrong from the start. I pushed my bike about eight miles in five or six hours. The trail had more or less completely disappeared. I knew it wasn't going to work anyway. With more storms coming soon, it was just a math problem. Really, it's all just math. I had slowed down to under one mile per hour. The trail wasn't going to get better anytime soon. The trail was gone. It was probably the wrong trail anyway. I was pretty sure of that. In the end it was the math that turned me around. I had five days of food. Not enough to go 120 miles at these speeds.

I spend a lot of time doing math on the trail. The most common math is just distance divided by speed. Time. Even when I don't care about time, I still want to know. I also spend a lot of time telling myself to stop doing math.

I turned around and went straight to the store in Tanana and bought as much food as I thought I could put on my bike. I figured I was good for eight days. Then a truck with a load of survey lath passed me. I knew right away that the lath would mark the Iron Dog Trail for the snowmachines that would race through on their way to Fairbanks later that week. I chased down the truck and asked the driver if he knew when the trail would be marked. "Nope."

I needed information. I needed a plan. I couldn't sit in Tanana and wait for the Iron Dog to show up in a week. I called Heather. She urged me to leave my stuff in Tanana and fly home for a week, then fly back after the storms and the Iron Dog had passed through. It was probably a good idea but didn't feel right to me. I wanted to see this through in one go or let it end where I got stopped. But I wasn't ready to stop yet. I didn't want to let the weather dictate all the terms. If I have an ethos at all, that goes against it.

Over two decades of winter biking in Alaska, I've just learned to accept that the weather will be the weather. Traveling by human power is simple: keep moving forward, and you get there. Sometimes you move fast, and sometimes you move slow. Take what you can get. You'll get there eventually. Other than what it does to pace, weather seems almost incidental to me. You've got to be prepared for it. But in an Alaska winter, on a trip of any length, weather generally averages itself out. I was pretty far ahead on this trip.

After restocking my food supplies, I went back to the school looking for Arnold Marks Jr., a teacher, to try to get some trail intel from him. Arnold grew up in Tanana, and he and his brother Aaron had raced the Iron Dog. They knew all the trails, cabins, and people in that country.

Arnold said Roger Huntington was snowmachining to Tanana that afternoon, from Kokrine Hills Bible Camp, located about sixty miles downstream. This was great news! It meant I'd have a trail to follow and could leave Tanana the next morning. He told me of a trail to avoid that would look like the main trail but would dead-end on the wrong side of the river. And finally, he told me that he'd let Carole Huntington, at Bible Camp, know that I was coming that way. This was a gold mine of valuable information. I was ready to take another swing in the morning.

When I got up the next morning, it was about negative fifty degrees in Tanana. I knew it'd be a little colder when I dropped down on the Yukon. I wasn't that excited to leave, but I slowly got my gear together and rolled out of the school by 8:30 a.m. It was *really* cold on the river. I knew that I needed to be deliberate with everything I did so that I didn't cause any problems for myself. Then decided to put air in my tires but instead let all the air out of my front tire. My pump was too cold to seal on the valve stem. I put the pump inside my jacket and pushed my flat tire bike for twenty minutes until the pump was warm enough to work. Then stopped, pumped up the tire, and pushed the pace for a half hour to get some heat going. Stopping is the enemy. You don't want to stop at those temperatures.

The day was a grind. Roger's trail was mostly rideable, but it was also mostly very slow. The cold combined with the high-effort riding really tapped my energy. The human body is not an efficient machine at cold temperatures. Bike tires also become very stiff and inefficient at cold temperatures. It's a double whammy. The upside is that working hard and traveling slowly is an effective way to stay warm when it's really cold.

Almost all the 275 miles of trail between Tanana and Kaltag is somewhere on the middle of the Yukon River. Since the trail is out on the river the entire way, you're pretty much stuck on the trail. The trail is always the safest place to be. The best thing that happens if you get off the trail is that you flounder in snow. Everything else is worse than that. These trails are put in by people who live and travel this country. They know the safe places to travel and the places you *must* avoid. I stick to their routes. There aren't many things less fun than putting a fresh trail in on a big river.

Around dark I stopped in the middle of the river to cook dinner. It was still plenty cold. I couldn't get my fuel pump to work very well. I tried putting it in my jacket. I'm basically a one-trick pony. If something doesn't work, I put it in my pocket. It didn't help much. It was too cold to try to take it apart. The stove would run but just barely. I let it flicker under a pot of water for a few minutes while I jogged and walked back and forth on the trail, then gave up and poured lukewarm water into a Mountain House packet and got moving again.

It was a struggle to get warm again after stopping. I knew I needed more food and water. It's easy to get behind on eating and drinking when it's cold. You don't want to take care of yourself. You just want to keep moving. So you don't do it as often as you need to. I managed to eat the cold, not-very-rehydrated meal. It was gross. But it was calories.

A couple hours later the weather began changing rapidly. Storm number two starting. It went from around -minus thirty to zero in an hour or two, and a headwind started gusting. Just like the night I got to Tanana, right as I arrived at Bible Camp, the storm was getting intense. There was one light on in the only building I could see at Bible Camp. I knocked. Carole Huntington came to the door. She was clearly surprised and uncertain about what to do with me. I guess Arnold forgot to let her know I was headed her way. All she knew was . . . some fool on a bicycle in a blizzard . . . in the middle of the night . . . on the Middle Yukon . . . not normal. She told me I couldn't come in, that her husband was gone. I said that was fine, that I was okay, and asked if she minded if I slept in her woodshed . . . it looked mostly sheltered and comfortable enough. She asked if I had food. I told her I was fine and had everything I needed. We chatted for a few more minutes. She told me to come in and sleep on the couch. I still don't dismiss what an act of kindness that was by her. She was all by herself, in the middle of both the night and nowhere, and welcomed a stranger, about whom she was most likely questioning the sanity, into her home. How many of us would do that?

Even though I knew it was futile, I tried to leave in the morning. Over a foot of new snow had fallen overnight, with plenty of wind. It was still coming down. Once again, there was no trail at all. I post-holed from the cabin on the north side of the river across to the south side of the river. I couldn't find a hint of a trail anywhere. I returned to Bible Camp. In five hours I'd gone less than three miles . . . more bad math.

I spent most of the next day and a half on the couch while storm number two played out. Carole and I chatted. I've always enjoyed meeting folks while I'm out on rides. Even when I only spend an hour or two with them, I try to learn a couple things. I rarely get to spend as much time with people as I did with Carole. She fed me cookies and moose ribs and filled me in on the river gossip. Which almost completely involves who is traveling where and when. Or why they had not shown up. People who live out there really try to keep track of each other. They send messages up and down the river on Facebook Messenger when somebody is traveling. They all stop at Carole and Roger's place. After they do, Carole sends messages, so others know their progress and start watching for them. It's a tracking system and a real safety net.

This gets at the reason I try to keep in mind that these rides are just vacations, no matter how long, what time of year, or how much wilderness they might cross. I'm traveling trails that get used regularly by people who live in this country. On this route there were a couple sections that aren't traveled much by locals. But for the most part, my "adventure" is somebody else's commute. It's their trapline access, the route they take to get to the basketball game or to go see their parents and friends in a nearby village. I suppose if you come from outside of Alaska, this is hard to recognize. It just looks like "wilderness." But if you're going any distance on a bike in Alaska, in winter, you're on the trail of a snowmachine. Most of those are put there by people who live in that country.

I keep in mind that I'm not some kind of "explorer" out on a bicycle. Even when I'm stuck in a blizzard or camping at forty-five below and it does *feel* like I am an *explorer*. In many people's eyes it's fair to say that I'm probably not even an adventurer. Why would I look like anything other than another fool with too much time on my hands? I've chosen about the slowest possible way to get from point A to point B.

I don't discount the value of . . . whatever it is . . . that many of us have found by the end of a bike trip. I'm just pointing out that some of that is not necessarily obvious to the casual observer, and I think it's important to consider that point of view. Especially if you are occasionally depending on help from that casual observer of your silliness.

Anyhow . . . on my second morning at Bible Camp, it was still snowing. I wasn't going anywhere. Carole told me that she hadn't heard of anybody traveling the river but that she expected the Iron Dog trailbreakers the next day. The last of the three snowstorms was coming the next day too. The timing wasn't great.

The snow and dearth of traffic were big problems. I needed to update the plan. There was another family staying at Bible Camp. It was a much larger group of buildings than I'd realized that first night. They have up to 120 kids there at times during the summer and have a mess hall, dorms, and such. But that winter it was just Carole and Roger and another young family. The family was a young couple with three young children.

I knew if I left Bible Camp on foot, with my bike, I was likely to get stuck . . . having to be rescued, stuck. I talked to the father about borrowing some snowshoes. He only had one good pair, and he needed them for his trapline runs. But his nine-year-old son had a pair of wooden snowshoes. They were small but seemed sturdy. He said I was welcome to them and that I could leave them with a mutual friend in Galena and he'd pick them up later.

I improvised an improved binding system, tying them to my cycling boots with p-cord. They worked surprisingly well. When the Iron Dog trailbreakers arrived at Bible Camp around noon the next day, I was headed downriver before they were to Carole's porch. There were eighteen teams (of two) coming through and after that nobody coming for a while. I had sixty-two miles to get to Ruby. It was snowing like crazy. Again.

Iron Doggers began passing me within two hours of leaving Bible camp. A team passed about every thirty to forty-five minutes. I was using their "trail," which helped my pace and eliminated the need to navigate, but it wasn't going to be rideable or even easy to walk. It was a mashed potato trail. Machines going that fast don't pack a trail; they just beat the air out of the snow. It was better than nothing. Take what you can get.

About fourteen hours after I left Carole's, I made a poor decision trying to cross some overflow. I'm usually careful around overflow. That makes it hard to explain how I fell into thigh deep water, along with half my bike, in the middle of the Yukon River, at 2:00 a.m., miles from anything. "Bad decision" seems to cover it well enough.

The overflow was obvious. The depth was astonishing. I didn't see a way around it. It extended off both sides of the trail as far as my headlight would shine. I thought with the snowshoes and leaning on my bike to spread my weight a bit, I would get across the twenty yards of wet, ominous-looking snow. Worst case . . . I get my feet wet. I almost made it. But 90 percent of the way across, just as I was starting to relax and think, "Made it," a trapdoor opened beneath me. When my snowshoes touched the bottom—which for a fraction of a second, I was afraid might not happen—I shot back up, almost out of the water. Then, on the way up, the snowshoes caught the underside of the snow slab on the edge of the overflow, causing me to fall on my face, breaking off a snow shelf, sending me and my bike back into the water a little farther than the initial dunking.

I crawled out of the water in a state of something between panic and rage. I shouted profanities. That didn't seem to help, so I shouted more profanities. Louder. More profane. I made up new ones. After fifteen seconds that passed, and I got to the business of surviving. I took off my shoes, socks, and pants and did what I could to wring them out.

I worked quickly, and in less than a couple minutes I was walking again. It was about thirty degrees out and snowing off and on. Not cold at all, but I was wet. I guessed the next twenty minutes would let me know if I was wet-and-uncomfortable or wet-and-in-trouble. Building a fire in the middle of the Yukon River wasn't really an option . . . I was wearing the only flammable materials within a mile. I wasn't nearly desperate enough to leave the trail to get to the edge of the river to find firewood. If I found something closer to the trail, maybe I'd try to build a fire. If I needed to.

Twenty minutes later I knew I was okay for the night. I was wet. But I wasn't in trouble. Nothing I was wearing, except my socks and boots, held much water at all. My upper body didn't really get wet, except one arm . . . right to the shoulder. My lower body was submerged, twice. Within an hour my pants barely felt damp. I was fine.

I walked until 6:00 a.m. I hadn't seen any Iron Doggers in hours. I figured they'd all passed. I'd made it about thirty miles from Bible Camp, and I needed to sleep. I had hoped that the trail would go near some willows or trees, but it never went close enough. Eventually, I stomped out an area barely off the trail and set my bike up with a flasher going so a snowmachiner would see me if they came through and hopefully not run me over. Then I crawled into my sleeping bag.

A couple hours later I was awake and I was cold! It was dumping snow again. Heavy, wet snow. It was *way* too warm! It was basically a downpour. I was sleeping in a minus-twenty-five-degree down bag with no rain protection. I was wet again. I got moving quickly. Right away I knew this was a bigger problem than falling in water the previous night. It was well above freezing and dumping snow.

The snow continued through the day. It was like napalm. It stuck to everything and melted, leaving me and every bit of my gear soaked. I had puddles inside of my packs. Through the day it gradually got harder to stay warm. My feet were taking a beating from snowshoeing in wet cycling boots. I stopped about every thirty minutes to try to wring my socks out and try to find some sock layering combination that would help with what was becoming very painful blisters. Nothing helped. Twice I took the snowshoes off because they were killing my feet. I couldn't go anywhere without them and had to put them right back on. By midafternoon I realized making it thirty-two miles to Ruby was not going to happen. I was traveling way too slowly . . . hurting too much. My average speed was well under one mile per hour. My physical condition was not great. I thought about a cabin I'd heard about somewhere on the north side of the river along this section of trail. With the snow dumping, I couldn't see anything. The only way I'd find a cabin was if it was in the middle of the trail.

Hypothermia was becoming something to consider. I could stay warm as long as I could keep moving. But my sleeping bag was already soaked. I wasn't going to be able to bivy. My feet hurt enough that keeping moving was going to be a problem soon. My choices were to either get to some trees, improvise a shelter, and build a big fire to try to dry some things out and stay close to the fire all night . . . no small task. Or find this cabin. I carry a satellite messenger but don't tend to use it very much. I decided it was time. I messaged Ed Plumb, who had told me about the cabin, to see if he could send me exact coordinates. If I was a better planner, I'd have brought the coordinates with me . . . but I'm not. I decided unless I heard back from Ed soon, I'd stop at the next trees I found and start preparing to survive a tough night.

If you do enough winter biking, especially this far north in the world, there are going to be times when things get tough. It's a given. This was one of those times. This was the worst of those times. Sometimes, during those situations, it's inevitable that you'll ask, "Why am I doing this?" Soaking wet, feet on fire from blisters, trying to decide how to fight off hypothermia without a dry sleeping bag in thirty-five degrees and nuking wet snow . . . not the time to answer that question.

Things were on the verge of being more than a "tough situation." It was becoming a full-blown ordeal. I was having a hard time keeping moving enough to stay warm. I wasn't in trouble yet. But I was less sure that I wouldn't be soon. There was a little more seriousness than I think I'd experienced before. Except maybe one or two forced negative-fifty-degree campouts, just because at those temperatures, things go sideways very fast and you don't really get a chance to recover from many mistakes. This was at least slower.

I started looking for a spot to try to hunker down. I wanted a spruce forest. But I'd take anything that offered shelter and flammable material. I couldn't find anything. After walking another hour, the InReach pinged. Ed sent the coordinates. I plugged them into my GPS and was less than a mile and a half from Sam's place. I could make that distance! Ed had messaged Sam too. Thirty minutes later he rode up on his snow-machine. I was incredibly happy to see him. But when he asked if I wanted a ride, I said, "No, I need to get there on my own." I felt like a giant asshole. I was really mad at myself as I limped across the river to his place. This wasn't a race. There was no rule about taking a ride. It felt like I'd violated my own rule that I was just doing this for fun by not taking a ride when I *really* needed one, and Sam had come out and offered me one on a really shitty day. It's not like he wanted to come out.

I thought about that during the hour it took me to walk the mile to his place. And more as we hung my soaking wet gear all over the place. I don't think there was enough space left to hang another sock. Everything I had with me was soaked. I poured water out of all my bike bags. I wrung water out of my clothing.

I wasn't walking very well. My feet were a mess of blisters. We chatted as I went about popping them. Sam asked how long I thought I'd stay. I told him I'd leave in the morning. He didn't try to hide his skepticism. I said: "I know. I look bad. But I'll air out overnight, tape everything up in the morning, and be good to go." I knew I didn't need to heal. I just needed a chance to hit "reset." I needed to not have to walk a razor's edge to get through the night. A night in a nice warm bed was all I needed.

The next morning that's what happened. Sam fixed me a breakfast burrito and asked if I'd take a ride back across the river to the trail. His trail from the previous day was gone. I gladly accepted and silently patted myself on the back for acting like a human being.

I limped into Ruby that night. The 120 miles from Tanana to Ruby had taken me a week. The temperature was in the negative fifties when I'd left Tanana. It was in the high thirties at Sam's place. I'd been caught in snowstorms. I fell into overflow. I learned a little about life on the river talking to Carole. I spent a solid day fighting off hypothermia. When Arnold Marks Jr. passed me on my way into Ruby, he told me that I'd had wolves following me earlier in the day. I never saw them. It was about as eventful as a bike ride gets. I'd averaged 0.7 miles per hour. Low-speed events.

Arriving in Ruby, I was surprised at how physically beaten up I'd gotten. Pushing a bike wearing snowshoes is essentially a form of torture. I'd done several thousand-mile rides across Alaska and generally come out of them feeling pretty good. Exhausted. But not this beat-up. I'd ridden 1,400 miles, and I was seriously leaking oil. But I knew I'd gotten through the worst of it. I'd made it through Ed's three storms with some help, some luck, some patience, and some gritting my teeth. I was back on heavily traveled trails. I had physical issues for sure, but I'd mentally rebounded and was ready to keep going.

Over the next couple of days, as I moved west, everything . . . the trail, the weather, my feet, my spirits . . . slowly got better. The trail was almost all rideable within fifteen or twenty miles of leaving Ruby. I was in tourist mode. I didn't care how slow or fast I went. I wanted to finish each day feeling a little better than I had when I started it.

In Galena I spent the night at a friend's house and ate ice cream. A day later I cruised into Kaltag during an incredible western Alaska evening twilight. I was easily moving ten miles per hour on bomber trails. The fast trail and beautiful sunset felt like a reward for my efforts. Like Alaska was giving me an "attaboy" and a pat on the back. This is some seriously cheesy shit, but I had Steve Earle's "The Other Kind" playing on my headphones as I pulled off the river and hiked up the steep bank into Kaltag . . . *There are those that break and bend . . . I'm the other kind.* Cheeseball, but pretty much how I felt . . . unstoppable.

I felt like I'd been hit with everything possible between Manley and Kaltag and I'd made it. I was euphoric. Even without the snowstorms and mishaps, getting off the Yukon River is a significant box to check. A milestone worth relishing on a long ride to Nome. Up next was a ninety-mile portage to Unalakleet, with its beautiful views and nice cabins. Then a couple hundred miles of Norton Sound coast riding. I didn't want the ride to end. I was having a great time. But I wanted to accomplish my goal of getting to Nome.

As planned, Heather flew into Kaltag to rejoin me for the rest of the ride. Riding the coast is beautiful. It's also exotic if you live in Interior Alaska. She wanted to see it on a bike. The riding was rarely easy, but the effort was rewarded with beautiful views and great friends the entire way.

We struggled the first thirty miles from Kaltag to the Tripod Flats cabin on a rough trail and spent the night there. It was in the negative thirties, and Heather had a hard time staying warm in the cabin with no firewood. It's hard to make the adjustment from comfortable living to life on the trail. Especially when it happens with the rudeness of a minus-thirties night.

We hit the Bering Coast during a beautiful, bright-blue, high-pressure weather pattern. It was in the zero to minus twenty range, with little wind most of the way to Nome. I finally got to spend a night in the Qwik River cabin, between Koyuk and Elim. I'd always loved the starkness of that cabin, all by itself in the middle of a huge river delta, but I'd never been able to stay there when I was racing. The wind howled all night, and the next morning we left the cabin with no sign of trail at all. We were surprised to find that we could ride wind slab anywhere we wanted to go. It was super fun and playful riding and seemed incongruous with a 1,900-mile journey. I got to use some navigational and memory skills to try to relocate the trail as it reappeared from the wind slab and windblown snow near Moses Point.

On the last of many gorgeous sunsets on the trip, we finished the

Topkok Hills and descended to the cabin that essentially marks the end of the topography for the route. It was a flat, forty-mile ride to Nome from there. Heather wanted to spend the night. I was feeling the accumulation of the miles and days. I had lost thirty pounds since the start of the ride. My clothes were all a little loose. I'm not sure everything hurt any worse than it had been, but I think the proximity to the finish allowed me to think about the discomfort a little more. To acknowledge it. Something you really can't do in the middle of the thing.

For the first time since Sam found me on the Yukon, I didn't feel unstoppable. At all. I knew I'd get to Nome. That was about all. It still meant something to me but not nearly as much as it did when I was struggling on the Yukon River. I was getting ready for the post-ride letdown. I told Heather that we had to cover another thirteen miles to make the last day as short as possible. I wanted the Tommy Johnson blowhole behind me too. It's an orographic feature that is hard to understand until you've been caught in it. We built a fire and ate dinner. Then rode two more hours to the next shelter cabin. The blowhole was quiet.

We finished the ride in Nome the next day. It had taken thirty-six days and covered 1,860 miles. Heather had ridden about 800 miles with me. I'd taken two days off during that time, one by choice in Dawson City and one due to weather at Bible Camp.

It feels good to finish a ride. Whether it's a ride, tour, or race, finishing is always the first goal. But finishing is bittersweet too. There is a letdown. I do rides like this because they're fun. But there is more to it than that. I can spend the whole ride telling myself that there isn't more to it than that. The focus kind of requires that. But when it's over, I can admit that there is more to it. I've spent a lot of time on trails by myself. Often in the dead of winter and sometimes in the middle of nowhere, with plenty of time to ponder "Why?" The answer is easy and obvious . . . kind of self-evident . . . but still difficult to explain. It's a combination of so many things. Things I see, people I meet, time alone, simplicity, beautiful country, absurd situations, horrible weather, sunsets, northern lights, the difficulty and the effortlessness. It's all of those things and so much more. It's the accumulation of all those seconds and minutes and hours, of peace and struggle, sights and sounds. The fatigue and the buoyant energy. It's the Experience. It's hard to let the

Experience end. Even when I need to get back to "real life" or when aches and pains can't be ignored anymore. Ride a hundred miles with me or a thousand or ten thousand . . . or better yet, do it by yourself. Then you'll understand it . . . or maybe you won't?

At risk of allowing a bike ride to become more than a bike ride . . . when I'm on the trail, the Experience becomes something tangible. It's hard to say goodbye to that because I know that once it ends, it will never happen again. Even if I did the same ride again, it would be different. Each ride is a unique experience. When it ends, it's gone. A memory. No longer the tangible thing that I spent that time with. That I shared that trail with. That I asked and answered questions of when there was nobody else around. There is a sadness to that. Even in the joy of accomplishing whatever it was that I had hoped to do.

Even on a mostly uneventful bike ride, things happen. You spend time thinking, singing, doing math, talking to the trail, or just pedaling. You get caught in a storm. You see new things and places and meet new people. You watch a slow sunset and semi-infinite twilight. You listen to an owl. You hit a wall. You stop and look at the stars. A wolverine finds you. You push farther than you thought you could. You push reset. Wolves follow you. You get scared. You laugh at yourself. Then have a slow dance with the northern lights. You have an adventure. It's Alaska . . .

The Government Sign   CORINNA COOK

I ride to the end of the road. A sign marks the place: END ROAD. At the end of the road, I turn around. That is generally what cyclists do on the North Douglas Highway. We ride to the end. Then we turn around.

The government made that sign, you know. It is a proper yellow sideways-square, with a proper black stripe all around it and proper black letters in the government's proper roadside size and font.

You know the adage about hiding things in plain sight? END ROAD, says the sign. As if there could be any mistake. So I think about that.

"The past walks through the present," writes Rebecca Solnit, who is also interested in what's hidden in plain sight. "We are ourselves ghosts of other times, not fully present in our own; and we see what is no longer here and feel the future as a wind through the streets, a wind that is for us who look backward always blowing away what we cherish."

This road ends in the trees where the END ROAD sign stands. These trees end in the muskeg, but there is no sign. This muskeg ends in more trees. Those trees end in the beach, which is rocky, and does not end. Yes, there is the sea, and yes, there is its salty froth kicking up steam at the sky, but the beach, it goes on. It dives down underneath all that.

Though there is, now that I think about it, a sign on the beach. It advises boats not to crash on the rocks. Because, as I said, the beach does not end: its rocky reef is out there in the water at every tide, whether you see it or not. It'll gut your skiff in a second. The beach, then, is marked not because it is an endpoint but because continuity, too, can be treacherous.

On a bicycle my body is also the most continuous continual continuity. On a bicycle my body is concerted rhythm and repetition, cold water crashing on black rocks all day and all night and all moon and all year while the continents shuffle, tectonic adjustments prescient as tea leaves.

I learned to ride a bicycle some decades ago on the paved shoulder of this same highway on this same island. Perhaps you know the place. Not at the end of the road but out by the boat launch. Where the road peels out of the forest and runs for two miles right alongside the sea, pavement flat and wide and quiet, sky large and cold and crisscrossed by eagles, glacier muscling out of the mountains across the water. I learned to ride a bicycle in that place even though a whale showed up, sending its plumes of breath up into the cold air. I was with my dad, you see. He marveled at the whale. My own focus remained on the bicycle. So I probably learned to balance on two wheels first by exhaling like the whale, loudly, then by requiring my dad to focus on the task at hand, yes, even though a whale, yes, even though the eagles, yes, even though the glacier. That is how I learned to ride a bicycle.

My family laughs about it now. How child-me said, *There's always a whale.* How child-me said, *What I'm trying to do right now is ride a bicycle.*

My grandmother physically startles when I ask her what she remembers of me at my youngest. *You were a ghostly child*, she says.

What a flaming gift, I think, even if I kept my head down for the sake of balance. Abundance breaking the skin of the sea to fill its pliable lungs, abundance slicing the sky with rounded wingtips, abundance muscling its blue and white curve between the mountains. And smooth pavement running right through it. Smooth pavement running all the way through to its own abrupt end.

Do you feel bad about that? The pavement running through it? For myself the answer is dense. I sense that where there is a road—any paved or trafficked road at all—something does, indeed, end.

We are ourselves ghosts of other times. We see what is no longer here. In a distant and heavily industrialized place, Alberta's Rocky Mountains, scientists have mapped genetically distinct populations of grizzlies, of mountain goats—animals whose habitats are cut by roads and who are stranded in discrete island populations. Populations whose isolation— because they cannot cross the roads—is genetically measurable.

We, too, live alongside bears and goats. What is the difference between marked ending places and unmarked ones?

The bicycle, of course, permits me to love pavement. Not just to hash out sightlines on my own complicity—to simply, senselessly, love it. Do you understand? I'm saying that flying on pavement flowers my heart straight open.

An ecologist, a professor, and a regulator travel one thousand miles, one-point-five thousand miles, and four thousand miles, respectively. But there is no punch line. They travel by invitation to tell a group of us what they, in their heavily paved places, learned of road planning and maintenance and development and design. Their echoes disperse.

Roads beget roads, says the road ecologist. *The world is building roads like crazy*, says the roads professor. *Calcium bedrock is the best indicator for where biodiversity is going to persist into the future*, says the roads regulator. That is what we learn from pavement experts about continuity and transience. Air pushes against the earth, and we feel the future as a wind through the streets blowing away what we cherish.

The pavement at the end of the road is a bit chipped, a bit uneven. There can be loose gravel, loose dogs. In other words, discontinuities abound. Often enough someone wants a photograph with the black and yellow government sign. We pose. The government sign—it's basically an old friend, though no one really knows why it's there or what it's really telling us.

One thing hidden in plain sight at the end of the road: a trailhead. It goes to the beach, of course. To raw rock and the salt that pounds it on windy days.

Plate tectonics could be happening right now, this very second. It's hard to tell. I hold my breath. Yes, I hope plate tectonics is happening right now, though it seems the air has gone suddenly still.

Maybe something ends at the end of this road, but it isn't my ride. For my ride the end is only a halfway mark. In other words, the end of this road is more a time than a place; it's the moment to double down. I make my lollipop turn and fly.

Last Ride of the Season

DAVID A. JAMES

Brilliant sunshine burns through the stand of denuded birch trees, one of my favorite things to witness in Fairbanks. It's one of those perfect late-fall days, when the reality of winter is closing in but the lingering promise of summer has not yet given up hope. When the sunny places feel warm but morning frost in shaded spots still loiters.

I pause to take a photograph and also to rest. I'm on my mountain bike, and I've just begun ascending Ester Dome, my fifty-six-year-old legs nearly as much on fire as the sun. They're tired from climbing the same hill the evening before by a different but equally challenging route.

I hadn't intended to go riding this afternoon. But the weather forecast is calling for snow, and I've lived in Alaska far too long to let a day like this get away. Because rarely will the next day be its match. I figure I can make the top of the Dome. It's only a 1,700-foot climb.

Coming down won't be a problem.

When I was four, my dad bought me a used spider bike that was my chariot. After a few spills, I quickly mastered the art of propelling myself forward and never quit doing so. The spider bike gave way to a three-speed and later a ten-speed. My grade school was close enough to my house that I began riding there in first grade. My junior high and high schools were farther away, but I kept riding anyway. Even after obtaining a driver's license.

I grew up on Vashon Island in Washington State and by my early teens had ridden nearly every one of its roads and frequently boarded the ferryboat to Seattle or Tacoma to ride through cities and rural areas alike. In the late seventies and early eighties, friends and I rode to campgrounds on the Kitsap and Olympic Peninsulas for overnight stays, bikepacking before we'd ever heard the term.

I rode all through college. And for three long years in Seattle after graduating, I continued riding everywhere. From my University District home, I could get downtown faster by bike than by bus and often even by car, given the city's notorious traffic. And I'd have more fun getting there, joyfully rushing past drivers who rarely looked happy.

A maze of old mining roads crisscrosses Ester Dome. Finding gold in this hill has been the goal of everyone from lone prospectors to multi-national corporations for over a century, but it's never paid. Meanwhile, private residences crept up its sides, and a few sprouted on the very top. These days it's a nearby recreational destination for Fairbanks' residents. From my house, at the Dome's foot, it feels like my backyard. I've spent thousands of hours running and biking it.

Right now I'm ascending one of those old roadbeds. The birch trees give way to aspen and spruce. My dog, Loki, springs back and forth, fruitlessly chasing squirrels and grouse, wondering why his companion is so slow. He's the third dog to join my Alaska travels and, after a lifetime of black Lab mixes, my first sled dog. His energy is remarkable. These distinctively Alaskan dogs have no lineage papers. They've been bred for one thing: speed. They're gangly critters with skinny torsos atop ridiculously long legs and can bound through deep snow. And unlike people, they never seem to tire.

A good sled dog can just as easily come from the pound, as Loki did as a puppy, as from a champion musher. Loki was spared a life in a dog yard and will occupy the living room couch with as much self-entitlement as the most spoiled canine. But the trail is his natural habitat. Observing his athleticism never ceases to astound me. I've often said I need to get him his own GPS so I can compare his mileage to mine. I suspect he averages about 30 to 50 percent more distance than I do. And if I stop too long to rest, he barks demandingly at me to get going again. It's advisable that I do so, if only to avoid hearing damage from his protests.

I didn't plan on becoming an Alaskan or a mountain biker. Both happened on their own, even if the roots extend back to my childhood. Growing up in western Washington, Alaska was ever present. On any visit to Seattle's waterfront piers, signs of Alaska abounded. Cargo containers heading north, ferries returning south, and tacky Alaskan mementos cluttering busy souvenir shops. As a schoolchild, I read Jack London and Robert Service and felt the lure of the North. During college, when friends returned from summer jobs and told stories of their adventures, they kept the seed alive.

I talked about heading north countless times. Then, rather suddenly, it happened in the spring of 1990. College classmates who lived in Fairbanks came to visit. I met them for dinner. While catching up, I told them that I was working an enjoyable but futureless job, my apartment lease was about to expire, and my latest relationship already had. I wanted money to travel, I told them. I wanted to get as far south as I could go. They suggested I solve both dilemmas by coming north. I could earn money and hit the road come fall.

That night, like so many times in my life, I went for a long bike ride and did a lot of thinking. Truth be told, I'd already made up my mind. But riding helped clarify plans.

Three weeks later I was in Fairbanks, having left Seattle, right then the hippest city in the known universe. "What a dump," I thought, upon seeing the Golden Heart City. "I'll bet I end up living here."

Eventually, I did, but first I would spend five summers and a winter in Denali National Park, meeting my wife in the process.

Continuing up the roadbed, I turn onto a narrow pathway worn in by mountain bikers over the years. It used to lead to a crumbling old miner's cabin. I once took a photo of my kid on its porch, holding his ski pole like a Sourdough aiming his rifle. A few years ago the Department of Natural Resources removed it and a few other old cabins that once stood scattered along trails on the Dome. Presumably, it was to discourage squatters. But it felt like yet another uprooting of our history, something Alaskans are as skilled at doing as anyone else.

From there it's a steep climb to another fallow mining route, then onto a bandit trail that will put me near the top of the Dome. The ground is littered with leaves, but it's dry. On wet days I can blame the combination of wet slippery leaves and roots snaking along the surface of the ground for destroying my traction and forcing me to push up the steepest parts. Today I don't have that excuse. But the fatigue I felt earlier has faded, and instead of a quick ride to the top and back to my house, I'm making grander plans.

My life has centered on Alaska for over thirty years now, and my Alaska life has centered on mountain biking for most of them. I was still fairly young when I first ventured north, expecting my encounters with Alaska's outdoors would mostly happen on foot. Mostly, they did early on and still often do. Hiking into alpine country is something I'll always treasure. What I didn't anticipate was that the time I would spend mountain biking would overwhelmingly outweigh time spent on all other outdoor activities combined.

I also didn't anticipate the trails around Fairbanks. My wife and I chose to live here for its proximity to Denali and for its slower pace and smaller population than Anchorage. And for the dryer weather. It was only after arriving that we learned that hundreds of miles of trails litter the Tanana Valley, where the city of Fairbanks lies. Many cross through private property, but owing to easements, long-standing right-of-way laws, and a generally accepting attitude from many property owners, it's a dreamland for recreational travelers, be they cyclists, skiers, hikers, joggers, mushers, skijorers, or ATV or snowmachine riders.

I took to those trails like nothing else in my life. As GPS units rose in popularity, I started tracking my miles, and every year they run into the thousands. In summers I'll frequently head up Ester Dome after dinner. The endless daylight from May until early August means there's no real curfew. In the shoulder seasons between summer and winter, it stays light late enough to allow lengthy sojourns. And headlights make winter night rides a joy. As often as possible, I'm out the door and in the woods.

It's become my default way of life. The urban cycling I did when young now seems drab and pointless. "Pavement sucks" has become my mantra. Even when riding into town, I know a system of trails that can keep me almost entirely off roads most of the way. In Fairbanks a quick trip to buy milk can turn into a mountain bike adventure. Where else is this possible?

I've often said that riding a mountain bike on Ester Dome is akin to those choose-your-adventure children's books. You can pursue any number of routes from bottom to top and back again. But it's good to know the seasonal variabilities. Head down the northwestern side in winter for one of the funnest descents in the Fairbanks vicinity. Try this trajectory in summer, however, and prepare to push though miles of muskeg and muck.

Most trails on the Dome lead to the top, and today the climb pays off both athletically and aesthetically. The workout has me energized. I follow a grassy four-wheeler pathway looping the north summit of the Dome and head for an outcrop that marks the final high point before the steep rutty unmaintained gravel road dropping to Goldstream Creek.

A couple of weeks ago, some friends and I headed this direction to connect with another old roadbed that ascends to the southern summit. Like so many rides I've taken, it bottomed out in a swamp. If you're going to mountain bike in Interior Alaska, plan on wet feet, wet legs, and possibly a wet torso as you shove through fetid water. Or try riding through it, with half your wheels obscured by mud and goop. Aim for the far shore and pedal like crazy and don't be surprised when you lose momentum and splash sideways.

But on top of Ester Dome, it's bone-dry. I prop my bike in a rock cleft and start taking pictures. Murphy Dome dominates to the northwest, and the White Mountains spill across the northeastern horizon. To the southeast, the city of Fairbanks, such as it is, is dwarfed by the immensity of this land. And by the endless sky as well. This is the reward in climbing. You gain perspective.

When I brought my bike to Denali, I discovered riding on the park road. The long climb from the entrance to mile 9 took me out of the forested creek drainages and up to the tundra, where caribou meander, bears lurk, and mountains span as far as can be seen in all directions. As you ride deeper into the park, you overlook valleys, cross rivers, climb and descend, climb and descend. And sometimes, when the wind is blowing hard, which it frequently does, riding downhill can require more effort than going up. Rarely have I pedaled as hard as I once did coming down the park road on the long downhill drop on Mount Margaret, hailstones peppering my face, driven by frigid gales hell-bent on preventing my progress.

This was in July. Summer in Alaska.

Once I found myself close to a grizzly lounging near a bend in the road. My riding companions and I pondered how quickly we could retreat down the hill and if we would be faster than a pursuing bear. We nervously made the requisite jokes about who the slowest would be. But the bear was more concerned with taking a nap on the tundra than feasting on a trio of seasonal workers. It barely acknowledged us. So we rode onward.

Decades after moving to Fairbanks, I rode beyond the Teklanika rest stop on a visit to Denali and noticed a large animal just ahead. Wondering who had let their dog off leash, I stopped. That's when I realized it was a lynx. The sizable feline noticed me and stopped as well. We stared inquisitively at each other for several magical minutes until the cat evaporated into the brush.

That remains my best lynx sighting, although a close second happened just two months later, on a September midnight, after darkness had returned. Barreling down the Equinox Marathon Trail on the University of Alaska campus, my headlight caught movement. It was a lynx scrambling across the path. I came to a halt and turned my headlights into the woods. There it sat, and again I found myself in a staring match with one of Alaska's more elusive animals. Eventually, it got bored and wandered off. I rode home through the night with a warm chill, if there could be such a thing.

I've come close to colliding with moose on several occasions while zipping down trails. Grouse, which almost invariably fly in front of oncoming traffic, have many times come fluttering toward my face, nearly leaving me with a mouthful of feathers. A scampering fox vanquished one attempt at setting a personal best time for descending Ester Dome Road. It dashed in front of my bike so quickly that only my instinctual swerve to the right prevented what could have been a badly injurious collision for us both. My dog at the time, Sugi, pursued it into the woods. My attempt at a land speed record was cut short not by the wild canine but by the domesticated one I had to retrieve.

Only once have I actually flushed a bear. While riding with friends on logging roads near the Tanana River southwest of Fairbanks, I surged ahead on the winding route. A black bear suddenly emerged a few yards ahead. It turned, stopped, stared, and snorted. I slammed the brakes and shouted, "No bear! Go away!" My friend Eric pulled up behind me, and the bear, perhaps realizing its was outnumbered, turned and charged into the trees. The rest of the group missed it entirely. We huddled in close together as we passed through those few yards of trail, hoping against—and laughing about—the bear's possible return. But we didn't see it again. Undoubtedly, it was eyeing us though.

After reaching the top and looping the cell and radio towers that are forever self-replicating on this hilltop, I opt to follow the Out & Back, a four-wheeler trail shooting off to the southwest. It's part of the Equinox Marathon route, an annual race in September that sends runners up Ester Dome then partway down this side of it so they can turn around and top the hill a second time. In the best years marathoners are treated to views of the Alaska Range, including Denali, dominating the southern horizon. It's entirely out today, and unlike runners racing the clock, I have the option of stopping and admiring this place I've called home for three decades, gazing at mountains of staggering beauty across the entire southern horizon.

I'm not running the marathon, so I go partway out but not back. Part of the adventure I've chosen is to go down the Gravity Trail, a narrow and very steep descent that pops out on the Tricon Road, which leads to Ester. Most people don't know the Gravity Trail exists. It's an open secret among mountain bikers.

The Tricon Road was the sight of my first ever mountain bike ride in Fairbanks. My first ever real trail ride. In the summer of 1998, I showed up for one of the Fairbanks Cycle Club's Tuesday night mountain bike rides, led by local cycling legend Doug Burnside. I'd read about them in the paper. It sounded like fun. I didn't realize it at the time, but this was when my road riding would succumb to trail fever. Before long I was avoiding roads. They're never so exciting as trails.

The ride began in Ester, west of Fairbanks. It was mid-May, so daylight wasn't a concern. We headed out the Ester Mine Road and onto the Fireplug Trail, the route of a since discontinued dogsled race. We hung a right at a steep ascent leading to the top of Ester Dome, some 1,600 feet higher. The trail was boggy and brushy and generally terrible, and our feet were soaked as we did a lot of pushing, eventually attaining the far end of the Out & Back. We rode that to the Tricon, which we bombed back down. Twice I was nearly taken out by other riders as I clung to my brakes on a very steep, deeply rutted descent. It was terrifying. It was gratuitously stupid. I was back for more the following week. And I've been back nearly every Tuesday night during every single summer since. I help lead those rides now.

It's no longer summer, so today daylight is a concern. It's already 5:00 p.m. It will be dark by 7:00. I can head back to the top of the Dome and be home in under half an hour by road. But what's the fun in that? I brought a headlight and a fully charged battery. Loki is barking furiously because he knows going downhill is the only time he has to keep up with me instead of the reverse. And he knows this descent. He has a sled dog's memory for trails. I've always felt confident that if he were to become separated from me anywhere on the Dome, he'd find his way home. But he always stays close.

The Tricon road is treacherous, and since I'm alone, I take it easy on the drop. This allows Loki to pull ahead. Three-quarters of the way down, he turns onto another four-wheeler trail, one crossing over to the quirky bedroom community of Ester. More downhill fun awaits and a couple of brief but virtually unrideable uphills, a creek crossing, and a swamp. It's a good thing on this chilly afternoon that my shoes are waterproof. Winter is the only time in Interior Alaska that you can mountain bike with reasonable confidence you won't get wet feet. Unless you fall through the ice.

Upon moving north, I'd assumed my bike riding would be limited to summers. But soon after arrival, I saw people commuting the roads around Fairbanks in winter and before long had bought studded tires so I could join them. People here ride in any conditions, and so have I, although I don't recommend riding at forty below zero unless both you and your bike are prepared. Human bodies slow down at that temperature, when simply going outdoors, much less moving in it for an extended time, can be an act of willpower and perhaps limited common sense. Bicycles don't like such extremes either. Over the years local mechanics have figured out which lubricants do best in the deep cold, but bottom brackets, wheel hubs, shifts, and brakes resist movement when thermometers plunge.

Winter riding has become a global phenomenon since fat bikes hit the market around 2000. The large tires, operated under low air pressure, roll nicely over packed snow trails. It's a great way to explore winter pathways that traverse the swamps and rivers, which present significant obstacles in summer but become superhighways once everything freezes and routes are broken in.

Winter biking long predates fat bikes in Alaska, however. The earliest gold miners brought bikes as transportation tools. A few rode the Yukon River from Dawson to Nome when gold was discovered on Alaska's western beaches. Imagine doing that in 1899.

Recreational winter riding came later. In the seventies and eighties, as mountain bikes surged in popularity, Alaskans learned that by reducing air pressure in tires, they could travel the more solidly packed trails. Soon winter races began to be held. Inspired by a competitive winter cyclist who had welded two rims together for each of his wheels, local cycle mechanic Simon Rakower speculated that with wider rims than those that came stock on mountain bikes, tires would roll better over snow.

Thus were born SnowCat rims. Twice the width of a standard mountain bike rim, they could be installed on most frames. Riders, including myself, adopted the biannual ritual of swapping out their wheels. There was no longer a single mountain biking season.

Fat bikes took it up another notch, and now the winter trails around Fairbanks are plied daily by recreational riders. Two decades ago trials were shared by skiers, mushers, and snowmachiners. These days fat bikers seem to outnumber all others combined. It's a transition I've watched and been part of. I haven't skied in years now. Biking is faster and more fun. And bikes have brakes. For an accident-prone athlete like myself, this is a major selling point.

The other big change that has expanded winter riding is in lighting. Halogen bulbs were the brightest things on the market when I commuted in Seattle in the 1980s and remained so into the early aughts. But when switched to full power, they discharged their batteries quickly. And rechargeable batteries suffer in extreme cold. This hampered Alaskan night rides.

Then LEDs came online, and the world opened up. A headlight ten times as bright as the halogen ones I once used can run for hours on a single charge. Cold remains a problem for batteries, but you learn tricks to insulate them. These days my biggest headlight issue comes when I get off of my bike and into my truck to go home. My high beams are dimmer than my bike lights. Suddenly I'm struggling to see where I'm going.

We reach the neighborhoods above Ester, and I'm forced to make more decisions. I can cut up to the Equinox Trail fairly quickly and from there head home. I'm burning daylight, as Jack London put it. The sun is drooping low in the southern horizon. I'll soon need that headlight if I don't hurry. But I know a fun trail nearby that drops most of the way down to Ester. And from there I can hop the Eva Creek Trail and still reach the Equinox fairly soon.

A week from now the trails could be snowed in, and until that snow gets packed down, the Eva Creek Trail won't be rideable. This could be my final chance for weeks. So farther we go, down one trail to climb another.

When I first arrived in Fairbanks, conflicts between motorized and nonmotorized trail users were rampant. In those days, before online comment threads became the medium for outraged debates, the local newspaper's letters page saw endless battles over who had the right to use the trails and in what fashion. It was especially fierce between skiers and snowmachine riders.

Then a curious thing happened. As more people took to winter cycling, trail disputes seemed to wither away. Relations between gasoline-powered travelers and the self-propelled became downright cordial. There's a good reason for this. We fat bikers need snowmachine riders to pack our trails for us. It's a parasitic relationship perhaps, but it's produced a much-needed truce between snow travelers. One I'm grateful for.

Even in my skiing days, I recognized the potential for injury and that the guy on a snowmachine could be the one to come along and render aid. That would leave me pretty embarrassed if I had devoted my efforts toward banning him from the trails (not an unfounded idea—banning snowmachines from parts of the valley was put to a vote many years ago and fortunately failed). So, I always chose to share the trail. All I ask is that people—including my fellow cyclists—be safe and respectful. And overwhelmingly, this has been my experience. Oftentimes, when encountering motorized travelers, they turn off their engines and we talk for a while, exchanging trail condition information and discussing what a fine day it is. Much better than animosity.

So, fat bikes haven't just made my life better. They've been part of an easing of tensions in my community. A bike might have a human engine, but with all its interworking parts, it's still mechanical. Perhaps the bicycle itself provides the meeting ground between the two formerly warring camps.

In Ester I spot a barely used four-wheeler path heading in the general direction of the Eva Creek Trail. Loki is already exploring it, so I follow. We pop out on what I briefly mistake for the trail, only to realize it's a section line. We bushwhack a bit farther and find our objective.

The Eva Creek Trail runs through a subdivision near houses, even crossing a driveway at one point. The resident dog runs out to play with Loki, and I pause to visit with its owner and marvel at this last shot of summer before winter sets in. It's one of the unique things about the trails near Fairbanks. They sometimes go right past people's houses, and many of the owners not only accept this gracefully; they welcome those traveling through. Despite having a strong compulsion for property rights, Fairbanks' residents can be surprisingly generous when it comes to allowing people passage. Many of the trails are protected by easements, but friendliness isn't. That comes from generosity and the sense of shared life in this outpost town surrounded by vast open lands in every direction.

By now the sun is behind the hills, and it's a race with darkness. Loki and I climb back up the Dome to the Equinox Trail. From here I have several options that can get me home quickly. Alternatively, I can continue up the hill to another bandit trail I know about. One that will put me on Henderson Road near the top entrance to the Ester Dome Single Track and a super fun downhill. There's some healthy climbing involved, and dusk is setting in, but I have a light, and the days of summer riding are dwindling to zero. So up we go.

I once rode the fifty or so miles from Fairbanks to Nenana with a friend who had strung together a course that followed logging roads, section lines, recreational routes, trappers' trails, and more. We wove our way through moss, roots, gravel, deep puddles, and one of the steepest hills I've ever climbed with a bike. I've ridden the pavement both ways in less time than it took us to go one way by trail. And burned far fewer calories doing it.

I couldn't retrace the route if I tried. It was too complex, too exemplary of the nature of trails in the interior. At one time or another, one person needed to get from where they were to just over there and beyond. So, they cut a pathway. Others, coming from different directions, followed. Over time travel corridors were connected. But traffic was never heavy enough to warrant putting in public roads. They remained well-used trails and nothing more. And so the mazes of passageways became playgrounds for adults. It's one of the things that's kept me here. It's immediately accessible.

It's been a strange summer in a strange and seemingly unending year, and I've spent much of it in the saddle. With a pandemic, political uncertainty, and postponed plans, mountain biking has been a beacon of normalcy. It's even been a relatively safe means of socializing. When riding with friends, we're generally far enough from each other that swapping viruses isn't a concern.

Today it's just Loki and I, though, and he's blissfully oblivious to a world in turmoil. All he knows is everyone has been home a lot. That means he's been getting out even more often than usual. He's been all over these trails and knows the choices. He stops ahead of me, at the cut-off to Ester, and looks back inquisitively. "Not today, buddy," I tell him.

The climb grows steeper. We round a bend, and Loki pauses again. A barely noticeable pathway leads into the woods. This is the one we're taking. I turn onto it and begin navigating a twisty single track. The trail traverses spruce roots, mud, and rocks. It threads between trees barely wide enough apart to accommodate my handlebars. It crosses a spring, where Loki drinks his fill and takes what might be his final splash in open water for the season.

The sun has now set, but the sky remains illuminated by its vanishing glow. I take a few more photos with my phone and notice the battery is nearly dead. Not from use but from the cold. On my next ride I'll need to pack it in a pocket under a couple of layers to insulate it. I try to take a drink from my CamelBak but can't. I forgot to blow the water back down after my last sips an hour earlier, and the liquid in the thin exposed tube has iced up. Further signs of summer's end.

I'm able to unclog the tube and drink deeply, then begin the last climb of the day. The news of the world hasn't been promising these past months, but right now none of this matters. I'm on my bike and in Alaska, and there's nowhere else I'd prefer to be. So, in this corner of the world, all is just right.

Riding has always been a stress reducer for me. In grade school I'd escape my childhood frustrations by hopping on my spider bike and hitting the trails the cows had worn into our pastures and woods. I'd pedal as hard and as fast and as far as I could go, and sometimes I'd crash, and sometimes I'd bleed. So, in a sense, I prepared myself for adult life as a mountain biker.

Long bike rides distracted me from studies in college, helped me ignore my perpetual lack of money in Seattle, and sustained me through breakups. More than once, when my kids were young and acting up and my patience was wearing thin, my wife would all but order me out onto the trail. By the time I got home, I was back on an even keel.

Cycling has helped me ride through the loss of family members. In early 2014 I spent several weeks in Seattle, tending to my sister during the final days of her struggle with cancer. It was made easier by her many wonderful friends. But I felt hemmed in by the city. As one of her friends told me a few days after she died, "You need to be home now."

When I got home, in late February, I went riding the next morning with my friend Tom. From my house we headed down the hill and onto the winter trails crossing between Ester and Murphy Domes. It was ideal weather, a bit below zero. The winter sun had sufficiently returned to create a blinding brightness beaming down from the sky and reflecting up from the snow.

Winters in Fairbanks, I've always said, are much brighter than in Seattle. The days might be shorter, the temperatures significantly colder, but unlike the dank and gloomy Pacific Northwest, in Fairbanks the sun can be seen most winter days. Even in December, when it's so very far away, it usually puts in an appearance. By late February it's well above the horizon and stays up long enough to put plenty of hours on the trail. There's nothing like it.

And because seven minutes of direct sunlight are added each day, it's intoxicatingly energizing.

Tom and I rode through subdivisions and into a stretch of woods along the Dredge Trail, putting us near his place. By then I was sweaty and warm, despite the cold, and smiling because we were having good dumb fun. It would be a long haul coming to terms with the death of my only sibling, but from a bicycle I began that process, knowing I could get through it.

In subsequent years, as first my father and then my mother died, I knew what to do. Get on my bike. Go find a trail. Ride. And in doing so, plunge into this beautiful place I've been lucky enough to make my home. This is how I've come to know it best. I can't imagine Alaska without my mountain bike.

It won't last forever. My own clock is ticking. It's been more than thirty years since I first came to Alaska. In thirty more, I'll be well into my eighties. I'd like to think I'll still be riding up steep hills and careening down steeper descents. But the reality is, should I live that long, I probably won't. Bones grow fragile. Hearts weaken. Joints quit cooperating. At some point mountain biking, which for me is completely entwined with the place I live, will become too difficult to continue, and I'll need to quit pretending I'm a kid.

Not today, though. It's downhill time. I've reached the Ester Dome Single Track, a network of loop trails and connectors that was built with volunteer labor over a decade ago. Busy with young children at the time, I wasn't involved in the construction but try to atone for this with trail maintenance. I always carry a brush saw for clearing deadfall and other obstacles that get blown in. But it should be clear today. And since it's just about dark, I will only have my headlight to alert me if something has dropped onto the path.

It's also getting colder. What little solar gain can be had from the sun this time of year vaporized as soon as it set. And spots like this one haven't seen direct sunlight for a couple of weeks now and won't again until late winter.

I stop for a few more photographs, but Loki is impatient. I put my phone away, pull on a windbreaker, turn on my headlight full beam, and climb on my bike. It's time to turn off my brain, let instinct take over, hurl down the hill as quickly as I can, and head home. The next time I come this way, it will be covered in snow.

A Winter Bike Commute

MARTHA AMORE

My snow bike is weighed down by two panniers: one contains my laptop, Brontë's *Jane Eyre*, and a change of clothes for teaching; while the other, which I affectionately call my feed bag, holds my lunch and snacks for the day. A perk of winter bike commuting is the immense number of calories one gets to consume in the name of survival. My water bottle cage holds a small thermos of hot tea, and this I twist open and sip at each red light, the steam continually warming and then freezing my face. It took me a while to figure out the best layering system for my ride to the university, but now I have it down. Each dark morning I don a suit of long underwear, an insulated jacket, waterproof pants, winter boots, plus my crowning victory over the cold, a downhill ski helmet and googles. A colleague tells me I look like a bobblehead. What do I care? The setup keeps me warm and safe, plus it prevents my eyelashes from icing over in the wind.

My commute isn't far, just about five miles each way, and I certainly don't go fast, though the clock sometimes gets the best of my better judgment. I know that riding through traffic in the dark of the season is dangerous. No matter how many lights glare and blink from my bike and person, Anchorage drivers simply don't see me. Yes, there are some who are out to get me—last week it was a MAGA-sticker man in a Ford F-350 super-duty gunning his engines as he cut me off—but for the most part it's an innocent right hook that threatens my life. Drivers look left to turn right, never expecting a cyclist to be there, legally crossing with the walk signal. I know these people aren't hoping to murder me. When they finally catch sight of my many reflectors, pulsing red blinkers, and blinding-white high beams, surprise transforms their sleepy faces, and they motion apologies. Some even roll down their frosty windows to holler: "Sorry! Didn't see you!"

It's hard for drivers to see what they don't expect. On a bike I never miss a thing. My life depends on my sense of sight, and because I'm not removed from my surroundings, I have an easier time seeing the world. In *Desert Solitaire* Edward Abbey rails against car travel, complaining that "you can't see anything from a car." Of course, he's not talking about bike commuters but, rather, the whole of life. He advises, "You've got to get out of the goddamned contraption and walk, better yet crawl, on hands and knees, over the sandstone and through the thornbush and cactus." I suppose that by jumping on my secondhand snow bike and slogging through the dark streets of Anchorage each morning, I am doing just what Abbey prescribes. I'm getting out in the elements, moving my body, but also slowing down, engaging my senses. Although this sometimes brings a bit of suffering, it feels good to be "out of the goddamned contraption" where I can be a part of the life around me.

I live in South Turnagain, and my commuter route takes me through Spenard and Midtown, where it's a straight shot down Thirty-Sixth Avenue to the university. If I added a few extra miles to my ride, I could follow a beautiful off-road paved bike path nearly the entire way, but I'm a woman, and—though I hate to admit it—I'm afraid. A good friend was attacked while riding one morning on that very trail. Although she managed to fight off her attacker, she was horribly beaten in the assault. Now every time I consider riding the trail in the dark, I picture her beautiful face as she looked the afternoon of her attack, how her eyes were nearly sealed shut within the bruises and swelling.

Once a colleague pointed out that, statistically, I would be safer on the trail. I knew he was right. Midtown traffic is heavy; cars are deadly. And yet there is a hierarchy to my fears, and violence against women tops the list. I hate that my physical movement is restricted, that I'm missing out on one of the best features of our city, but that's how it is. What I see during my morning commute, therefore, isn't a gorgeous frozen coastline, ice-coated creek, and quiet spruce and birch forest. Instead, I bear witness to urban Anchorage.

My ride begins near Balto Park, where shadowy figures cluster together on the hilltop and dots of colored lights dance and shoot beneath them. It looks like something from a sci-fi movie, but these are just the morning dog walkers and their pets, whose lighted collars glow so eerily in the dark. I marvel at how quiet they are now compared to after dinner; even the dogs seem reverent of the predawn hour. The cold begins to penetrate my layers, so I pedal quickly through the park until I hit the paved path along McRae Road. Many houses are still dark, but the winter air carries a lovely scent of coffee and weed, which is the mark of morning in Spenard, not unlike the crow of a rooster. At the firehouse near the corner, I slow down, hoping to catch sight of a fireman or two in the driveway. They are ever friendly, ever strapping, in their wide-legged turnout pants, suspenders, and T-shirts. Yes, even in the deep freeze of winter, T-shirts. But sadly, no one is out today. I ride on.

The next stretch of road is a tire popper in nicer weather. The problem isn't so much the shattered glass, which is everywhere along Spenard, but the broken screws, nails, and staples that litter the sidewalk. However, in winter a good firm coat of snow and ice solve the problem. I've never had a puncture during the cold season.

Soon I hit a big intersection at Minnesota and Spenard, where seven or eight homeless people group by the traffic light, their signs leaning useless at their feet in the dark: ANYTHING HELPS, GOD BLESS, WHY LIE? I NEED A BEER. The people used to sit along a low wall in front of the gas station, but it was removed in an effort to disperse the crowd. This did nothing to address the main issue, which is homelessness, so the wall is gone, but the people remain. They're just a bit more uncomfortable.

As I brake for the red light, somebody calls out, "Top o' the morning!"

I don't know how this greeting took root. I assume one of them caught sight of my red hair and Irish features in the warmer months, and now we have a refrain.

"Top o' the morning," I reply. "Keeping warm?"

"Trying," says a guy in a red-and-black checkered flannel hat. His hands are bare, causing me to flex my fingers inside my thick mitts. He clears his throat and shrugs. "But it ain't so bad now."

We smile at one another, and I can't help but consider what it would be like to have no home during the long Alaska winter. My ride is only about half an hour, and I move from a bowl of hot oatmeal in front of my fireplace to a toasty office with a plug-in kettle. How would it feel to be out in these elements at midnight, 2:00 a.m., 4:00 a.m., night after night?

"Blue must be your favorite color." A small woman, wrapped babushka style in a tattered scarf, points from my bike to my helmet. "Pretty."

"Thanks."

This is typical of the types of conversation we have at this corner. Nobody has ever asked me for money or said anything unfriendly. Often I ride away amid a chorus of warnings: be careful, watch out now, keep your eyes open.

Today the traffic light is slow to change, and now the woman grins at me, her eyes crinkling as she tilts a brown papered bottle my way. "One for the road?"

This gets a round of laughter.

During the ride down Thirty-Sixth, I'm stopped again and again at busy intersections. I find myself peering into the cars and trucks as I sip my hot tea, studying the drivers, their faces lit up by cellphones. Most of the people are alone in their cars. They appear ghoulish in the cast of light, hunched over their cells, their expressions ranging from uninspired to sad. I can't help but think how strange modern life is. What are we doing to ourselves?

On my route it's only the homeless people who are smiling and laughing. Well, the homeless people and me.

A friend once asked me why I ride to work when I could drive. In my reply I mentioned all the financial savings, exercise, and of course my reduced impact on the environment. The truth, though, is that I simply love to ride. I always have. As a kid, long before I got my own bicycle—a red, white, and blue Stingray knockoff called the American Spirit—my mother rode me around on hers. She had a beauty: a single-gear Schwinn cruiser with glittery red handgrips, a rear wheel cargo basket, and back-pedal breaks. She adored that bike, and because she did, so did I.

One of my earliest memories is sitting on that wide Schwinn two-tone saddle, legs dangling, arms wrapped around my mother's waist while she helped my brother climb up to her handlebars. I suppose it wasn't the safest way for the three of us to travel, but it was the 1970s, and standards were different back then. I don't recall where we were going that day, to the store or library, maybe to visit a friend, but I certainly remember how it felt to be on her bike, the mixture of excitement, physicality, and joy as she pushed us off down the sidewalk, yelling her standard, "Hang on for dear life!"

That bike is long gone, and now so is my mother, but I still have my love of the ride. It's a legacy I hope to pass on to my own kids.

After one moderate climb along Thirty-Sixth, it's all downhill to the university. This is a stretch with no intersections, few driveways, and rarely any other pedestrians, so I can finally put in some real effort. As I crest the top of the hill and begin to hammer away at the pedals, I look toward the mountains. It's still dark, but the sky to the east is easing into a deep shade of indigo, making visible the black outline of the Chugach Range. What can I say about these mountains? I ride this route in every season. Day after day here they stand—Near Point, Wolverine, O'Malley—permanent fixtures of the landscape. What I witness on my commute, though, is not permanence but constant change, as light, clouds, and snow shift across these peaks. They contain a sense of the rare, the miraculous. No wonder the ancient Greeks placed their gods on a mountain. Today I know I'm lucky to be here, in this very moment, as the Chugach Range is born into a new day.

My heart feels big in my chest as I hit campus. I pass all the cars circling for parking spots and cruise right up to my building, where I dismount with a flourish and then wheel my bike into my department's office suite. My nose is running, and my goggles are fogging, but my body is buoyed as though filled with helium. I feel too big to be contained in this space. Fortunately, a classroom full of sleepy college students awaits me.

"Top o' the morning!" I bellow into the white and beige suite.

From behind the front desk, the admin assistant studies me over the top of her reading glasses. She's close to retirement and tends to regard me with that special blend of exasperation and delight a mother feels for her problem child.

"If it isn't the abominable snowman!" She shakes her head. "I bet you're glad to be out of the weather."

I grin at her with my cold lips, then wheel my bike down the hall. The truth is, I don't want this ride to end.

The Bike Thief

DON REARDEN

The Edwin I knew stole bikes and rode them to rust around the dusty pothole laden roads of our sprawling tundra town of Bethel. A decade older than me, I didn't really know him so much as I knew his reputation, or rather his proclivity for locating and pedaling off with any and all unsecured bicycles. He'd often be hanging out in front of the grocery store, where I worked through high school, which in retrospect I now understand was the perfect place for him. The store functioned as the heart of the community. All the roads lead like dusty veins to the store, and all bikes would wind up leaning against the metal fencing skirting the building side or lying beside the boardwalk leading to the steel grates of the steps leading inside. You forgot to lock up? Or if you figured, why would anyone steal a bike in a remote town with no road in or out? *That bicycle was as good as Edwin's.*

You'd be inside the store paying for overpriced groceries, perhaps filling your mom's last-minute request for a recipe's ingredient, and Edwin would be pedaling like mad out of the parking lot. You'd see Edwin again but never the bike. Or at least not the whole bike.

I'm not sure where Edwin lived or if he even had a home, but I know that he frequented a plywood shack off Schawlbe Street. Behind that shack, in the shoulder-high grass, lay a massive boneyard of bicycle parts. Frames. Wheels. Gears. Seats. Handlebars. Rusted chains. Part of your bike was certain to end up there if you weren't careful. The other part of your bike would become a master creation of Edwin's making, something along the lines of that Johnny Cash song "One Piece at a Time" about a custom-made Cadillac made with parts from several

136

different models. Each iteration of the bikes he built seemed stranger and more outlandish than the last.

For a little town surrounded by tundra and lakes and no roads in or out, Bethel had no shortage of bikes, but as far I knew, we had only one master bike thief. I never really questioned how everyone knew who stole the bikes and yet no one did anything about the constant disappearing bicycles. A level of acceptance existed in the town for a bike thief, but that might be because there were bigger criminal offenses happening too regularly. As far as I knew, Edwin wasn't one of the *bad* guys, and I grew up hearing about bad guys.

My dad was one of the many probation officers Edwin would have during his rather short life. He called Edwin "the runner." As far as my father knew, Edwin *ran,* or delivered on stolen bikes, 750-milliliter bottles of vodka or whiskey, for local bootleggers. The going rate back then for bootlegged booze he would deliver? Fifty dollars a bottle. I didn't have the heart to tell my dad that he had the name all wrong and that he should call Edwin "the biker" or "the bike thief" instead. I can't exactly say why, but I felt bad enough for Edwin as it was.

It wasn't until I'd graduated from college and returned to Bethel to teach high school that I owned my first bike of any value. The shiny black Novara mountain bike shipped from REI Outlet and cost around $450 and probably a cool hundred or so for freight. Once I put it together and clipped in with my fancy new bike shoes, I raced off to speed around the town for my first big ride.

At the first stop sign, I forgot about my clipped-in shoes and tipped straight over. *Bam!* The fine black paint job instantly hidden beneath the grime that is a tundra road. I dusted off my bruised ego and continued on, glad no one saw my silly wreck. My goal that day consisted of making my first epic loop around the town, perhaps stopping somewhere to buy a Gatorade or some other cold beverage. I planned a stop by the home of a friend or two to show off the new bike and see if anyone wanted to grab dinner at Snack Shack. I didn't make it too far when a moment of dread hit me harder than the wreck a few minutes earlier.

A lock! I didn't have a lock!

Edwin!

I could not escape the vision of Edwin racing off down the road on my Novara.

How could I be so stupid? My bike wouldn't be safe until I had a quality lock.

I couldn't stop anywhere to purchase a lock because they likely wouldn't have one at the store, and if I left it outside? *Edwin!* I realized I wouldn't be able to bike anywhere that required me to dismount from the bike for several weeks, or at least until I had a lock shipped out from Anchorage.

I spent that whole first ride thinking about the lengths I would need to go to make sure my bike wouldn't get stolen. I hadn't even thought about how I would protect the bike once I got home. I couldn't leave it out on the porch. I would need to bring it inside. All of this because I couldn't bear the thought of Edwin racing off down the road on my new wheels. When I got home, my ride cut short, I ordered two heavy-duty locks.

I liked that bike enough that when I left Bethel to further my education and try to make something of myself, I decided to take the Novara with me. I could have easily sold it to someone who would have then left it somewhere for Edwin to steal. I moved to Anchorage, a mecca for biking. Incredible trails. None of that tundra grime. But it didn't take long for me to learn that the place crawled with bike thieves, and none of them had Edwin's charisma or charm. I carried my caution of those with Edwin-like skills to the big Alaskan city and to this day haven't had any of my bikes stolen. I've retired the Novara but still keep it for guests to use.

A few years ago I learned that Edwin had died living on the streets here, and that loss still haunts me. I didn't know he'd moved to the same town as me, but I suspect his relocation coincided with incarceration. I know for certain he didn't move here for the bike trails or to make something of himself. For all I know, I could have ridden past him.

How great would it have been for me to catch him stealing my fat bike? I might have said, "Hey! Hey you!" and then, "Edwin? Is that you? *Edwin!*" I certainly would have hugged him or given him a high-five. I think if I would have seen him taking off with someone's sweet Cannondale, I would have most certainly cheered.

The last time I ever saw Edwin on a bike in Bethel, he was riding this Frankenstein's monster of a circus-like ride with a modified frame, handlebars, and seat. At this point Edwin, in his bike thief career, was making some pretty cool bikes for the middle of nowhere Alaska. The bicycle he rode stood at least eight feet off the ground, and it was speeding down the street toward the store. As goofy as the bike was, my last vision of Edwin makes sense to me now. Edwin deserved to be on a bike that no one else could ride *or steal*.

I hope they let Edwin into heaven so he can ride the hell out of the gold paved streets behind the pearly gates, and when he's done, ditch God's bike in the long grass beside a salmon stream.

The Killer Hill

It was my perfect sporting event—brief, brutal, and relatively un-popular—and I was determined to love it, as long as it didn't kill me.

First, let me assure you, in case your wardrobe isn't 90 percent Lycra, that this essay isn't just about sport. It's about an experiment that started with one activity and expanded into a larger quest to understand how we spend our time.

But it starts with cycling. It starts at the bottom of a steep hill, looking up toward a hairpin curve with trepidation.

I first decided to bike up the hill behind Anchorage's Potter Marsh one early-summer day in 2006. The road, a favorite racing venue, rises about seven hundred feet in just under two miles, zigzagging past mansions and stunning views of Turnagain Arm.

Winners of the race climb the 7 percent–grade hill in under ten minutes, "sport" or intermediate cyclists take twelve to fourteen minutes, while novices might hyperventilate their way to the top in something under eighteen.

Ten to twenty minutes of anything: how bad could it be?

On my first attempt, garbed in sweatpants and naive optimism, I planned to give it my best and use that time as a baseline for potential improvement.

Making sure no cyclist or observer of any kind was in the vicinity, I pedaled up the hill in my lowest gear, panting and straining. I muscled my way around a tight curve, climbed again, and finally pulled into an expensive neighborhood that I assumed to be the hill's end.

I looked at my watch, and then I spent several minutes coughing and recovering my breath, feeling if not gleeful, at least reassured: *Twenty minutes, without any training. Take that!*

In the victory speech my mind played on the easy ride down, I thanked the genetic heritage of my supremely fit grandfather. Not long before his death, "Papa Coach" broke his hip on an icy winter day while cycling at a steep-banked velodrome north of Chicago, leaving me to inherit his fondness for questionable training routines as well as his extremely bulky calves.

Except that when I retraced the hill a few days later, in my car, I realized I hadn't finished the course. In fact, I'd barely started it. The road doesn't hairpin once; it hairpins five times, for a total of six steep, straight sections, ending where the asphalt becomes gravel. I'd cycled under one-third its length and height in more time than it takes most beginners to pedal the whole thing. Turns out that without a lot of cardiovascular conditioning, bulky calves don't do much more than hold up knee socks.

Even my Subaru resented the long, steep ride that day, nearly overheating on the drive up. Back at sea level, I felt a little grim. And—perversely—inspired as well.

Later that summer, pacing myself and taking several rests, while tolerating the fact that my heart seemed ready to break through the walls of my chest like Sigourney Weaver's 1980s alien foe, I managed to do the entire hill in eighteen minutes.

Two weeks later I shaved another forty seconds off that time—an act of sheer will, rather than a result of training.

The physical effort of each climb was hard enough, but for a novice the mental effort was even tougher. On my second try I didn't stop for any rest, and I had to bargain with myself around every hairpin: don't quit, don't stop pedaling, keep hands and neck loose, don't look too far ahead, and most of all, don't worry—this isn't really going to kill you.

Having climbed the hill only twice, without witnesses, I found the nerve to enter a three-stage women's beginners' race series called the Posies. The first stage was Potter, which I finished in sixteen minutes, twenty-eight seconds, taking a minute off my previous time.

At the top I could barely breathe and felt the blood drain from my whitening face. People glanced my way, probably wondering if I was going to pass out. I hurried home to recover in private.

A few years earlier, prior to owning a decent bicycle, I had started along the path to becoming a novelist. During this time I took up jogging with a friend. As our labored steps added up to miles, I took the lesson to heart: even the slowest, most incremental progress will get you somewhere. I repeated that lesson to myself as a creative writing mantra. I finished my novel. It was published, nationally and abroad. I had some good luck with reviews and publicity. Frankly, my life changed.

But it didn't get any easier. The year my first novel came out was one of the hardest in a decade, filled with high expectations and stress, work-related travel, tricky financial decisions, minor health issues, and two family deaths.

Work, during this year, was not one of my comforts. I started a second novel, but it proved more difficult to write than the first. In the shadow of midlife pressures, I had lost some easy joy, spontaneity, and faith. Oh sure, I knew more small steps would get me somewhere again, but in the meanwhile I wasn't sure I could take the angst of each baby step.

Plus—and this is no metaphor—my knees had really started to hurt. Running wasn't going to help me get through this rough patch.

On December 31, for the first time in my entire life, I wasn't looking forward to New Year's resolutions. That's saying a lot for a goal junkie.

Trouble was, I'd been making the same resolutions for a decade: the cello thing; the Spanish thing; the exercise and weight thing. There was never any time, anyway—for me or any other person I knew struggling to balance work and school-age children. It was hard enough just to meet deadlines and balance a checkbook. Or get out of bed in the morning.

Wait a minute—was I depressed? When had it started? When would it end?

When had I learned something about learning to suck it up, just a little? Ah yes, Potter Hill.

So, on January 1, 2008, I pledged to climb that hill again the right way, with training and a plan.

But first, I wanted to sort out some bigger lifestyle issues. I spent a few weeks analyzing my life by keeping a detailed time diary. Quickly, I realized how little I knew about my own life patterns. I sleep a lot—and seem to need it. When I exclude time-wasting tasks, and even though my workdays feel plenty full, I don't work nearly as many hours as I think. (Few people do, researchers say.)

I spend a fair amount of time cooking and eating: at least two hours daily for those combined activities. (The French would approve.) But the American in me spends much more time than I would have guessed shopping, doing errands, and chauffeuring children.

My time diary showed me that I don't know the basic patterns of my own life. When I try to plug the holes in my time-leaking schedule, I go after little cracks while ignoring entire sewage tunnels through which wasted time gushes forth, carrying away the unrealized moments that matter most: returning a call to a friend, reading literature, listening to the joke my daughter is trying to tell me, taking care of my own physical health. I should know this life of mine better. It's the only one I'm going to get.

"I have seen an essay, 'How to live on eight shillings a week,'" wrote the British novelist Arnold Bennett, a contemporary of Virginia Woolf. "But I have never seen an essay 'How to live on twenty-four hours a day.' Which of us lives on twenty-four hours a day? And when I say 'lives,' I do not mean 'exists,' nor 'muddles through.' Which of us is free from that uneasy feeling that the 'great spending departments' of his daily life are not managed as they ought to be? We shall never have any more time. We have, and we have always had, all the time there is."

Bennett's 1910 musings on time would give birth to the self-help revolution. He advised an emerging white-collar population, working at city jobs they didn't necessarily enjoy, that they should claim ninety minutes, three evenings a week, and use that time for self-improvement. "All depends on that. Your happiness—the elusive prize that you are all clutching for, my friends!—depends on that."

Around the same time I stumbled across Bennett, I discovered the research of John Robinson and Geoffrey Godbey, authors of *Time for Life: The Surprising Ways Americans Use Their Time*. When the book was published, Robinson was director of the Americans' Use of Time Project. According to their analysis of national surveys covering three decades of time-diary data, Americans don't have less time than we used to have. We actually have on average five *more* hours of leisure time per week than we had in the 1960s.

Those five hours are not our only leisure time; they are just part of the total forty or so hours of free time people have in a week. (The researchers define free time as any time when one isn't committed to work, family, chores, or personal needs like sleeping, eating, and grooming.)

But if so, where are those forty leisure hours hiding? In small pieces scattered mostly throughout the workweek, the *Time for Life* authors contend. These little pieces are often spent in low-satisfaction activities that are readily available, such as watching TV, the main activity that gobbled leisure time increases since the 1960s, or in more recent years, going online. The result is that we don't perceive true leisure, that tranquil time best used in larger chunks, during which the spirit and body recharge. In surveys most people report feeling more harried than ever.

Even away from screens, we slice up time, layer activities by multitasking, and muddy our own abilities to perceive time's passage. The desire for greater efficiency may in fact be depriving us of what we most need: the purposeful pursuit of truly regenerative activities and a break from the *perception* of time pressure.

My own winter funk began to lift when, lying in bed one night, I tried to imagine what I would do if I had some extra hours each week to spend any way I pleased.

Just the thought of spending newfound pockets of time—"golden hours," I began to call them—cheered me. I also sent out an email that was forwarded to dozens of strangers in which I asked people how they would spend three to four hours a week of guilt-free "extra" time. Working more was an option I specified in the email; so was sleeping. No one had to pick something oriented toward self-improvement. Yet often people did.

The top answers fell into a handful of categories. Pursue a physical activity (often solo) for health and pleasure. Read the long-ignored pile of books stacked alongside one's bed. Get outside and be in nature. Pursue some kind of art, whether by learning guitar, taking a dance class, or taking a fine arts class. Travel or prepare for a trip. Journal or write.

One woman said she wanted to document family history for her son while her own parents are still alive. No one singled out cleaning or getting more organized. Plenty of people thanked me just for asking.

I was particularly touched by the answer of a thirty-eight-year-old single mom with three teenage kids who said she'd spend the imaginary time exercising. In reality, though, she called such extra, guilt-free, leisure time "unthinkable."

I thanked her for her time, even more rare and precious because she is a single mom. In her follow-up email, she said that no one had called her time "rare and precious" before. It was a wake-up call for her, an aha moment.

Her email and others like it convinced me: we should talk about this. It matters just as much as financial planning. We need to have time *and we need to feel as if we have time.*

But the selection of how best to use this time is difficult, I quickly realized. I found myself wishing for a consumer's guide to leisure time even if I knew such a guide was bound to be idiosyncratic and whimsical. And yet we comparison shop before buying a refrigerator or a car. Why not hear from someone else what a hundred hours of leisure dedicated to a specific, regenerative activity yielded over a year's time? Which is more rewarding, in the end: building Habitat for Humanity houses or going for solo walks or taking one's teenager on a weekly date to the local bookstore?

If no one else was going to create such a leisure comparison guide, I decided, then I would make some comparisons myself. Cycling would be just the start.

One of the first things I liked about Matt Novakovich was his heavy breathing over the phone. He apologized, but I understood completely: he was biking as we talked, multitasking so that my interview wouldn't cut into his workout, safeguarding his own "golden hours." This was just Matt's easy warm-up—I'm sure by the time he really got going, we couldn't have talked at all—but he needed to get it done before his wife and three young children got home.

Though Matt, a top Anchorage record holder, bikes about twelve to fifteen hours a week (peaking at twenty hours weekly in March), he didn't laugh at me when I said I could do maybe three or four. Barring any serious weight or health issues, "every person is four months away from the best shape of his life," Matt told me.

At his house Matt set me up on a bike in his garage, linked to a computer trainer that monitored my cadence, speed, power output, and heart rate. The results of my test on a simulated racecourse were unimpressive. Even the warm-up phase had felt uncomfortably hard.

Later, in his kitchen, Matt penciled a weekly workout plan for me, including sessions that targeted long bike rides as well as intervals of high-cadence and high-pulse pedaling as well as some cross-training. Most of these workouts would be done on an inside trainer that had been gathering dust in my basement.

The first twenty- and thirty-minute workouts were hard, even at an "easy" pace. My rear end, unaccustomed to the bike seat, let its discontent be known.

As winter months progressed, I was able to bike 60 to 120 minutes and pedal with enough intensity to make a racket, drowning out any music or movie I was using to distract myself from tedium. I'd always thought of myself as someone who didn't perspire very much. Now I realized that it was only because I'd never exercised long or hard enough to really sweat. It's a little embarrassing to realize, midlife, how much you've been sparing yourself.

At the same time, it was hard to stick to the routine and find time for the multiple new hobbies I'd recently added to my life. As part of this larger time study effort, I volunteered for a political campaign, which included a trip out of state. I bought a pawnshop electric guitar, which proceeded to gather dust in a corner. I tinkered with yet other pastimes, but most of them didn't stick.

In the end I missed about a quarter of the cycling workouts. I'd meant to train for one hundred hours, but I managed something like seventy-five. I stressed about it, of course, and I cursed the irony of my own stressing about lost "leisure."

Where did three to four hours a week on a bike get me? Not far, I thought in April, when I tried to climb Potter Hill again and discovered that I still couldn't get all the way to the top. Even after months of indoor cycling!

Not far, I still thought in May, noticing that my weight hadn't budged one bit since January.

Not far, I thought even in early June, as I struggled to bicycle up steep DeArmoun on a weekday night around 9:00 p.m., having found no time, yet, to make dinner.

Finally, on June 11, I did the Posies Potter Hill Climb race, the same race I'd finished in sixteen minutes and twenty-eight seconds, back in 2006. This time I was hoping to do it two minutes faster, in fourteen minutes, thirty seconds.

I finished in thirteen minutes, fifty-nine seconds.

I was met at the bottom of the hill by my husband and smiling thirteen-year-old son, and I didn't even feel overheated, sick, or woozy; I felt great. I didn't hate the hill. It wasn't trying to kill me; it was trying to save me. I loved the hill.

But that wasn't the best hill climb. The best one was the one a few days earlier, when I finished a slower-paced ride up Potter's 700-foot climb and impulsively decided to take a different route home. I turned right on Rabbit Creek Road, instead of left, and kept pedaling uphill another six miles, for a total elevation gain that day of 1,646 feet—just for the pleasure of it.

I'd started out cycling Potter Hill because it was something hard that I could do quickly. *Ten to twenty minutes: how bad can it be?* But it had led me to a level of fitness where I could stay active for hours. It had prodded me into the best shape of my life.

At the top of most of my hill climbs, I had started to experience a "cyclist's high," during which my energy soared, writing ideas came easier, and everything seemed possible.

My experience made we want to tell others: yes, really, three or four hours a week doing anything new. Find the time. Make the time. As Arnold Bennett said in 1910, "All depends on that."

Cryo-Cave!

An Ode to Indoor Training in Alaska

Cryo-cave is not a pretty sight. It is not for children. It is not scenic. Mountains it has for backdrop, could one see out of it, and small woods around. But it is shut upon the world.

Shut, not sealed, for cryo-cave is drafty, besides being cold.

Cryo for "cold" and *cave* for "hole (horizontal), rock recess, paleo *doms*, ur-shelter post-arbor, hunter's canvas, bone midden place, shadow screen, dire wolf tomb, hermit hovel, sanctum." Truth be told, it is a foursquare garage annex, with cathedral ceilings for hanging bikes and a large, upward rolling door for machines—mostly horticultural—to exit and return. But when cryo-cave is cryo-cave, this door remains fasted against the elements, since any cave worth its salt will blunt the winds and nudge the blizzard, moderate the temps and protect the traveler.

This last assuredly, as the altar here, called Emonda (the world) in the Roman fashion, fixed at the rear to a flywheel device, is surmounted by a salty drifter seeking relief, claiming asylum on the threshold. This he is granted, reprieve to bounce in the saddle to the very worst European techno, covered in nothing more than a strappy unitard, a diapery bum pad sewn inside (the chamois, once a goatskin hardly more elegant), the ensemble properly a "bib short," to complete the infantilization. Pedaling begins with scant regard for decency, though perhaps we have improved upon the state of nature.

Our caveman has woken in the Eternal City, has ambled seminude through suburban palestrae, has exchanged his loincloth for a disused wrestling singlet unattended by its owner, has wandered into the training grounds of the hippodrome, has climbed aboard the mechanical horse and halloos now, in precincts sacred to Zeus, under the sway of

148

local vines. Little else can explain this rapid assimilation of technology by Neolithic man, unless it be the manifest indifference of play—I had almost said, of fun—to time and the ages.

These are not the most savory precincts, the raw drywall tagged with toilet stall apothegms doubtless akin to the worst forms of classical graffiti. "Don't be a bitch," sexist we'd now say but for the addendum, "Don't be a dick," straight after, then the stale affirmative "Be a hero" superposed in belts of Catholic red. Cryo-cave is full of sage advice, most of it crossed out, all of it cribbed, but still useful in the pitch of agony.

The withering pitch. Our agon is never far to find, our cloistered agon. The agora is elsewhere. For this cell, monkish in fact, is where the training happens, almost the only real training, in the so-called off-season. The bike, a supple-brittle Martian thing in gloss black and viper red, hooks into the aptly named Kick(e)r, a direct drive ergometer with ample flywheel, one able to register so many thousands of kilojoules of encyclic motion and primed to track the luminous outflows, given as watts, for the power and the glory, forever.

The Kick(e)r connects via wireless protocol to a small black box running any number of simulations, each offering enticements to training. Most notable among them are the other riders, or "users," whose on-screen avatars one can race. These sims display on a large, flat, high-definition screen, a bargain model but fancy for an annex, its images close, but the cave isn't spacious.

Here is a cavern mystery worthy of Plato, absent the prison or the play of the shades or their failing adequation in the light. This cave is real yet virtual, in fact as well in form; the avatar an ideal self whose faults are yet one's own. For upon the screen there does appear a man, alike in body to the one astride the bike, himself astride similarly, yet of a tan-ness of calf wholly out of season and of a tan-ness altogether unlikely in the original, whose essential paleness goes sheet-white in the drafts. This avatar, tintable, moldable after a fashion, dressed and redressed like a well-appointed doll, responds with barely perceptible delay to each downstroke and upstroke of the pedals. The actual pedals, which must be got going if blood is to flow through our ashen model, not nearly so inspirited as his manifest puppet, though sanguine of his prospects could he only *get* going.

It will hot up presently; fans will be engaged, to evaporate. But for the moment it is cold; it is winter above the forty-fifth parallel, even above the sixtieth; snow is blowing and darkness feels permanent. Where the outer world is hostile, the inner must suffice. Yet the northern blood is sludgy, the legs leaden in the first barrage, the core creaking, the breath visible. The soul, an ingle under bellows, must be coaxed. Breath raises a low flame, makes it respectable, decent, almost hot. Sharp cold lingers in the far extremities, so hands and toes are covered, at least at first. Wrapped steel (more wan putty), the rider in repose browses his music, loafs unimpressively, fiddles with earbuds and sundry techne, drops something and has to climb down, remembers something (water probably) and has to go fetch it, returns to toggle screens and babble pique—a spoiled troll accustomed to the luxuries of his barrow, wanting only the sobering privations of the bridge. At last our little monster settles, forgets all, becomes more beautiful, provokes his avatar. Briefest delay, span of an echo, and his thera-self spins up, threading, under load, an island world, counterpoint to the one outside, chosen for its volcanoes and peerless palms.

A choice of worlds is to hand, and we choose the one most populated. Cryo-cave is social, at least nominally. Really, we are hunting humans and just cause they are there; antagonism obtains in every idle pass and vengeful overtaking. A perpetual bike path sprint waits in readiness, in a world teeming with adversaries made more terrible by their foreign flags and in-game handles—"BathSalts69" up ahead, "Epstein_didn't_kill_himself" back a bit but lively on the chat. And yet the general bloodbath, the war of all against all, never materializes; words of encouragement predominate, chummy groups tout each other's talents; in the teeth of international competition, the social bond. And the cave, erstwhile emblem of the insular hunting band, shines out global, a portal onto a vast cardiovascular nexus touching all nations. Doomed to dissension probably but touching in the moment.

This utopia is not long in faltering. Some, it is alleged, have cheated, have made their projected selves lighter or smaller than the truth, to the benefit of their speed. Some have marred their ideation with the rank criterion: success. Some have profaned the sacred competition who profane again once accused. Ever more ingenious forms of cynical manipulation are advanced to explain the world-beating power of random avatars, named by nothing more than a pair of letters or a string of numbers—bots, obviously, or hackers or something worse. Campaigns of denunciation leak out of the simulated world; exoneration is sought via real-world efforts. Amid the turmoil, some retreat into the ludic, claim the sim is just a game. Others bristle, maintain there's nothing ludicrous about it and that cheaters must be shot. Indeed, the best lack all conviction, while the worst are full of passionate intensity, as the poet says. Each rider, each "player," looks from their respective cave upon a fallen world, of mixed merit, not unlike the one outside their doors.

And what an outside for cryo-cave! Better to fly to it? Environs are a sporty town, a sporting state, a great land, extensive of hunter and fisher and flyer and climber. And beautiful. It is God's own light upon them hills. Nature has her holidays, in the far corners. Of the factor and the grade, the less said the better, but everything's extra. So our athletes play to suffer, bleating (triumphantly, it must be said) in their hurt boxes, torture chambers, and pain caves. But these are integuments of the mind, states of mind comparable to dark enclosures, wherein the masochistic focus would allow the jocks to suffer better. Suffice to say, none of these is cryo-cave, where the pain is met. Our chilly confines give the lie. Here we exceed the limit and decline, or we come up to it and hold it there, betimes forever. The ready state is the steady one, the metronome a motto, the robot no ghetto of the fulsome body's pride, but aspiration. For there is naught of nature in cryo-cave that would not merge with some machine, that would not thrill to those smooth mechanical powers made flesh, the sign of a good day being *not to feel the legs* for the duration. Put culturally, one would not be an American original but a Euro-bot, a hard man of the Old World and even, to the scandal of local politics, the Eastern bloc.

Ah, but nature is out there, you know! The big wild life I know I know. Predatory wastes. When the bears sleep, the cold stalks. These threats are real. During a recent, particularly frigid midwinter race, a friend of mine stopped halfway—luckily, the route passed twice by hospital—to check himself into the emergency room. His eyeballs were frozen, he said, their light failing fast. We can never lose sight of the dangers. His vision regained, he swore never to test the cold again or never so brazenly. Others their water froze or their food; few could eat and drink enough. Frost-nipped cheeks threatened permanent disfigurement. Tires lost pressure, their seals failing. Whoever touched metal, inadvertently as they tried to eat, paid with fingers so numb they must fall off in the hour. None were at their best or spared mishap, though some were saved from oblivion.

Cryo-cave knows none of this hardship but is a stack of cookies and a doppio, spring water and the aforementioned techno. Deliciously cold, sooth, and energizing, like the best crystal—the addicts say—it releases potential. Nothing like that cruel adrenal focus, in the first flights of transcendental synth, the smooth draw of the viscous psychostimulant in the traction of the throat, mingled wide with buttery solids and the serotonic chocolate. A doped beginning, if not plainly drugged, but in our defense we do not have to steer. Can you get a ticket for riding your bike drunk? Indeed, you can but not for riding indoors thus augmented. Verily, cryo-cave is safe and cold, allowing its dweller to suffer best.

One needs no crash course in cryonics to understand the benefits. Besides the mood music, ease of eating, gratifying efficiency, and general time savings, there is the nearly perfect temperature. For performance the ambient optimum is fifty degrees, just below which, after a decent warm-up and a few hard ramps, cryo-cave settles. Thereafter, the stable cool lowers perceived effort, giving a psychological edge. It is thus much easier to push much harder, the breath curling from nostrils flared to a purpose, like a bit of dragon's fire, then dissipating in the chill stream of our work—that feint of flame being but the reign of cold showing out, declaring itself for heart and lung and aerobic glycolysis. That avian reptile, cold-blooded, is not in store, but a beast far hairier will be unchained and curried, in the cave at last.

Of course, real cryonics, the cryonics of the future, has no truck with us. Life extension, or resurrection, is no part of our program. In the far perspective we may die in cryo-cave, having finally pushed too hard, our corpse thereby preserved somewhat better, discovered more in the pose of action and not its sequel. In the far perspective cryo-cave may be a tomb, not thermostatically controlled, not a morgue, but suitably cool the year round, like an Etruscan crypt, its walls painted with scenes from the life, mostly of sporting and feasting. Our beliefs in the underworld notwithstanding, we deny ourselves nothing. Like the inhumers of the ancient Medi, we pile in such provisions as might prove useful "elsewhere." Clearly, calorie restriction, that other pillar of radical life extension, is not for us (unless "puke intervals" count in the negative—depends, did you?); we scorn the fast as we do ketosis, for we must stay nourished for the longest journey. That journey, some days, feels nigh; exerting to exhaustion cannot be healthy; we are likely running down the mortal coil in here.

Appropriately for an engine room that would bank eternal rest, it is often hard to tell the time. There is only one window in cryo-cave, a milky aperture made blond by errant sawdust—for the garage must be a woodshop, when the rest of life calls. And when cryo-cave hits its seasonal prime, it is already dark here most of the time, above the sixtieth parallel: to the detriment of reality. We stare again at our island world, tilting against avatars based halfway across the globe whose pilots are just waking up. Really, this circadian clash enlivens; we draft the morning energy of our European confreres. It is 9:00 p.m. Alaska time, so we are stealing a march on the sun, but thus surcharged, we find it hard to sleep and wake next morning much later than normal. To the detriment of reality.

So far, time in the virtual has enhanced the hyperborean life, keeping at bay those wintry doldrums, especially when the snow is low. That could change. One day soon a visor could descend, nesting over the eyes and face, with other inputs athwart the skin, divers cold instruments reading the blood. Then the machine will be complete and the outside cease, and even when the snow is bountiful or the earth shines green, we will hold fast to the cave and its illusions, riding through palaces yet undreamed. The virtual, so supplied, does feel inevitable.

An eerie fate but not a useless one. This VR nightmare may brook the green solution yet, without low sallies into verdure. For in the visory future so imagined, we may see ourselves pedaling up some magic battery or amplifying instrument, productive of sufficient wattage to run the appliances, heat the house, give light to the loved habitants, though we rarely come out. They rather visit us, at intervals, to bring refreshment as we flag, the flickering of kitchen lights indicating the need. Then we ourselves are perceived like the cabinet cards of the

Horse in Motion, first film already ancient, until we are supplied with something like food. Then the full radiance descends again and we are so beheld. A lamp-lighting ritual, a keeping of the eternal flame—it justifies the blind provider in his banishment: he has found the future of work.

Of course, he is not blind but sees thoroughly whatever he wishes. To know this is to know all. A single spot of light, hoarfrost running out in all directions, the world smoking nearly in its white soil. A luminous cube projecting such banners of light as to exceed any thought of a man's having done it but for the shadow of a skull laying high on the light, shot from the roof and flapping on the sky.

Nothing so gothic, or so cruel, awaits us. What a waste that would be. Our cave is not a prison but a haven for Anchorites, power hungry and glad. Perhaps one day our work will bank some watts for the city, the indoor work of thousands in the so-called off-season—power recycled—but that is a long way off. For now we do no public good but a private. A quiet quest for dominance, notwithstanding the cold, indeed because of it.

Cryo-cave is on a mission. We have humans to destroy, in their virtual incarnations. All so we can vanquish others more local, in their analogue versions. It is thus that cryo-cave treats splendidly of Outside—the proper noun Alaskans use, with slight provincial malice, to nominate the out-of-state—with a view to succeeding in the local out-of-doors. We climb digital volcanoes and blooming alpine groves to prepare for dirt tracks and shitty gravel roads in our own fair season, in the so-called real mountains. We ride on winter weekends with hungover Australians who are sweltering in their summer heat, preparing for our snow-girt battles, our cold spring races, the marquee contests of our own mellow summer. We are becoming cosmopolitan, for cavemen; we paint stories of the hunt for all to see, in the afterglow of international competition, on linked digital fora; we ping our cyber rivals and offer kudos, follow their exploits, weave them into our networks. We are becoming more human.

And when the green kicks it up, it shall all be shuttered, practically abandoned. An antisocial act, considering what friends we have made. Conceivably, we are embracing nature. Nature is certainly in evidence, is indeed so vast and boundless that we cannot grasp it. Nevertheless, we stumble from our burrow like a dazed bear, begin the laying up of debris and the backfilling with stone and dirt, disguising our portal, almost as if we were hiding our shame. The beautiful world beckons, we must fly to it, we must resist the mission creep of the virtual, we must we must. Yet coincidence conspires to detain us. I am only just reading, in latitudes cousin to ours, in lands westerly once contiguous, reindeer herders have recovered an Ice Age cave bear, perfectly preserved with intact organs, from the retreating permafrost. This is a comfort; we feel ourselves properly placed, immune to the vagaries of time immured just as we are, or were. If we are discovered some years hence, like the bear twenty thousand years after our demise, we are sure the discovering life will be different, perhaps not organic at all, perhaps not of this world. To the master machines as to aliens equally, our little hovel becks an unbecoming enigma, its crude picture box propped askew upon a ski waxing table, its sweat-stiffened towels hung about like shrouds, banded with dried salt no doubt the consequence of weeping, its jolly skeleton lying beside this workhorse contraption of carbon fiber and costly metals and circuits and wires, highly engineered yet asked to do no more than crank in place.

But actually they would find an empty tomb, for were death imminent, one really would ride without. And should I get a bad diagnosis or fall on dark days, I would ride outside, where I could be alone. Let the world end with warning for a few, and I among them, the very first thing I would do, also then the last, would be to pull my bike out of the garage and ride through the apocalypse upon the lawless roads. I would not be caught dead in cryo-cave should life pull up short and not stretch out, as it does now, in endless green-gold profusion, so big and woodsy and mountainous that I can spare a thought for Inside without losing track of the great outdoors. Let others, plump tourists, heed the call of the wild. There is wilderness on our doorstep; the wild world starts with a cave. Survival begins with a bit of shelter and a fire. Haven't you seen the television shows, pretending to be our local reality? I am watching one right now as I pedal to keep warm.

The Iditarod Trail and Me   CLINTON HODGES III

We made our way into the snow. Right away, it became apparent to me that we were going to have a slow first day. Tyson Flaharty, Kurt Refsnider, and I were riding but with a decent amount of effort and not very fast. My attention quickly turned to body temperature. The slower conditions, warmth, and snow could cause me some issues with sweating in my gear too much. Because of these conditions, I decided to just keep those two guys in sight. It sounds like the three of us made it through this first part of the race in much better shape than others.

From the Iditarod Trail Invitational (ITI) website in 2020:

> The Iditarod Trail Invitational is the world's longest running winter ultra-marathon. One of the most challenging experiences on the planet, participants brave extreme physical, environmental and mental challenges as they travel along the historic Iditarod Trail on bicycle, foot or skis. Requiring self-sufficiency and the considerable resilience to make it through up to 30 frozen days and nights, the Iditarod Trail Invitational has built its reputation on notoriously inhospitable conditions and minimal outside support.
>
> A true test of human endurance, adaptability and mental fortitude, competitors travel 350 miles on the historic Iditarod Trail under their own power while hauling all of their survival gear with them. Only six checkpoints with food and minimal sleeping quarters are offered prior to reaching the finish line in McGrath, Alaska.

My name is Clinton, and racing has been my life's work. Some people's life work is art. Others it is their profession. My story has always been racing. It has always been my passion and a foundation for happiness.

I grew up in the now hip Spenard area on West Twenty-Seventh Avenue in the early 1980s, a mere block away from what is now Bear Tooth Theatrepub. I was born at the Third Avenue Alaska Native Medical Center. I lived in a cozy green-and-white trailer with my father, mom, and our two Newfoundland dogs, Jeremiah and Pepper. Spenard has a close place to my heart. After almost thirty years, moving back to where I was raised, I've watched Spenard and Anchorage change and grow.

When we got to Yentna Station, we were drying out, having cheese sandwiches, chicken noodle soup, and a couple of Cokes while chatting nicely. Tyson and I have spent time talking together, but this was the first time that Kurt, Tyson, and I were together in close quarters, and we took this time to just talk and enjoy what the trail was like at this point. About an hour after showing up, we each made our way out the door and back on the trail.

We were evaluating each other, much like players in a poker game. The three of us were comfortable and confident with ourselves and were looking forward to the trail. We were starting to get the "feel" for it and how fast we could finish the event.

Jeremiah and Pepper were majestic animals. Newfoundlands are mostly gentle giants. I remember they had warm, calm, and welcoming temperaments. An ideal day for us was to go through the Burger King drive-through and play in Lake Spenard. In the winter they would pull me around the neighborhood in a wooden sled, much like what we see on the Iditarod Dog Sled Race. Those two were my consistent friends when I was little. The little neighborhood I lived in had a very transient population, so friends came and went with regularity.

The sensation of speed came rather subconsciously. As a young child, I would develop these complex tracks and cities that I would push my Hot Wheels toys around in the dirt. I would imagine the sensation of speed and drifting around corners. I always would "drive" my Hot

Wheels smoothly around the corners. I enjoyed playing in the dirt driveway. Seeing how gravel roads develop started to tell the story of speed and provided me content for my imagination.

I had a rather impressive collection of automobile type toys, couldn't stand eating spinach (my father would remind me about Popeye and his strength to get me to finish eating); I loved Mickey Mouse and the shows *Knight Rider* and *Transformers*. Looking back at this point in my life, I realize that the mechanical characters of *Knight Rider* and the *Transformers* may have helped drive me to develop certain maintenance habits and care for my bike and cars.

The trail was in really good shape outside of Skwentna. I've never seen the Shell Hills in the daylight. There is a contractor who built a SnowCat trail that you could probably drive a large tired vehicle on. A common theme this year on the trail from multiple competitors is seeing sections of the trail in the daylight. Sort of a side story/experience that develops each year on the Iditarod trail and what brings many of us back for more. For sure, slow conditions are hard, but with them come their own set of positives.

I think I was four years old, and one day we were at the store, and I saw a Mickey Mouse bell that you mount on the handlebars. I was stoked to put this bell on my bike! My dad and I made a deal that if I learned how to ride my bike without training wheels, he would mount the bell. If my memory serves me right, as soon as we got home, I requested that the training wheels be taken off and that my unassisted riding begin immediately. It didn't take long; I had that bell on within a day.

My father was a racer. He has a competitive spirit that began probably around the same age it started for me. He played baseball, football, threw the javelin (and almost qualified for the Olympics), and raced dirt bikes. As a young boy, I remember his Husqvarna CR250 and riding on the gas tank at our cabin in Wasilla. I remember the unique noise the big two-stroke engine would make and how it gave me a rush when we would accelerate. Not long after he sold his dirt bike, he bought a beautiful Harley Davidson 1200cc Sportster that I absolutely loved to ride on the back with him. Heck, I used to fall asleep on the back on those long summer days. I really enjoyed the feeling of having my breath taken away.

I remember when my dad got his first serious remote-controlled (R/C) car, a ¹⁄₁₂th-scale Kyosho Plazma pan car. I had never seen anything accelerate so quickly before. I was speechless watching him drive the car up and down the street. I felt a rush from all my senses experiencing this little car rush up and down the street. I could hear the chassis and body magnify the sounds of the road. The noise the motor made as it was under load while accelerating.

I moved out of Shell Lake and started to make my way out of the wooded areas that surround it. I had a feeling that as soon as I hit the first swamp after Shell Lake Lodge, I was going to have some walking to accomplish.

It took us over eight hours to get from Shell Lake to the Finger Lake checkpoint. We were now over thirty hours into the race. The wind was immense and had drifted in the trail heavily. The three of us had grouped back up, and we were all thankful for that, I think. We each took turns breaking the trail. Each time we were able to get into a wooded area, we would take a small break and just allow ourselves to loosen up. We would stuff our faces with some food and water, zip our jackets back up, and cross the next swamp. As the sun went down, our route finding became more and more difficult. Some of our footsteps were met with a surprising drop up to our knees and thighs. Tyson had a strong handlebar light to allow us to see the small reflectors that dot the side of the trail so we could get an idea of where the trail was. When we started getting close to the checkpoint, I could tell that we were happy to be done with this section of trail. We were greeted by the great checkpoint workers, and they set us up with our choice of chicken or veggie burritos, donuts, and other baked goods. They also grabbed our drop bags for us. All three of us were thrashed from the wind and slow trail. We ate our food, then headed down to the wall tent on the lake, where it was surprisingly warm. Might I even say comfortable.

Many hours later there was a rustle outside the wall tent, and in walks Pete Basinger. He made a comment about how tough the conditions were. Anybody who knows Pete knows he has been through just about every kind of trail and weather condition. When he made a comment about the wind, I knew that we had been through some tough stuff.

When I entered the third grade, my father and I moved across town to the east side. He started allowing me to ride my bike to school. I was so excited to have this freedom! I would explore my neighborhood and all the dirt trails that I could ride to. If my friends and I found something to jump, we would spend hours sessioning until the sun went down. One summer afternoon I was playing in the street with my friend Skippy, and he told me about BMX racing. We used to race up and down the street, and I was one of the faster kids, but I think what really hooked me was the rush of adrenaline from competing.

I had not done much organized sports or racing when I was young. But the BMX racing community during this era was very welcoming to young kids who were interested. We raced behind the YMCA on a nice track. I really liked BMX racing and picked it up quickly. It wasn't long before I even had my first race bike. My dad built me up a sweet GT Mach 1 (from Paramount Cycles when it was on Northern Lights Boulevard). The YMCA felt differently about the BMX crowd. I guess we were just a little too "bad boy" for them. To many people of Alaska, it has been known as the Last Frontier, but sometimes the people of Alaska are the First Objectors.

We started packing up our gear, loaded up our food and supplies from our drop bags, and one by one, we left Winterlake Lodge. I took a moment to chat with Aaron Thrasher and the first woman competitor, Kate Coward, after they came into the checkpoint, and both looked a little thrashed. They had each had quite a night getting to the checkpoint. Kate had lost her GPS unit along the way.

The wind had died down, and the trail is also mostly protected until you're just outside of Puntilla Lake and the Rainy Pass Lodge, so I was hopeful that the trail would be in decent condition.

It didn't take long for me to pick up another competitive hobby. This time it was remote-controlled cars. Some folks may think they are toys, but there is a legit, serious crowd and market for them.

It was with R/C cars that I started to learn the intricacies of racing. Thousands of setup options are available on competitive-style R/C cars. *Roll centers, toe, bump steer, ride height, spring weight, anti-roll bars, electric motors, battery matching,* and *tire compounds* are all common words thrown around in the world of R/C car racing. There were many different classes of racing, 4WD touring cars, Pan cars (prototype bodied, light, quick, and high grip) for indoor-outdoor racing, and 2WD/4WD off-road classes. During the summer I would play baseball, but as soon as the temperatures started to drop, I would turn the heat up and charge the batteries on the R/Cs.

R/C car racing is really competitive. Adults and well-behaved children race in four-minute heats that lead to aggressive racing tactics and high tension. I started racing against grown men when I was nine or ten years old. Many of them were the same age or older than my father. It was here that I started developing my racing technique and was beginning to get accustomed to racing strategy. I also was able to develop strong friendships and fun rivalries that would carry on well into my twenties.

Eventually, the R/C club started to peter out. It has enjoyed a resurgence at various times in Anchorage. When I got into high school, I started to follow various types of motorsports. A guy I met through a church youth group had a Honda XR100 and also raced R/C cars, so we obviously became best of friends.

I wanted to catch back up to Tyson; giving him any gap is pretty dangerous at this point. When the trail conditions are good, you need to cover ground as efficiently as possible. I once again started to gap Kurt while attempting to chase down Tyson.

Riding loaded fat tire bikes is hard work. It is particularly hard chasing after someone as fast as Tyson. I knew that putting out too much effort would cost me, but I had to stay close to the leader at this point. It was a goal I aimed to accomplish this year. In past years I thought that you could save enough energy to cover gaps later in the race. And perhaps that works in regions of the world where the weather has less of an abrupt impact on trail conditions and speed. In 2018 I gave Neil too large of a gap and got hung up in a couple of storms. In 2019 I counted on my speed getting me from Rohn to Nikolai faster than Tyson. I did not count on freezing my boots. Both times my decision ended up biting me in the rear.

I did not catch Tyson, and Kurt ended up catching me once we got out into the swamps and open areas just outside of Puntilla Lake. I was not so concerned with my speed but more at the thought that we weren't going to be staying at the next checkpoint for too long. As the wind continued to blow, I knew that we were going to be in for a long night with minimal rest. I allowed the sunshine to power my attitude and soul. I let the mild temps keep my mind at ease. I tried to stick with the game plan: eat, drink, and conserve energy when possible.

I really enjoyed riding dirt bikes. At high speed the bike moves underneath your body, and you have to work with the bike. You become a single unit, covering any ground you come across. I pleaded with my father to let me get a dirt bike. He made a deal with me: I had to work for it. I learned how to perform the maintenance and upgrades and take care of the other responsibilities that came with owning a dirt bike. I got my first job, and the payments were made by me. I remember riding the bus to work, going to the bank to make payments. I even did a couple of motocross races. They were really tough. I wasn't that strong when I was younger and continued to try and ride often to get better and stronger. Not long after, I was sixteen years old. You know what that means—time to get your license! I was already looking at pickup trucks to carry my dirt bike.

My dad helped me buy a 1992 Nissan Hardbody pickup for my first vehicle. I spent a lot of time washing my truck and dirt bike. If I wasn't adding some new speakers or changing the oil, I was busy vacuuming and wiping down the interior. I was hooked. I loved driving. It gave me a sense of freedom, independence, and a need to explore. Not long after that, I inherited my dad's 1988 GMC Sportside pickup. We lowered it, put some cool tires and wheels on it and a nice exhaust. It felt great customizing vehicles; it was a way to express who I was to the outside world.

The next part of my life is a bit of a blur. My mother and stepmother had some difficulty with alcohol consumption, and I was grappling with growing up, rebelling against anyone who knew better than I, and experiencing difficulties negotiating with my feelings. I didn't take very good care of myself, emotionally and physically. I continued racing and schooling. But I took a lot of risks. I ended up getting a DUI, lost my job, got removed from my associate degree program with only one semester left to finish. I hurt many of my friends. I hurt my family. I was hurting myself. It was a dark moment. I felt really lost and like I had let myself down. I felt like that wasn't what I wanted for my life.

The wind was screaming once again. I took my hands out of my pogies, and I realized that they were extremely cold after accomplishing just a short task. After putting them back in my pogies, I was met with some Screaming Barfies. I could also tell that there was some wind leakage happening on my face system. I was getting a little down on myself. "C'mon Clint, get your act together!" I would tell myself. I tried to seal up the cracks, but there is only so much you can do at this point without causing more harm than good. I could feel spots on my face getting that dreaded dry feeling, I knew I was going to have some windburn or maybe even a little frostnip/bite. It's so difficult adapting to changing conditions quickly and efficiently when you're tired. Seeing Kurt handle the conditions well, I didn't want to show any weakness to him. I made it so I was somewhat comfortable and rode on.

After some stellar parenting by my dad, I got a job at Young's Gear building driveshafts and doing bench repairs. I got back on track making my car payments. My dad continued to let me stay with him while I got back on my feet. I worked on developing a set of more sustainable habits. I had been racing Autocross time trials for a few years at this point, so I started to focus on becoming a better racer. Eventually, I wanted to branch out to more advanced forms of motorsports.

One of my best friends and I decided to build a race car. We had grand visions of road racing and ultimately racing the Fur Rondy Grand Prix (RIP). It was all I ever thought about. I traveled across the United States to watch the 12 Hours of Sebring and the Petit LeMans and still dreamed of going to the grandest race of them all, the 24 Hours of LeMans. I worked, daydreamed, raced, and built cars. I always thought about how I could better my skills. I thought of ways to make the 1986 Mazda RX7 my friend and I developed handle better. I thought about how I could adjust my 2006 Mitsubishi Lancer Evolution to get a little closer to the quickest car up here, a Nissan Skyline GT-R driven by Ryan Guthrie. I spent two winters in Laguna Seca at Skip Barber Racing School learning the ins and outs of race car driving to sharpen my skills. It was there that I learned I was out of shape and needed to trim unnecessary fat. I was trying to compete with younger, smaller, stronger, and better athletes. I knew that if I wanted to go faster, I had to lose some weight and get into shape.

Right about this time in my life, a really adorable blonde came into our lives, Palmer the yellow Lab. At this stage of my life, I didn't care for being outside in the cold, dark, and snow. I had never really understood what it meant to go for a hike or a bike ride on trails. But Palmer needed exercise and interaction. My dad and I started to learn about dog training, and one important part of training is exercise. With that, Palmer helped my father and I discover our love for exploring again. Just like getting my driver's license or when my dad would let me ride my bike farther and farther from the house in third grade, I felt a need to go farther and farther.

Being Kurt's first time up Rainy Pass, I looked for the sign marking the top of the pass. It was really windy again, and night had fallen after we entered the valley. Not knowing it was right there off the trail, I started my tromping around. I walked about a bit, went back to him after giving up.

He took a picture of me with the sign, and I attempted to put a Fatback sticker on the post and failed because it was so cold and the sticker wasn't sticking. Kurt started making his way down. I had mentioned to him earlier that there usually is not much riding down the pass if it's been windy, and this time was no different. I was struggling to hang with him now. In a tired stumble, I noticed he had stopped, and his body language had changed to one of heightened awareness. I looked in the general direction his head was pointed and saw a flash of green lasers point back at me. It was a wolf!

In 2011 I bought my first fat bike, nicknamed the HULK. A green 9:ZERO:7. I started to look into racing fat bikes and one day stumbled upon the Susitna 100 and the Iditarod Trail Invitational. Guys like Tim Berntson, Jeff Oatley, Kevin Breitenbach, Pete Basinger, Jay Petervary, and John Lackey all seemed like rock stars to me. Like many others, I watched and followed those guys and events in awe. I knew that one day I wanted to take this event on. And so I developed a plan.

The trail outside of Rohn is a mountain biker's dream. It's a wonderful backdrop—rolling hills, usually a nice bit of dirt, and even some high-speed swoopy turns. The sun was out; I was totally buzzing. The rest and recovery at the Rohn checkpoint was just what I needed. Near the climb up Post River Glacier, I rode past the carcass and innards of a bison. Maybe I would see some bison on the trail this year. I continued down the trail, building momentum as the sun continued to charge my internal battery. I have visualized myself riding this section over and over. I remember large swaths of it. I have a sweet, light bike to ride. A gear setup that allows me to stay warm yet not hot so that I can push the pace when I need to. I am much better about staying on top of food and water intake. I was enjoying the great conditions.

One year after my first Susitna 100 finish, in 2015 I decided to try the Iditasport 225. Man, that race really showed me a new world. Sleep deprivation, cold weather, general route finding, gear setups. I had a close finish with the winner, Kevin Murphy. Not long after that, while in Boston to watch my significant other at the time run the Boston Marathon, I sent off my application to participate in the 2016 Iditarod Trail Invitational. After that I patiently waited to hear whether or not I was qualified enough to participate.

What a year to sign up. John Lackey had just set the bike record to McGrath, faster than the dogs. A year earlier Jeff Oatley had hauled butt all the way to Nome in ten days. It was a time of growth for the race for sure. Trackleaders website was really starting to catch on for all the different bikepacking events, including the ITI. The "dot watchers" were born.

I got to Sullivan Creek, filled up my water bladder, and made sure that it was sealed well. I checked and adjusted my gear, tightened down my boots, and put on another layer as the temps were dropping quick. I went up the trail a bit to take a pee, then filled up my tires with a good amount of air in preparation for the nighttime trail conditions. I continued to ride, and wouldn't you know ... after chasing Tyson all morning and afternoon, I saw where he had pulled over for the snowmachines and calculated that he was only about thirty minutes in front of me.

I was so excited at this. Kurt and I had been chasing him for over a day since leaving Finger Lake more than a hundred miles back.

The Iditarod Trail Invitational is a world-class event. It brings competitors from all over: from professional athletes to elite amateurs. Ask anyone who has raced the ultra-endurance events, and they will tell you that they would love to participate in the Iditarod Trail Invitational.

Over the past five years, I have raced the best ultradistance cyclists. I have learned so much about myself and racing technique. Each time on the trail, I picked up more experience and continued to better myself. But something else happened along the way. My life felt like it had found some purpose. Each time on the trail, I pushed myself to new limits. I had been so tired at times that I could barely walk, only to be awakened by the most amazing northern lights. I had felt weather that I never would have considered going out in if I wasn't racing. I started organizing my life and training with a purpose. I began to look at things in my life with a new priority. The quality of my life has improved drastically. My senses are greater; my passion and understanding are at a level that I never would have thought I could get to.

There's something about a race. The chase. There's a spark in your gut that happens. The world around you begins to slow, and the outside conditions no longer grab your attention. I knew that I was going to catch Tyson. I began to think that perhaps this was my chance. I needed to make my move when and if I caught him.

Guess what? While crossing one of the many swamps, I saw a light flicker ahead. My heart rate must've spiked twenty beats. I paused, closing in on him for about half a mile or so. I just followed him at his pace to see how he was doing. I was super comfortable, so I knew that he was starting to get tired. I started to get myself hyped up, knowing that I was in for a long push. If I made my move, this was it. No turning back. He started to slow down, and I think he may have been waiting for us to catch him. When I pulled up to him, he sounded very tired. I passed him and wished him luck, took another look back to see Kurt, and decided to light it up.

Rediscovering bikes has been life altering for me. And having the opportunity to participate in the Iditarod Trail Invitational has been amazing. To think that I've been able to race on the trail that we read about when I was in elementary school is so cool.

Then he was gone. It happened so fast; after many days it almost didn't seem like it was real. I rode up to Tyson, and he mentioned that we were a long ways out and that we would probably catch Kurt. I just remember thinking, I don't know, man, he's a strong dude, and if he didn't think he could hold the lead, then he probably wouldn't have done it. I told Tyson that I had to at least try to catch him.

I didn't catch Kurt that day. And even though I didn't, I feel like I had fulfilled my needs. I felt complete, full, and happy. I love sharing my experiences riding bicycles in Alaska with my friends and anyone who listens. I feel ready to tackle new and exciting challenges for the next part of my life. That could be more riding in Alaska and in other parts of the world. The lingering fear or uncertainty of life doesn't seem so heavy now.

I may not have won the race, but as I rolled into McGrath, I felt accomplished. I no longer am searching for the finish line. I left everything out in the swamps, lakes, and tundra of the interior. It's as if the wind picked up my worries and swept them away. This race was what I needed—it was a spark, even if, like Bruce Springsteen wrote, we're just dancing in the dark.

So here we are now. I've had an incredible time getting here, and I wouldn't change a damn thing. My dad, family, and friends have always supported me and continue to. I've met amazing people, seen amazing things, and experienced parts of myself that I don't think I would've found had I not been daydreaming as a little kid on West Twenty-Seventh Avenue.

That One Magnetek Time I Jumped Over Five Cars

M. C. MOHAGANI MAGNETEK

The ride is almost over
You still have a chance to win.
Dig deep. Breath in
And you are gone with the wind
Swiftly down city streets
Pedaling over your own heartbeats
Focused on one hundred miles of peace
Letting the negativity and toxins be released
From your brow and opened pores
Above you . . . along your side the raven soars
Giving you a bird's-eye view of one love.
Slow down. Take a break. Tranquility thinking of
Absolutely nothing, just being one with humanity
Not, the insanity
Of unrequited phobic overextended kindness
Secretly doubting your very existence with blindness.
Let it go. The finish line is right there.
Just take in another big gust of air
Push. Pull. Keep on pedaling around the sun
Don't stop until the race is done.
Even though the crowds may not shake and scream
You would have won, simply by living the dream.
Magnetek seems to think you deserve a medal for participation in life.
What do you think?

—"Magnetek Believes You Can Win" (2015)

Did I accomplish my mission? Yes. I rode one hundred miles. I raised $600, all for the National Alliance on Mental Illness. I elevated the collective consciousness about transgender, nonbinary identities. Although I am not sure if anyone remembers my ride as much as they remember the time, I jumped over five cars. Yep, that is what I said. You read that right. I jumped over five cars a week before my "We Are Human Too Century Ride" in August 2015. It was all my idea, but my friends set the stage with a rickety makeshift ramp. I needed to get people excited about my challenge, and I saw no better way to hype up an ambitious bicycle ride than with a spectacular stunt. Impending danger did not concern me. At the time I was in the grips of a full-blown manic bipolar disorder episode. No fear, no inhibitions, and no limitations.

First, I made a little spiel for the recording camera: "Hi. I'm M. C. MoHagani Magnetek, and I'm here to promote my one-hundred-mile bike ride for human rights. I am going to jump over not one, not two, not three, not four, but five cars!" Holding up five fingers to accentuate my announcement, I then proceeded to mount my 2006 Coda Sport Hybrid bike and clipped into the pedals to begin pedaling, gaining as much speed as possible to hit the ramp. My audience of five stood on the side of the road to cheer me on as I launched myself through the air to jump over four Micro Machine cars and one helicopter before a safe landing and a great sense of accomplishment. Yeah, and so what that it was not real cars, rather toys, but there are not too many people in the world who can say they jumped over four cars and a helicopter.

A week later Alaska's rainy season did not look too good for Kid Magnetek. I knew I might have to ride all one hundred miles in the rain, but that was nothing compared to the thirteen transgender people who had been murdered so far that year in the United States. That was nothing compared to the number of suicides among people with mental illnesses and their families, who endure the torment with them. I may have been battered from a bee sting and an awful bike crash a few days earlier; however, I knew I would help honor the deceased, missing, and ill people by completing my campaign goal in spite of the rain. I had to dig deep down for strength, endurance, and fortitude because it was bigger than me. There were smiles in jeopardy of being lost forever.

Furthermore, the world needed to know that we are people, too, and all we want is peace, love, and respect, as everyone else, and that we just don't lie around being transgender all damn day long.

Would I ride one hundred miles to reduce mental illness stigma and raise awareness for transgender-nonbinary human rights again is a serious question I am contemplating. More so because of the difficulty I experienced during my "One Woman Crusade" (as labeled by a news reporter). *Miserable* is the one word that captures all of my emotions on that fateful day, yet that feeling resulted from constant discrimination and harassment in my daily life as I moved around Anchorage among people . . . a population that had had very few previous encounters with an African American transgender woman.

At the time I had been hospitalized in the mental health ward a total of twelve times for PTSD and bipolar disorder. From what I understand, most people who are diagnosed with some form of mental illness are hospitalized once or twice on average in a lifetime, whereas I had had so many stays for behavioral health, I knew all too well what stigma felt like. I had been hospitalized with others who were given a plethora of diagnoses ranging from severe depression to dissociative identity disorder to schizophrenia. In group therapy sessions, at the lunch table, making arts and crafts, or in the television room, I heard many stories of people being neglected, shunned, and shamed by their families and communities at large for having been clinically diagnosed as mentally ill. Not only did I empathize with their plights, but I also understood the struggle and the need to reduce stigma as much as possible. A means to accomplish this was to raise awareness about mental health issues through some type of action. I remember speaking with a sister-friend of mine during the spring of 2015 about my idea to raise awareness and my goal to ride my bicycle one hundred miles. It was a feat I had dreamed about for many years but was never afforded the time and opportunity to embark on such a strenuous physical task. In that conversation my idea and goal merged to become the "We Are Human Too Century Ride."

I trained by spending more time on the seat of my hybrid bicycle, which was not the best type of bike to have for cycling long distance, but it was all I had at the time. Besides that, the bike and I had many good rides behind us, such as participating in the New York City Five

Borough Bike Tour three times, which was a forty-mile ride through the city. A good friend of mine who lived in Brooklyn would often meet up with me at the beginning of the Westside Highway near the Staten Island Ferry Terminal to begin a forty-mile ride up to the George Washington Bridge and then down the shoreline of the Hudson River, weaving through Weehawken, Hoboken, Jersey City, and over the Bayonne Bridge to get back on Staten Island to the ferry terminal for a full round trip.

When I arrived in Anchorage and had the pleasure of having nothing to do in the summers of 2013–15 with the exception of a few college classes, I cycled daily anywhere from twenty to forty miles . . . sometimes pushing myself to fifty or sixty miles. Over the 2015 summer, I planned my route. Not an official ride sanctioned by the municipality nor sponsored by some nonprofit organization, there really were no rules for me to follow other than the traffic laws.

I must say when it comes to cycling traffic laws, I break some rules because I know damn well I am not a car protected by front and rear bumpers, so I do not ride in the street and stop at light intersections. I have always thought that it was a bit strange to pretend I am a car. The other thing that I do not do at all, unless there is just not enough road on the right-hand side, is riding with traffic because I am afraid of being hit by a car from behind. By riding on the left-hand side of the road against traffic, I feel comfortable with the ability to see the vehicles headed toward me. I figure I can swerve or jump off my bike with relative ease in the event an out-of-control car looks like it is going to strike me. Of course, I wear my helmet and remain vigilant throughout my rides.

No official route existed other than the one I created by simply riding around the inner geographic basin, or bowl, of Anchorage. One trip beginning and ending at Earthquake Park was forty miles, thus my route for my Century Ride was two and half times around the Anchorage bowl to reach one hundred miles and end at Valley of the Moon Park.

I began my heroic adventure at 6:00 a.m., thinking it would take me ten hours, considering my average speed was twelve miles per hour. My bike odometer marked the five hundred miles I have traveled so far during the summer and the start of my Century Ride. I was grateful to the Most High for giving me the strength, courage, and tenacity to make this dream a reality. It had been my goal for almost ten years to do a one-hundred-mile ride, but life and four knee surgeries had kept me out of the game. However, I felt good about my training and practice and trusted that they would carry me through my personal challenges.

I used social media to update all of my followers, and after I reached my first twenty-five miles, I had to put in some dedicated work for my friend who was going through hard times. Thus, I rode twenty miles for him and took more requests from people who were in need of prayer and positive vibrations. Then I dedicated the next ten miles for all the animals that had to deal with the drama of humans.

All was going as smoothly as planned, but after thirty miles, one of my back tire spokes broke, so I had to ride seventy miles with a substantial drag. And then it rained more, yet I was mentally prepared for heavy August rains. Good thing I had a riding partner for about thirty miles to push me, encourage me, and keep me company. Whenever I grew weary and questioned my motivations for riding one hundred miles, I thought about all the transphobia I suffered, the hundreds of African trans women around the world who had been murdered and slaughtered. Why is there no justice and no peace for us? Whenever I wanted to quit, I reflected on the many people who had died by suicide because they felt alone, isolated, and stigmatized. Mental illness resides in every culture, every population, and all people, cutting across the board and stabbing deep into the fabric of families, communities, and relationships, with very little if any compassion for the inflicted. All of those atrocities against humanity fueled me to keep pushing pedals. The ride was never about me because we are all human, and we need to be more aware that love is a viable option instead of hate. As for me, I knew the mind quits before the body does, but it sure was no longer a cakewalk with a dragging back tire.

Shit got real for the Kid after sixty miles of riding in torrential rains. The most I had done all summer was fifty miles, so now I was sucking up all kinds of oxygen to catch my breath. With only forty miles left to go, the struggle and fight for willpower continued to grow tougher. I guessed I had read too many cycling stories about cyclists peeing on themselves so as to not lose time, so I started to piss Gatorade after seventy-five miles. The first time it was weird and difficult to do it, but once I broke the seal of my bladder, that fifth, seventh, and ninth time of peeing all over myself became easier; besides, it was a torrential downpour so that was just as good as a shower as far as I was concerned.

Ninety-five miles and sixteen hours later, on my last stretch heading toward Valley of the Moon Park, where a small gathering of my friends and supporters gathered, I crashed out of nowhere. Nothing made sense. What in the world did I hit to make me topple over my handlebars, striking my chest so fast I did not know I had a bruised sternum until weeks later, when a doctor pointed out the bruise on an X-ray slide. Relentless, the rain did not care that I had fallen, and if anyone in cars passing by noticed me stretched out on the sidewalk, they were not going to stop driving toward their destination in the midst of Alaska's monsoon season. However, it was not long before I got up. Maybe a minute, but I think it was much less before I got back on my bike without accessing anymore of the whys in regard to my crash to get my feet back on those pedals and *push push* until I made it to the finish line with 105 miles on my cyclometer for the day. Among the claps and cheering, I collapsed onto the ground, wet, sweaty, and pissy.

In the end I completed my first Century Ride, jumped over four cars and a helicopter, and raised $600 for the National Alliance on Mental Illness. Not sure if I raised much awareness about transgender people or human rights, but I did attain legendary status for my Century Ride, and the five-car bike jump is still a legendary tale people often remember the most. I did not sleep that night because I couldn't stop the heavy breathing. It was like I was still out there on the road feeling every sensation and vibration from the roads. My legs took another three days to realize they were not pushing pedals anymore. I was blown away by the outpouring of support from all the social media likes, comments, and congratulations. It was the hardest thing I had ever done until I chained myself to a tree for twelve hours in full Wonder Woman gear for peace, justice, and equality, but that is another story for another day. After cycling around Anchorage, Alaska, on August 17, 2015, I celebrated by dancing because I did the damn thing like hot sex. However, I am going to stick with jumping over cars. That was much easier than riding one hundred miles on a wack-as-fuck bicycle with a broken spoke in the rain for sixteen hours.

When There's No One Left to Fight

RACHAEL KVAPIL

In the summer of 2019, just after finishing a multiday ride from Fairbanks to Anchorage, the motivation to ride suddenly disappeared. After five years training for triathlon and ultra-fat bike races, cycling no longer appealed to me outside of the few miles I rode in the morning to exercise my two-year-old chocolate Labrador, Java. At first I attributed it to the stress of buying a new house and moving after twenty-two years living in the same place. I blamed the disruption of my routine, the newness of my environment, and the distance that quadrupled my commute time to work. I blamed the darkness, even though I'd done many overnight rides miles away from the nearest race checkpoint or even the nearest rider. And when I realized how ridiculous I sounded blaming wildlife for my lack of motivation, I simply accepted that some form of depression had settled in.

I probably would have given up cycling if it wasn't for Java. She has an admirable tenacity when it comes to waking me up for 5:00 a.m. training sessions. If I don't respond to her gentle cuddles, she will paw my face. And if that doesn't work, she will lick me in the eye. She lies there, unflinching, as I shout in disgust as if to make it clear that it's my fault I didn't get up sooner. Far away from my regular trail systems near my old house, Java and I biked the hilly dirt roads around our new house, where we adjusted to off-leash dogs charging out of their yard after us. The aggressiveness of these dogs made me hate living up there more. In my old neighborhood people kept their dogs fenced or on leashes. In this neighborhood people seemed completely unaware of their dogs until I showed up at their door because of an unpleasant encounter that left my dog with an injury. But Java persisted, despite getting bitten by a German shepherd, tackled and pinned daily by a food-aggressive Akita, and bum-rushed by other territorial dogs. So I persisted too.

During this time I would frequently wake up and think about the most psychologically terrifying fat bike ride of my life. The temperatures had dropped to forty below that evening, and I decided to solo it around a five-mile loop in the Goldstream Valley to adjust to conditions I would face in the White Mountains 100 ultra race. I peeled off from a group ride down a well-used albeit narrow, snowy trail. I weaved through the woods two and a half miles until the bike grew difficult to pedal on flat terrain. My rear tire had gone flat in the cold, and I had to fill it with a small hand pump in my frame bag. Unfortunately, the downtime made the bike stiff, and given that I'm a terrible hill rider, I would spend more time than I wanted pushing the bike for the last two miles of the ride.

I decided to turn around and head back before things could get any worse.

I often wonder if my disappointment set up the terror I experienced on the way back. A dense fog settled in the area, and my bright headlamp reflected back so that it was difficult to see the trail ahead. A wispy mist knit tight into a gray blanket around the aging trees and closed on me until I no longer could breathe. I wasn't in any real danger. My brain communicated this clearly by pointing out sights and sounds along the trail: the railroad tracks that paralleled the trail for the last quarter mile; cars along Sheep Creek Road crossing the tracks a few feet from the turnoff; and the tire tracks from the bikes that had returned early too from their ride.

One truth about type A personalities that often makes people uncomfortable or even irritated: we must have goals. Goals are how people like me survive. It's how we build structure into our lives. Without them things go downhill pretty fast. This applies to biking as much as anything else. Riding for the sake of riding? Meh. Riding to complete a commute challenge, train for a race, save gas money, improve the environment. That's more my speed. Sure, the thrill of peering down gaping valleys, staring up at rigid peaks, and winding through trees partially revealing Mother Nature's great mysteries is incredible. Or on the road, fully engaged in the pace of afternoon traffic and the placement of cars as you ventured into a crowded intersection. Dodging pedestrians who step off the bus right in front of your wheel. And laughing at cars racing to the corner so they don't have to wait for me only to turn so hard their tires come off the road.

Biking is active meditation at its best. Still any enjoyment I get from riding is always through the lens of the primary goal.

One would think knowing this would make it easier to overcome depression. However, there is a lot of guilt that comes with being a type A personality. Not everyone is on board with the sacrifice to family time, the adjustments to schedules, or simply the reminder that you are dedicated to something outside of them. As the primary caretaker, housemaid, cook, and errand girl, the house falls into disarray quickly when training takes over. Not to say my husband doesn't do his part when it comes to house and vehicle maintenance, land development, and technology. The management hours are truly even. Yet it's hard to overcome guilt when people are digging through dirty dishes, tripping over three sets of running shoes, and can't find clean clothes to wear. Moving to Ester cut into my training time by adding a commute for work and errands with a dog who refuses to stay home peacefully, and the added floorspace tripled the housework.

Then there's the backlash to my ambitious nature. For years my husband assumed my ambition reflected some type of neurotic dissatisfaction with life. Family members would ask with annoyance how long a thirty-mile bike ride would take, pointing out they now had to delay family plans that meant more to them than they did to me. And friends often grew more demanding the less time I sacrificed listening to their personal problems. I begrudgingly assess every goal through the Spectacles of Guilt to determine if I can withstand the level of selfishness someone will ultimately assign.

Things changed in the spring of 2020, when we all had way more important things to worry about than chores, training, and getting stuck behind a fleet of crawling Subarus on the Parks Highway. News of the pandemic hit a month after I suffered a three-week illness I now suspect was coronavirus. Within twenty-four hours of the first Alaska Health Mandate, swim camp and my trip to Hawai'i were canceled, it snowed twenty-four inches, and I was filling out paperwork to work from home, one floor above where my husband set up his home office. I joked about this new goal to go a whole year without seeing my coworkers. My husband joked about avoiding the office until he retired in 2025. Neither of us realized how long this pandemic would drag out while people fought mask mandates, travel warnings, and social distancing. It became apparent some weeks later that if I had forced us to stay in our tiny little house off College Road, my marriage would have suffered or even ended in divorce.

Things sorted themselves near the one-year anniversary at the new house. Java and I biked our normal neighborhood route under a sunny June morning sky, blue and cloudless. A rare ride undisturbed by other dogs, we flew through hard shadows cast by trees. I don't often take photos or videos during our rides. I hate stopping to pull out the camera. I think it's a waste of my precious ride time. But that morning I threw an ancient GoPro on a mount to capture such a beautiful day. The video shows my silly chocolate Lab sprinting down our dirt road, darting in and out of the forested hillside chasing squirrels and flushing birds, careening down hills and around corners unconcerned about what's ahead. In the picture, taken from the video footage, is the moment all the frustration and resentment finally broke. I'm petting Java as she wraps her body around my legs, wagging her overexcited tail.

"I know, Java Bean," I remember whispering as I gave her a treat. "I'm happy too."

Despite the unknown future of the pandemic, I returned to the occasional Ladies of Leisure (LOL) group ride. I ended my summer with an eighty-two-mile ride from my house to just outside of Healy. I also retired from several activities to compensate for the training time lost to my commute and housework. As much as I enjoyed my board of director positions for the Fairbanks Cycle Club and the Fairbanks Arts Association, I no longer had thirty extra hours a month to volunteer. Besides I had been volunteering for twenty-plus hours a month since I was a six-year-old Girl Scout. It was time for someone else to take their turn.

Not long after, I registered for the 2021 Ironman Coeur d'Alene. Despite the uncertainty of a persisting pandemic, I pulled together a training plan that would allow me to rebuild the structure I had lost in the move. My husband and I negotiated finances and schedules for the next year, and isolation has kept my long training hours from affecting my friends and family.

I wake up to much happier memories now. One is where it is thirty-six below at 11:00 p.m., and I'm riding alone on the White Mountains 100 racecourse. The crystal-clear sky glitters with white twinkling stars, and thick green bands dance in the sky. Taken away by the view, I stopped, not for a picture but for a moment to watch Mother Nature's encouragement, those green lights arching toward the finish line.

The Books I Carried

"Hardship sells," Pete remarked, his comment in response to my announcement that I was going to bicycle from Fairbanks to Valdez, Alaska. Implied, my twenty-two-day, six-hundred-mile trek might make for a good story. I, now sixty-four, had completed my last solo tour in 2002, bicycling the Great Divide Mountain Bike Route from northern Montana to southern New Mexico. After that, I took up long-distance horse trekking. I was a fit horseback rider and an unfit bicycle tourist.

I postponed trip preparations until mid-June, a week before leaving Palmer. Pete tuned up my mountain bike, and I pulled my dusty panniers and trailer out of our gear cabin. I then gathered together travel items. Essentials consisted of a toiletry bag, a bear-proof food container, a repair kit, and cooking paraphernalia. Nonessentials consisted of two cardboard boxes containing hardcover and paperback books.

I stashed the heavier gear in my trailer and the lighter gear in my front panniers. I slipped two remaining nonessentials into the side pouch of my front pannier. These consisted of a journal and Tim O'Brien's *The Things They Carried*. I'd read O'Brien's book several years previously; this time the title and introductory pages were a readerly hook.

O'Brien initially writes about the objects that he and his Vietnam War buddies carried into battle, the essentials being a function of rank, mission, and field specialties, and the nonessentials being a function of their personal wants, needs, and compulsions. For instance, 1st Lt. Jimmy Cross carried letters and photos; Kiowa carried a New Testament, a hatchet, and moccasins; Dave Jenson carried night vitamins; Lee Strunk carried a slingshot; Rat Kiley carried brandy and M&M candies; Ted Lavender carried tranquilizers and pot; and Henry Dobbins carried his girlfriend's pantyhose. Alys Culhane would carry twenty-plus pounds of books.

Friends dropped me off on the outskirts of Fairbanks, where I set up base camp in a cabin owned by Suzi Lozo. Suzi was the remaining member of what, thirty years earlier, was a quasi-commune.

We spent the evening on Suzi's outdoor porch traipsing down memory lane. Her porch was enshrouded in mist and mosquito netting, thus giving the surroundings an ethereal feeling. We sat in wicker chairs, surrounded by geraniums.

Suzi had been a homebody who hoarded furniture, clothing, bicycles, and vehicles. I had been a traveler who scorned material possessions. Our one commonality was books. I accompanied her on thrift store forays. We returned home with boxes of books, which we read, swapped, and further discussed.

Suzi's interest was piqued when I told her that I now salvaged books and made them available to potential readers. I'd appointed myself Bright Lights Book Project Outreach Coordinator after discovering twenty chest-high boxes of books at the Palmer-based recycling facility, Valley Community for Recycling Solutions. The paperbacks were to be shredded and the hardbacks to be sent to the mill. I circumvented the process by passing free books on to community members. Books began appearing in the VCRS entryway when the COVID quarantine went into effect. By March 2020 the supply exceeded the demand. Come April, I decided to do an in-state bicycle tour and along the way distribute books.

I told Suzi that I was reading *The Things They Carried*, adding that like O'Brien's counterparts, I was also on a mission. The American soldiers were battling the Communists, and I was combating illiteracy.

I set out at eleven the following morning. I alternated slapping at mosquitoes and wiping the rain off my glasses with my index finger. I cursed, for I'd erred in not having taken my overloaded bicycle for a test ride. A front-end wobble was exacerbated by potholes.

I coasted the mile downhill stretch to the Parks Highway and turned right. A mile or so later I turned right, onto the Old Nenana Highway. My destination, Old Ridge Trail Road, was seven miles distant. I alternated walking uphill, riding downhill, my jaw set, my shoulders rigid.

Old Ridge Trail Road was a mess. I slid sideways into a muddy rut and toppled over. I had one and a half miles remaining; nevertheless, I considered backtracking and borrowing one of Suzy's vehicular junkers. However, traveling by car would be akin to retreating from the front lines. I'd set out to pedal my wares by bicycle, and this was what I was going to do.

Sarah and Fran Bundtzen met me at the base of their driveway and escorted me to their bug shelter. The homesteader artists reside in Ester in the summer and in the Goldstream Valley in the winter. Our friendship spanned twenty years, our common interest being Icelandic horses.

The two botanists watched as I wheeled my bicycle and trailer into their bug shelter and wiped the mud off my face. I regained my composure and rummaged through my trailer. "Here, these are for you two," I said, handing Fran two bird carving books and Sarah three digital photography books. Fran's eyes grew wide when I then gave her a copy of *The Alaska Flora and Fauna*. This, she informed me, is *the* guide for field botanists in Alaska. That evening the pair, book in front of them, assisted me in identifying plants I'd see on my trek.

I spent the evening of the summer solstice in Fran and Sarah's refurbished camper. Rain beat down on the metal roof as I resumed reading *The Things They Carried*. The next morning Fran asked me why I was doing this trip.

"Because," I said, "I need to get the word out there."

"The word out there?"

"Yes, about the book project."

I kept mum about the fact that I was seeing parallels between O'Brien's situation and my own since this would weaken my already shaky resolve. However, there was a parallel. O'Brien, a reluctant Vietnam draftee, confesses that he's caught up in a "moral split." If he went to war, he'd support a morally reprehensible endeavor. But if O'Brien fled to Canada, he'd be labeled a traitor. Conversely, my returning home would make me a long-distance bicycle touring has-been.

I finished my conversation with Fran on an upbeat note, saying that distributing books would provide me with what my previous bicycle tours lacked, a much-needed sense of purpose.

The Bundtzens dropped me off on the Old Nenana Highway at eleven o'clock the next morning. It was a short distance to the Parks Highway, the main thoroughfare between Fairbanks and Palmer. I'd left my bicycle lock behind. However, the wobble remained. I progressed, by walking up and riding down the roller-coaster grade.

Skinny Dick's Halfway Inn is located halfway between Fairbanks and Nenana, a distance of fifty-four miles. The thought of passing on Louis L'Amour's books to bar patrons gave me a warm feeling.

I donned my N-95 mask and entered the single-story dwelling. The dozen or so patrons glanced up at me, then resumed talking. I told the bartender about the book project as he filled my water bottle. He returned my container, stood tall, and proclaimed: "Lady, people don't come here to read. They come here to drink!" I backed out the door as the patrons nodded in agreement.

A passage from O'Brien's book came to mind that afternoon as I walked up yet another hill. O'Brien defined a "leg," or "grunt," as someone who is "humping it." In his words, "to carry something is to hump it, as when Lieutenant Jimmy Cross humped his love for Martha up the hills and through the swamps. In its intransitive form, to hump [means] to walk, or to march, but [this] implies burdens far beyond the transitive." Indeed, I, now chilled and humping books, qualified for transitive status.

I arrived in Nenana at 7:00 p.m. and followed the signs to the town campground. The rain had penetrated my threadbare rain gear and running shoes, yet I'd remained in good spirits. I paid for my site, showered, then perused the laundry room book selection. It was what we book trade experts call "thin." Several Jehovah Witness tracts and a handful of romance novels were piled high on the windowsill. I left a copy of Madeleine L'Engle's *A Wrinkle in Time* and a dozen Bright Lights flyers beside a well-worn edition of the *Alaska Milepost*.

The following morning's drizzle was, by noon, a downpour. I had presumed that there would be minimal traffic on the Parks Highway, for out-of-state tourists were homebound. However, in-state travelers and truckers were taking advantage of the lull. For the next two days, I pedaled into the wind, stayed to the right of the rumble strip, and twisted my head sideways so as to avoid the spray of passing semis.

I hadn't made any project appointments for I figured that libraries and lodges would be open. I soon discovered that most establishments were either closed or boarded up. Even Denali Park Lodge had a CLOSED DUE TO COVID sign posted on the main entrance. If there was any consolation, it was that the rain stopped and the sun appeared as I passed through what I in the past had called "Denali-Land."

The privately owned Carlo Creek Cabins, located thirteen miles beyond the Denali Park Road turnoff, was open. I grabbed a handful of book flyers and entered the main office. It occurred to me that Martha Stewart would reside here if she became an Alaskan lodge owner. Her middle-aged doppelgänger wore a freshly pressed blouse and pants. I took in the smells of fresh coffee, baked goods, and clean laundry, then stepped back in order to spare her the combined smells of sweat and road grime. Martha told me that the tent site fee was $50.

"Thanks. I'll keep going," I said.

I exited the lodge, slipped the flyers back into my front pannier, and picked up my bicycle and trailer. The door behind me opened.

I turned and faced Martha.

"I won't charge you for a night's stay," she said.

I stood, deep in thought. I'd gone, in a nanosecond, from being a tight-wad traveler to a woeful charity case. How would Martha have reacted if I had arrived at her doorstep pushing a shopping cart full of books?

I followed the well-coiffed lodge owner back inside, slapped $15 on the counter, and remarked that this was the going rate for long-distance bicyclist tourists. She uncapped a Sharpie, picked up a campground map, circled the tent site area, and pushed the piece of paper across the countertop. I grabbed it and hustled out the door.

I located the camping area, hung my moldy socks on the shelter railing, then sauntered back to the main office.

"This is for you and your customers," I said, handing her a copy of *The Alaska Bicycle Touring Guide*. I added, "I coauthored it with my husband, Pete. It contains information on every lodge in the state." Martha thumbed through the book. I explained that the book was thirty-plus years old; this was why most of the contact information was out-of-date.

"We'll do a revision next year," I said.

Martha handed me a business card and a towel. I was, she said, welcome to use the lodge shower. I bounced down the lodge steps, for I'd raised her estimation of bicycle tourists yet another notch.

It was 4:00 p.m., still early. My references to our book prompted me to give Pete a call. I listened carefully as he gave me a livestock update. However, my attention wavered as he provided me with a garden status report, for weed pulling isn't in my DNA.

I said that I'd just set up camp at the Carlo Creek campground, which was "under new management." I then had his undivided attention. We met in Denali Park in July 1987, and our first date took place during the Carlo Creek Music Festival. I then spared no details in telling Pete about my Martha Stewart encounter. I hung up feeling unsettled, for I wasn't sure if I'd gotten the facts correct and in the proper order. This was important; otherwise, Pete might think that Carlo Creek had remained a gathering place for locals and music lovers, this as opposed to what it now was, a high-end tourist trap.

The importance of detail in relation to truth was on my mind as that evening I read the chapter in *The Things They Carried* titled "How to Tell a True War Story." O'Brien determines that "true war stor[ies] are never moral . . . The angles of vision are skewed . . . cannot be believed . . . do not indulge in abstraction or analysis . . . comes down to gut instinct . . ." Finally, what seems to happen becomes its own happening and has to be told that way.

O'Brien's definitional criteria seemed to me to be applicable to narratives in which the storyteller is attempting to convey a specific feeling, emotion, point of view. Details might be altered or left out. This is permissible if the writer unearths central truths. This was my intent. A second call, in which Pete empathized with me about the changes at Carlo Creek as a personal loss, affirmed that I'd gotten my point across.

The wind abated as, at noon the next day, I veered left in order to check out the defunct Igloo Motel. I sat on a rickety filling station bench and gnawed on a carrot. Five minutes later I was down to the orange nub when a motorist parked his van beside a concrete barrier and ambled across the gravel parking lot. He was wearing a beige shirt, beige pants, and a beige canvas hat. A bulky beige camera bag pulled his weight to the left, giving him a lopsided appearance.

I felt giddy, this being a combination of my having stopped in a surreal setting and having eaten a light lunch. And so, rather than introduce myself, I asked the man if he was on safari.

"No," he said.

"Well, where are you from, and what are you doing here?" I asked.

"I'm from England. I'm taking photographs. And you?" he asked.

"I'm here on business. I'm going to purchase the Igloo and turn it into a bookstore."

"Great idea," the photographer said, taking several steps backward.

I told him about the Bright Lights Book Project and added that the Palmer recycling center warehouse contained thousands of used books on every imaginable subject, including photography.

I sprinted over to my trailer and returned with a copy of Susan Sontag's *On Photography* in hand. "Here," I said, slapping it into his open hands. "I'll check out this place on my way to Anchorage," he said, turning and trotting back in the direction of his vehicle. I left the Igloo feeling energized for I'd again gotten an obscure book into the right reader's hands.

My afternoon ride reminded me of what I most enjoyed about bicycle touring. The sun shone brightly, and a strong tailwind pushed me southward. I gazed in awe at Alaska Range and watched as small spindly spruce gave way to thicker stands of birch. A fox darted across the highway, and two hawks played on the updrafts.

Change is a constant when one is bicycle touring, and this time was no exception. A succession of orange road signs came into view. I slowed down in order to give myself time to prepare for a long wait and a bumpy ride through displaced terrain.

The flag person at a distance grew larger as I approached what I dubbed the war zone. When, finally, we were the government-mandated six feet apart, I was informed that bicyclists were to be transported to the far end of the road construction site, in the bed of the pilot car.

I asked the flag person if she had any extra water. She nodded, walked over to her truck bed, and returned with a bottled water. I consumed the contents in seconds.

The woman was petite, blonde, and quick moving. My reflection materialized in her white-rimmed sunglasses. I looked like shit. My lower lip was blistered and scabby, and my glasses (from having rolled onto them the night before) were askew. "Helmet hair," I said, tapping my orange helmet. "Helmet hair," she said, tapping her white hard hat.

Introductions affirmed that we'd crossed paths five years previously. Haley had spent several months working on a road construction project in my area. We had struck up an acquaintanceship in the course of my comings and goings. We picked up where we'd left off, my trip and Haley's job taking precedence, the woof of her barking dogs and the beep of road machinery being incidental distractions.

A pilot car stopped on the left side of the road, while the cars it had led through the construction zone passed by. Haley held my bicycle while I rummaged through the cardboard box. I handed her a copy of W. Bruce Cameron's *A Dog's Purpose* and hoisted my disassembled bicycle and trailer into the pickup bed. I waved my hand, and the driver hit the gas. Haley, increasingly in the distance, grew smaller and smaller.

I arrived at the Hatcher Pass turnoff, located on the outskirts of Willow, turned left, and where the paved road surface turned to gravel, set up camp and crawled into my sleeping bag. I awoke to the sound of hail pummeling my tent fly. I pulled back the tent flap and groaned, for Hatcher Pass was enshrouded in low-lying clouds. It was most likely snowing on the summit, so bicycling over the pass was now a no-go. Rather than ride through Wasilla, I took a ride home with Pete, who met me at the Parks Highway / Hatcher Pass turnoff. I finished the first part of my trip on June 28, eight days after leaving Fairbanks.

I prepared for part two of my bicycle trek in a more judicious fashion. I jettisoned a second spare tube, several packages of dehydrated beans (circa 2011), and an extra stove fuel cartridge. This left ample room for an additional dozen paperbacks, *The Things They Carried* included. My literary itinerary again included post offices, libraries, roadhouses, and campgrounds.

I rationalized my still-heavy load by reminding myself that I didn't have far to go. The distance from Palmer to Glennallen on the Glenn Highway is 136 miles; the distance from Glennallen to Valdez on the Richardson Highway is 120 miles.

I left home on Saturday, July 11, after the day's rain abated. I'd planned on clandestine camping on the far side of Sutton, which was twenty or so miles from home. I was a few miles beyond Sutton proper when a tall man pushing a small wheelbarrow appeared on the left-hand side of the road. The Ichabod Crane lookalike was my friend Bill Schmidt-kunz. He was spreading horse manure that I'd given him on a strip of land adjoining the Glenn Highway. His gardening efforts had paid off: wildflowers were in abundance.

I agreed to stay for dinner and sleep on his couch. I'd dubbed the poet/carpenter/gardener/handyman the Bright Lights Book Project Jack of All Trades. His job description included distribution; his target audience was Anchorage homeless shelters and rescue mission residents. His home resembled mine in that poetry, art, and literature books covered all flat surfaces. COVID had put a damper on our efforts, providing us both with lots of reading time. We agreed that it was time to get the recycling center books back into circulation.

Bill cooked up brown rice and made a garden salad. My contributions consisted of a can of tuna, sundried tomatoes, a chocolate bar, and trail mix. His wife, Charlene, joined us for dinner.

A look of surprise crossed Charlene's face when I mentioned that I was rereading *The Things They Carried*. She and I recounted our experience together back in 2010. I taught a community-based writing and reading course titled Memory, Memoir, and Memorabilia. Both Charlene and Bill Long, her stepfather, were my students. At the class where we were to discuss this book, Long swept the book off the table with a gnarled hand, raised his bony six-foot-six frame to its full height, and sputtered, "This book is full of lies." "Then," Charlene interjected in her recounting, "you resumed talking."

Yes, I said, adding, "I, like O'Brien, and unlike Bill [Long], believed that the Vietnam War was unjust and immoral. But I didn't want this to be the focus of our discussion. There were other things here to talk about. Such as—"

I yanked my copy of *The Things They Carried* out of my pannier and went to the chapter titled "Notes." The couple listened as I noted that O'Brien's point of reference is Norman Bowker, a former war buddy. Bowker writes O'Brien a seventeen-page postwar letter in which he suggests that O'Brien write about what it's like to be a civilian after engaging in combat duty. Bowker, by way of self-example, describes himself as being "a guy who can't get his act together and just drives around all day and can't think of any damn place to go and doesn't know how to get there any way." Bowker adds, "The guy just wants to talk about it but he can't . . ."

"Here," I said, citing the passage in question. Bowker's letter "hits [O'Brien] hard" because he's made "the shift from war to peace." However, O'Brien concedes that he attempted to make sense of what happened in his writerly endeavors. "And yet, ever since my return I had been talking about it virtually nonstop through my writing. Telling stories seemed a natural, inevitable process, like clearing a throat."

"You see," I said, "there are numerous books out there in which the writers have attempted to determine whether or not the Vietnam War was or was not a political sham. But few, if any, of these authors have done as O'Brien has done and asserted that past memories are an integral part of memoir."

Charlene then resurrected another memory. The week following his outburst, Bill Long had come to class with an excerpt from a memoir-in-progress, one in which he'd summited Mount Vinson in Antarctica. "And yes," Long said, "while I have drawn upon notes from my journal, a lot of what I wrote is what I remember." I recalled thinking that he and O'Brien were kindred spirits but wisely kept my mouth shut.

With that, Charlene, her husband, Bill, and I called it a day.

I crawled into my sleeping bag but remained deep in thought. My discussion with Charlene and Bill had brought a truism to light. Book talk is intellectual fodder. And readers, deprived of this form of sustenance, remain hungry. By making books accessible, the likes of those involved in the Bright Lights Book Project were exercising metaphor in our attempt to feed the masses.

I arose at dawn, dressed, ate an apple, rolled my bicycle and trailer out of the Schmidtkunz greenhouse, and repacked my gear. The most dangerous portion of my trek, the winding, narrow, and shoulderless thirty-five-mile stretch to Hicks Creek, lay ahead. I left Schmidtkunz's place at 7:00 a.m. in hopes of staying ahead of the later, heavier traffic flow.

I gazed in awe at the swiftly flowing Matanuska River. My belief, that riding the next section was foolhardy, resurfaced when, at 10:00 a.m., the traffic markedly increased. The surge coincided with the return of the wobble. I deliberated about calling it quits but dismissed this idea; a mere shimmy wasn't going to deter me from finishing my trek.

The next few days summarized: sunny skies, slight headwinds, and innumerable ups and downs. I continued to hump it over the Puritan Creek, Caribou Creek, and Sheep Mountain Passes. And I celebrated my summiting Eureka Pass by consuming a bag of dehydrated fruit.

I stocked up on food in Glennallen, then turned right onto the Richardson Highway. I was 120 miles from Valdez. A stiff tailwind pushed up and over the undulating hills. I couldn't get Traffic's "The Low Spark of High Heeled Boys" out of my head, so I instead sang it loudly. Yes, this was the life. I envisioned boarding a ferry in Valdez and continuing south.

My euphoria lasted until noon the following day. I was moving at a good clip when my bicycle bucked several times, then lurched to a stop, nearly tossing me over the handlebars. I dropped both feet to the ground, dismounted, and pinched the sidewalls of my rear tire. I'd have to fix the flat. But where? The shoulder was narrow, the traffic fast, and the shrubbery dense. I scanned the Richardson Highway portion of my bike book. The Grizzly Lodge was two miles distant. I'd be best off changing my flat tire there.

I walked in seemingly slow motion. The midday heat, the roar of passing motorcycles, the *thump, thump, thump* of my rear tire, and the goddamn wobble felt as though they were conspiring against me. I arrived at the Grizzly Lodge forty-five minutes later. I pushed my bicycle up the gravel driveway, and at the top of the rise looked around. There were two junkers in the driveway and a CLOSED sign in the grimy window. A feral cat scooted across my path. The place gave me the willies. I leaned my bicycle against the edge of a rickety picnic table and sighed.

My repair bag contained a patch kit, Allen keys, a Presta valve converter, and a four-way bolt remover. Pete had assembled my kit, conceding to my insistence that I travel light. I'd opened the lid of my bear-proof container with my tire irons, then left them on a picnic table at Sheep Creek.

I disconnected the trailer, removed my front panniers, flipped my bicycle over, unscrewed the rear axle, and pried the tire off the rim, using two pieces of metal that someone had left on the table. I replaced the tube with the one I had on hand. The rear axle of my trailer was bent; perhaps this was the cause of the wobble.

I glimpsed a shadow out of the corner of my eye. I sat still; the hair on my neck stood on end. The shadow's owner was large, very large. I attempted to make eye contact, but the man appeared to be looking two ways simultaneously. He hauled himself down the creaky porch steps, lumbered down the driveway, checked the roadside mailbox, turned around, and lumbered back up the driveway. He reentered the lodge and closed the door. I skittered down the driveway, pushing my bicycle before me.

The ride to the top of 2,678-foot Thompson Pass lay ahead. It was eight miles from the base to the summit. I pedaled a hundred or so yards, then after almost colliding with a guard rail, hopped off my bicycle and began walking, slowly placing one foot in front of the other. It had been sunny, warm, and breezy the day before. It was now overcast, cold, and windy. Every hundred yards or so I did an about-face. The wind buffeted my back as I admired the alternate view.

Vehicles passed, the drivers oblivious to the tiny figure pushing a heavy load up a steep hill. My snail's pace enabled me to take in the vast landscape, the most striking feature being the Cal Worthington Glacier. The harsh wind blowing off the ice field's north side took my breath away.

I took refuge in a roadside shelter at noon and devoured a package of apricots. I yelled to a passing bicycle tourist, hoping that his bulk would serve as a wind block. Head down, he hammered up the steep incline.

Wispy, low-lying clouds and the scarcity of trees indicated that I was closing in on the pass. I resumed riding and passed a mile-long line of vehicles. I'd follow the pilot car after cresting the summit. *Bump, buck, bump, buck, bump, bump, buck.* The lurching of my bicycle meant one thing and one thing only. I at first refused to believe that I had a second flat tire. However, I accepted this as fact when I looked behind me and saw that the rear tire was wedged between the rear brake pads and the rim. I gritted my teeth and dragged my bicycle and gear over to where the flag person was standing. She indicated that the Blueberry Lake Recreation Area turnoff was one hundred yards away, then held the traffic line, allowing me to safely make the turn. I pushed my bicycle to my alternative destination, the Blueberry Lake campground.

I rested my bicycle on the far side of the shelter area and pitched my tent on the near side. Midway through dinner preparations, I ran out of gas. Dinner subsequently consisted of crunchy pasta and crispy dehydrated tomatoes. I watched as a midsized RV pulled into an adjacent site. A leashed dog emerged from the vehicle and was followed by a couple who appeared to be in their late sixties.

I met up with the pair at the water pump, adjoining our respective sites. Rather than ask, "How long might you be running your generator?" I instead offered them some trail mix, which they declined. My interest in their dog prompted an attitudinal about-face. Kyra was not, as I first thought, a miniature husky but, rather, a Shiba Inu, a breed that originated in Japan. She zoned in on a squirrel hole beside the pump.

We talked dogs, then introduced ourselves. Brian and Judy were Anchorage residents traveling around in their refurbished 1977 Chinook. He was tall, lanky, and talkative. She was short, compact, and reticent. Brian shifted from one leg to the other as we chatted. Judy remained grounded.

Judy's fleece coat logo read "Alaska Humanities Forum," which I presumed meant that she also had academic leanings. Thus, the framework of our subsequent conversation was: "Do you know so and so?"

Brian inched his way over to my campsite. Judy strode in the direction of the camping fee kiosk. I followed Brian. He then explained to me that he and Judy were avid sports enthusiasts. The former bicycle repair mechanic looked with interest at my bicycle and trailer. I shook the contents of my repair kit out onto the table and fingered my patch kit.

"Got a flat?" he asked.

"Yep. This is the second blowout this trip."

"You have the tools to repair it?"

"Uh-uh. I left my tire irons on a picnic table."

"How are you going to get the tire off the rim?"

I showed him the two pieces of metal that I'd previously used in place of the irons.

Brian picked up my pump. I picked up my tube. My thought, that he'd give me an assist, was short-lived. A squirrel emerged from a hole by the water pump. Brian set the pump back on the table and ran to retrieve Kyra. I set the tube on the table and sat down. Kyra caught the animal and flipped it in the air, snapping its neck. Brian, Judy, and dog reentered the RV.

I decided to fix the flat in the morning, rightly thinking that I'd do a better job if I was rested. I had, before embarking on my 1980 cross-country tour, vowed to arrive at my final destination under my own power. Having Pete pick me up in Wasilla was the sole exception. Chaucer was right: the tongue returns to the aching tooth. This analogy came to mind as I obsessed about every single repair-related step.

I crawled out of my tent at 4:00 a.m. and picked up where, in my near dream state, I'd left off. I filled the two tubes with air and submersed them individually in the nearby lake water. Two streams of tiny bubbles indicated that both tubes had valve leaks. I knew from previous experience that valve stem leaks are impossible to patch. No matter, I'd be the first cyclist to accomplish this task.

The faded price tag on the patch kit cover read "Beaver Sports." The patches were crumbly and the glue in the tube hard. Pete, who in 1989 worked as a bicycle mechanic at the Fairbanks shop, had most likely stashed this kit in his old toolbox.

I managed to squeeze some glue out of the tube, rolled it into a half dozen tiny balls, and squished them around the base of one of the valve stems. I pumped the tube to full capacity, correlating the rate of my breathing with the number of pump strokes. "No-o-o-o," I wailed, as I heard the hiss of escaping air.

Brian and Kyra emerged from the RV and zigzagged over to my shelter area. "I have two valve leaks," I said. Brian remarked that I must have been riding on a tire with low air pressure, the inference being that I'd been remiss in checking my tire pressure.

I watched Kyra pull Brian over to the squirrel hole. He led the dog back over and into the RV. Moments later he reemerged minus dog. We resumed talking, with me saying that I was going to fill the tire with sand.

"We'll give you a lift to town," Brian said. I agreed, having now exhausted all my repair options. A dark cloud rolled in and hung above my head, when fifteen minutes later I assisted Brian in loading my gear into the RV. My dour mood brightened somewhat as the Chinook chugged down the far side of Thompson Pass, for I conceded that that bicycling down the narrow, winding, rain-slick road through a construction site would have been foolhardy. I envisioned being squished by a front-end loader and pressed like a bug into the asphalt by a steamroller.

My mood brightened further as Judy and I talked. I soon learned that her primary literary interest was also personal narrative. My words gushed forth as I elaborated on the challenges inherent to promoting the Bright Lights Book Project while bicycle touring. When finally, I'd had my say, Judy asked me if I was going to write about my adventure. I said no, I didn't think so, adding that "nothing out of the ordinary had occurred."

Brian assisted me in selecting a new tube at Mr. Prospector's Sporting Goods Store. We then backtracked, the couple dropping me off at the City of Valdez Campground. Noisy locals kept me awake. I finished *The Things They Carried* then, flipped through my pasta-stained copy. I focused on the fate of the characters who'd endeared themselves to me. Ted Lavender had been shot in the head outside the village of Than Khe; Kiowa was hit by a mortar shell and died in a cesspool swamp; Lee Strunk had stepped on a mortar round and had his leg blown off; Rat Kiley was shipped off to Japan after being wounded; and Norman Bowker had died by suicide.

I, like O'Brien, had lived to tell my story. I'd humped my essential and nonessential load six hundred or so miles, averaging fifty miles a day. My story didn't compare to his in terms of the degree of hardship. However, there was a parallel. The things O'Brien and his characters carried shaped their identities as soldiers. The gear I carried shaped my identity as a reader and bicyclist.

I bicycled the final five miles to Valdez the next day. I was pleased for I'd completed a challenging trip, mostly under my own power. Mostly. I rationalized the exception to my ironclad rule. Riding through the construction zone would have been a dangerous proposition.

I spent the afternoon looking for possible book distribution sites. The Keystone Motel was one of the few businesses that was open. I rang the front desk bell. The clerk, a pencil-thin fellow in his twenties, sauntered over to the counter. I told him about the book project, then asked if he'd like to pass my remaining books on to motel customers.

This, he said, was a good idea. I retrieved my cardboard box, placed *The Things They Carried* on top, set it on the counter, and handed him O'Brien's book. "You should read this. It's quite good," I said. He opened the book, began reading, then stopped in order to tell me about his uncle, who was a Vietnam War veteran. Affirmed again, good books connect people, sometimes in unexpected ways.

Going Long, Going Solo   CORRINE LEISTIKOW

I love the Denali Highway.

This 135-mile mixed-surface road runs from Cantwell to Paxson. Lying east of Denali National Park, the Denali Highway has a different feel from the Denali Park Road, where tourists ride buses to see Denali, North America's highest peak, and the park's typically abundant wildlife.

I love the park road too. But it is highly regulated, whereas the Denali Highway is open to anybody. Running through the beautiful Alaska Range, the highway has big open vistas, mountains, glaciers, and typically much less traffic. I try to bike it once a summer. But here it was August, and I still hadn't ridden it.

The weather looked good for the upcoming weekend, so even though I was tired from several weekends of hiking and biking trips and should have stayed home, I decided to do another trip. I would go solo, which is often the case when I do the Denali Highway. It's hard to convince friends to bike two really long days with lots of climbing. But that's how I like to bike it.

No worries, though. I enjoy solo bikepacking. Others ask if I'm afraid when I go by myself. "Afraid of what?" I usually ask.

Of bears? I have bear spray and a whistle, and I'm on a road. I feel safe in that regard.

Of people? I feel that most people are basically good, and besides, I have my bear spray for any random weirdos.

Of being bored? That happens occasionally, but I bring music and podcasts to entertain me. Mostly, I enjoy just letting my thoughts go where they want. And in Alaska there is always amazing scenery to look at.

Of spending that much time by myself? I'm an outgoing introvert, so although I have no problem socializing with others, I love having time to myself.

Riding is relaxation. As a family physician, my days are fairly high stress. At work my mind is going constantly. Does that patient have palpitations from anxiety, or is it a heart condition? Is this patient's bone pain due to arthritis, or could he have multiple myeloma? Have I missed something about that boy's abdominal pain?

Talking with patients, which fills most of my days, can be exhausting. I question them about their past histories, both medically and socially. I teach about disease processes. I do motivational interviewing to help patients make healthy lifestyle changes. I try to educate patients about their misguided beliefs and the fallacies they find on the internet. I love the majority of my patients, but all that can be mentally exhausting.

I also get frustrated when so many patients want me to fix them with a pill or procedure instead of doing the hard work of living a healthier lifestyle. By the time I get home somedays, I just want to zone out. Facebook or YouTube, here I come! That might be zoning out, but it isn't relaxing. And that's why biking is so important to me.

Riding my bike alone for hours is a great way to zone out and relax. I don't have to help "fix" anybody; I don't have to be responsible to anybody but myself. And the decisions are simple. Do I want to ride farther or stop now? Should I eat soon or wait a while? Where do I want to sleep? Of course, exercise and being out in nature both help reduce stress. (I keep telling my patients that!) Long bike rides help me truly relax and rejuvenate from a busy, stressful job. I can't imagine my life as a doctor without having a stress reliever like that.

While I enjoy trips with other people—it's great to share the good and bad times with somebody else—I have no problem traveling by myself. I really enjoy that time with just me, my bike, and Alaska. So, when the weather report was good for the weekend and my husband had other plans, I decided I needed to visit the Denali Highway again.

I snagged a campsite in Denali National Park for Friday night. That was a bit north of my starting destination, but it would allow me a little time in one of my favorite national parks. I packed and had everything in my car so that I could head down right after work. I made the three-hour trip to the Savage River Campground with time for dinner and a hike before bedtime.

I was up at 5:00 a.m. Saturday morning, as I had to drive thirty miles to Cantwell, where I would start my bike ride. I had an ambitious plan to bike one hundred miles to the top of Maclaren Summit and camp. Then I would get up early Sunday morning, bike back, drive home, unpack, and get some sleep before work on Monday. A very full weekend.

While the question of being afraid to travel solo didn't rattle around in my brain, another one did. Why did I want to go big? Most summers I'm training for a race. I've done several long-distance bikepacking races, such as the Smoke 'n' Fire 400, BC Epic 100, Tour Divide, and Alberta Rockies 700. All are 400 miles long or more. This summer the races I planned (the 350-mile DKXL and the 750-mile Trans South Dakota) were either canceled or out of reach due to COVID travel restrictions.[1] I didn't need to train for anything, but here I was cramming a lot of miles into a weekend. Not the first time either. I had done other long bike rides earlier in the summer. Was I trying to prove something? Did I just want to see a lot of country, or was it something more?

I pondered while biking. Many athletes do endurance training to help with their anxiety or depression. Luckily, I have neither. I'm fairly even-keeled, mostly optimistic, and only need a short, hard ride to deal with any stress I may be feeling. However, I now have a reputation for going long, so do I feel I have to do something epic to keep up that reputation? Or do I do it for bragging rights? I admit that it feels good when people say I'm an inspiration to them, but it's also embarrassing. I'm not doing anything special; I just keep turning the pedals. And to be honest, just as many people think I'm crazy as inspiring. Do I even care what others think? I don't know. Maybe?

Thinking aside, the Denali Highway ride was great. The road was in good shape overall. There were *lots* of hunters, and every pullout was packed with RVs and ATVs. But most drivers were considerate and slowed while passing me. And even though there was more traffic than usual, I still had a lot of alone time to just bike and enjoy the views.

One reason I like long rides is that they are a type of meditation. My mind empties, and mostly, I'm just in the moment. That feels good. Worries drop away. And I love being able to see what is around the next corner or over the next hill. I like to keep moving forward. I like to see as much as I can in the time I have.

I also like to see wildlife, but I saw almost none on this ride. I think the traffic scared the animals off. However, I did see two moose, two beavers, and I heard loons calling at 50-Mile Lake, about fifty miles from Paxson and not too far from where I camped. No bears this time either. I rarely see bears while bikepacking, and they have always run off as soon as they see me. So, while they induce fear in other people, my experiences with them while bikepacking have always been fine. The exception is in Denali National Park, where they tend to ignore people and go about their business, which is often near the road. It's the law—and good sense—to keep your distance, so at times I've had to turn around or flag down a bus to get around them. Still, I always carry bear spray, just in case.

But my long rides are about more than meditation and nature. I also like to challenge myself. My friends think I'm competitive. And I am, though mostly with myself. I don't really care where I end up in a race—although I'd rather not be last. But I do like to set challenging goals and see if I can meet them. I want to see if I'm tough enough to finish what I start. That is more important to me than beating somebody else.

For biking my first really big challenge came the year I turned fifty. No fancy vacations or spas for me. I wanted to do something epic, so I entered the Fireweed 200, a two-hundred-mile bike race from Sheep Mountain on the Glenn Highway to Valdez. I had done several hundred-mile rides before, but I had never tried riding two hundred miles in one go. I knew it would be a real challenge and would take a lot of time to train. I was hesitant at first. That goal seemed selfish, since our kids were preteens. But my husband encouraged me to go for it. So, I spent that spring and early summer going for longer bike rides.

When we headed down to the race start, I felt I had trained well. And I did it. I finished. But . . . But . . . I left somewhat unsatisfied. During the race my stomach shut down. More than halfway through, but still many miles from the end, I threw up. I felt awful. I had to lie down by the side of the road to rest and recover. In fact, I felt miserable a lot of the race, which slowed me down. But after I finished, I was hooked. I had set a challenging goal and accomplished it! But . . . But . . . I knew I could do better.

I had to figure out how to fuel smarter so I didn't get sick. I spent a lot of time researching the issue. Over the following year I tried some new things. Then I did the race again and finished an hour and a half faster. And didn't throw up.

But . . . But . . . I still felt I hadn't done my best. The second year I finished in twelve and a half hours. I felt I had it in me to finish in under twelve hours. A new challenge. A couple of years later, I tried the race again and finished in eleven hours and fifty minutes. I set another more challenging goal, and I did it!

But then I was done. I didn't have any other goals for the Fireweed 200. I have never gone back to do that race again. I don't even remember in what place I finished in any of those races because that didn't matter. What mattered was that I did what I had set out to accomplish. That's my kind of competition. It continues to drive me.

After my first Fireweed 200 finish, I started looking for other goals. I had heard about Leadville 100, a one-hundred-mile mountain bike race in Colorado. Could I do it? I knew it would be a stretch for me. The course played to my strengths, as it required a lot of endurance but wasn't too technical. However, it started at ten thousand feet and had pretty tight time cutoffs. I wasn't sure I could make them. But that's what makes it a challenge. I wanted to try.

I entered the lottery and got in! We decided to take a two-week family vacation in Colorado that would culminate with the race. During the race I started strong and made it through the first checkpoint with a bit of time to spare. But then we had a long climb to the high point, at thirteen thousand feet. I bonked. I had to push up a lot of it and felt terrible. Once again, I threw up, but I was near the high point of the course so managed to continue, thinking I would feel better as I descended. I kept checking my watch and saw I would be close on the second cutoff.

And I was. But not close enough. I was about the third person who got stopped at the checkpoint. I was relieved to not have to keep suffering, and I knew I would never have made the third cutoff. But . . . But . . . I was disappointed that I hadn't made my goal. It was unfinished business.

So, I broached the subject with my husband about returning the next year. As usual, he totally supported me. In fact, for that race we left the kids with Grandma and both entered. I got a new bike and trained harder and smarter. I biked longer and rode more hills. We spent the two weeks before the race in Leadville resting and checking out parts of the course.

The race day came, and I felt good. I made each cutoff with a little time to spare. I was able to eat and drink. No vomiting this time. And I finished the race tired but feeling pretty good. Eric finished just a few minutes in front of me. I made my goal, and I haven't been back to that race either.

But I wasn't done with challenges. I started learning about bike-packing races and became intrigued. I've done several of those races, culminating in 2018 with the 2,700-mile Tour Divide. I have finished every bikepacking race I started, even though there was often pain and suffering along the way. But I didn't give up even when I wanted to. My competition is more about seeing how tough I can be.

And I'm not done. This past spring, when a lot of races were canceled, Rebecca Rusch, the Queen of Pain, put out a challenge for riders to try to Everest—that is, ride up and down one hill until you have climbed the height of Everest, just over twenty-nine thousand feet. Could I do it? Should I even try? I'd once ridden twenty thousand feet by riding one hundred miles up and down Ester Dome for a worthy cause, but doing an Everest was an extra nine thousand feet of climbing. I wasn't sure I had it in me. Which means it was a great challenge. I had already been training for a 350-mile race, which had been canceled, so why not try?

I decided to try on the hill from the Felix Pedro Monument to Cleary Summit on the Steese Highway. That hill climbs 3.6 miles, with 1,100 feet elevation gain. I'd have to do about twenty-seven laps. That seemed like a lot, but it felt within my reach.

I started at 6:00 a.m. on a perfect Saturday morning on Memorial Day weekend. I felt good for about the first half of the ride, but then at around 3:00 p.m., my stomach started to shut down again. I started vomiting. But I had experience with this and felt confident I could recover, so I continued.

But I didn't recover. I kept riding, but by 11:00 p.m. I had eaten very little for hours. I was getting weaker, and the temperature was falling. I knew that if I kept going at the pace I was biking, it would take me all night to finish the seven more laps I needed. Could I do it? I don't know. I knew I just didn't care enough to keep suffering. So, I quit.

That bugged me. I don't think I had ever quit just because I didn't want to keep suffering. What did it mean? Was I done pushing myself? Was my toughness fading? I still haven't quite figured that out yet, but as time passes, the Everest feels like unfinished business. I'm thinking that I'm going to have to go back and try again. I've got some different ideas about how to fuel better that may help. I have plans to do a couple of races this coming summer, but if they get canceled due to COVID, I'll try to Everest again.

There are still other challenges out there waiting for me. My failed Everest attempt didn't shake my confidence for long. I haven't quit pushing myself. I've still got that competitive drive to see if I can set goals just on the edge of my abilities. And then see if I can achieve them. I'm that kind of competitive. This Denali ride wasn't anything special in that regard, but it was a reminder that I could go long two days in a row. Positive reinforcement.

On Saturday I ran into a biker, Paul, from Anchorage. He had been riding the highway for several days and was just finishing up. We stopped to talk, and the no-see-ums started swarming. I bemoaned the fact that I had forgotten my head net, and without missing a beat, he offered me his. He said he was just about done with his ride and was fine with me taking it. Fellow bikepackers are the best! He then said that his good friends, David and Jan, were camped at 50-Mile Lake, another thirty miles up the road. I should stop, say hi, and tell them he sent me. He assured me they would feed me and give me anything I needed.

I felt a little weird, but I did stop and say hi, and Paul was right. Dave and Jan were amazing. They didn't know me, yet they immediately invited me into their RV, even though I was muddy and a little wet. They even invited me to have dinner with them. I had to say no as it was getting late and I still had fifteen miles to go, but I told them I would be headed back that way the next day. They invited me to stop by in the morning. I wasn't sure I would, but I was inspired by their hospitality. I showed up quite early, 7:30 a.m., but once again, they invited me right in and offered me hot water and fresh fruit while I made my oatmeal breakfast.

One of the things I love about solo bikepacking is that you can have incredible interactions with amazing people just by chance. I've had similar encounters on other trips. Random strangers have stopped and offered me ice-cold water or snacks or just wanted to talk. Visiting with David and Jan was one of the highlights of my trip. There are so many good people out there with interesting life stories. It's fun to have these serendipitous encounters and make new friends. I find it happens more frequently when I cycle alone. Yet another positive for going solo.

Overall, the weekend was very satisfying. I put in two ten- to twelve-hour days—each with one hundred miles of riding and 6,500 feet of elevation gain—with full bikepacking gear. It was hard but doable. When I finished, I had no regrets. Anything but. I had spent a wonderful weekend in beautiful country and met some delightful people. As always, the experiences, both inner and outer, gave me a break—and a contrast—from my everyday life.

But maybe those reasons don't really matter. Maybe I go long and go solo because I just like to keep turning the pedals.

Notes

1. The full (and offensive) name of the DKXL race, the Dirty Kanza XL, was changed in 2020 to Unbound Gravel at the urging of the Indigenous Kaw Nation and other activists.—Ed.

Physical Education

It's their last day in Alaska, and I'm taking the interns out for a flight
in my Cessna 182. They've earned it, working hard on a couple of civil
engineering projects at our office this summer. Annie is staying downtown near Merrill Field Airport, so we decide to load her bike into
my car at the office. I lean down to take off the front wheel and notice
there's no quick release.

"Annie, is there an easy way to take your wheels off, or do I need to
go get a wrench?"

"Oh, I have no idea!" she says with her characteristic earnestness.

"No idea? You've been riding this bike for two months!" I guess she
never had to take the wheels off.

"Yeah, sorry, I just borrowed it from the lady I'm renting from."

"But you've been riding over thirty miles a day!" I shake my head.
This bike is definitely a Walmart special. I'm impressed it lasted this
long, but that's the thing about bikes. You don't really need to spend a
lot of money just to get home and back, especially when you're young
and poor and your body is resilient enough to get around on something
that doesn't fit particularly well. In my forties now, my back and knees
hurt just looking at this thing. Annie is tall, lean, serious, and twenty
years old. She's from Illinois, with long, auburn hair, and her wiry limbs
wrap perfectly fine around this heavy, cheap bike.

Serena is small and curvaceous, the same age as Annie, with a light
drawl of northern Georgia and curly, dark hair. She is serious, too, but
a bit more outgoing. At the start of the summer, I loaned her my classic
Terry that I'd found up in Fairbanks, when I first moved to Alaska. It
is silver, with bar-end shifters and a smaller twenty-four-inch wheel

on just the front: a beautiful little road bike and one of the first made for women, by a woman, Georgena Terry.

Terry is herself an engineer, a polio survivor, and a visionary. Her simple idea was to make cycling more accessible to women by making the frames fit our bodies. On this one there is still writing in orange nail polish, from the previous owner, announcing this was Ernie's racing bike. I would have liked to meet Ernie. I didn't find Fairbanks a very hospitable place to ride road bikes, with its chip-sealed roads and short season and pickup trucks throwing beer cans out the window, but I did figure out that this Terry fit perfectly in the back of my airplane and could get me around wherever I flew.

When I dropped it off with Serena at the start of the summer, she was unsure about riding a road bike. I adjusted the seat height for her and showed her how the shifters worked. There was no indexing—this was old school; she'd have to listen and feel for the gear she wanted. I watched her work awkwardly around the parking lot and thought: Good, she'll learn something. As we parted, I saw a large man pass by the door in her rental.

"Is that your roommate?" I asked.

She chuckled. "Yeah, and my landlord. He just rents the extra room. He's army, so not around that much."

My eyebrows raised. "Hmm . . . well, you've got my number. If for some reason that doesn't work out, don't hesitate to call. I'm just down the street."

"Oh, thanks, I'm sure it will be fine. He's already invited me up to the hot springs in Fairbanks."

My heart started beating a little faster, like a weather-worn house mother in the sorority of life. "Well . . . be careful." I gave her the bike, but that's obviously not what I was worried about. She pedaled all over Anchorage for two months and I think never once shifted the gears on that Terry.

If I had to point to a couple of decisions I've made over the years about who I was going to be, they predated Alaska and flying airplanes and almost going to outer space, but they would make those things possible, later on. Learning to ride and fix bikes was really an important step, let alone all the places they would take me. Those places weren't so exotic—largely parks, city streets, and trails—but these quotidian rides were the places where I found I could think about who I was and what I wanted. The bike was also a place where I could stop thinking about anything at all.

I'd ridden bikes growing up in Nebraska, usually a hand-me-down or garage sale special—enough to get me to school, to the library, and to work at a handful of restaurants and just enough autonomy to stay sane. There was a long rail-to-trail out of Lincoln, called the MoPac Trail after the old Missouri-Pacific line, which led to a town-turned-grain-elevator called Walton that had a little bike shop. The MoPac Trail was a great place to ride away from my family and high school, neither of which suited me very well at the time. The sun beat down like a torch, and just east of town, the only shade I remember on the route was an occasional mulberry tree, staining the limestone gravel.

In Walton, at the bike shop, I could get an iced coffee and rest in the shade. Old railroad shrapnel caused a lot of flat tires, so I could also replace my spare tube if I'd already used the one I carried. Early on, I'd learned how to change a tube, adjust the brakes, replace and maintain the chain. With Dad gone in those years, no one was there to show me—I just figured it out by looking, reading a book, and getting the right tool, or at least one that would suffice for that moment. I also learned the hard way about a pinch flat and getting solvent in places where it didn't belong, but it was a space in which to make errors when the consequences were hardly more than a day's wages or a long walk home.

In New York City, though, in college and graduate school, I fell even more in love with cycling. The tree-lined loops of Central Park saved my life. When my eyes couldn't read another word of Kant or my understanding of geophysical fluid dynamics hit a wall, there was the park, night and day, however many six-mile loops I could do. Sometimes there, at night, I'd see wildlife. Not watching frozen like a bird and birder in the Rambles but glimpsing a raccoon diving down a storm sewer or a coyote's tail trotting toward the reservoir—animals that were moving as I moved, making their own path. When that wasn't enough, I figured out the route over the George Washington Bridge to New Jersey, along the Palisades, and Upstate. I had to overcome my fear of heights on the bridge, but then I'd watch the serious riders in their candy-colored spandex, men chattering in Spanish and English, and I'd follow behind them to learn the routes. It took me a long time before I decided to bike with other people, and now, more than ever, I prefer to bike alone.

In my freshman dorm, in northern Manhattan, our floor was co-ed. It was the only dorm where you could live in a room by yourself, which is why I chose it. There a cheap Gary Fisher hybrid leaned up against my bed. One of the engineers living down the hall, Felix, would whistle at me in my robe, on the way to the shower, which was creepy at best. But later, in grad school, he'd actually become one of my cycling coaches, and I'd try my hand at racing. Felix probably even helped me pick out my first adult road bike—a sturdy, gray Bianchi—but I don't really remember. Maybe by that point I had the confidence and savings to just go to a store and buy one.

Back then I still believed that a lot of guys who seemed creepy at first were mostly just awkward. I think Felix was all right, but I don't really know. His family was Jewish, from Tunisia, and he had a pretty girlfriend whom he wanted to provide for in a traditional way. He had a head shaped like a football on a thick, stocky body, and he was the kind of guy who stared at a woman's chest when he was talking to her. He rarely looked me in the eye.

In the early morning in the park, Felix would teach me, and the two other women on our intramural team, bike-handling drills. He understood that we could fight our way to fitness on our own, but it was manipulating the bike in tight packs and different road surfaces with sand and leaves and loose soil and crazed taxies that we needed to improve. Later, when he was struggling, I would get Felix a computer programming job at my oceanography lab, which didn't pay very well, and he would default on his college loans. When the school started garnishing his wages, he disappeared. I'd see him once more on a city bus, years later, when I was back visiting from Alaska, and then the next message from him would be a few more years later, from Hong Kong: a lonely note through LinkedIn. I never wrote back but for no reason in particular. Maybe I don't think I'm the person I once was, but of course I am.

We had an old man coach, too, named Happy, but he couldn't actually ride a bike anymore. He'd had some kind of accident, and nerve damage left him wearing shorts 365 days a year and limping along with a cane. Mostly, Happy just talked, sometimes about bike racing but not usually. By day he was some kind of foot doctor's assistant, but he also gave really expensive massages to wealthy women. He would offer to give the women on the cycling team free massages if they just bought him dinner afterward and tolerated his self-centered monologue. Before my first time, I asked my teammate Kirstie if he was a pervert. He might be, she said, but I think he just wants someone to be his wife and he doesn't know how. If you don't want a free massage, don't go. Those were the rules for our generation. Be smart. Accept what might happen. Have a backup plan. We weren't children: I was twenty-four years old. Happy was dull, but he was not inappropriate, and by that time, frankly, I could really use a massage. He would go on to marry Felix's sister and father her child, and I have no idea how that worked out. The sister bought my Bianchi before I moved north, and I still miss that bike.

The one who did move my heart just a little bit was Jason. He was funny and smart and full of personality. He was short, from New Jersey, and had a weird hair that only grew on the top of his head and not the sides. He was the captain of our informal team, which only meant that he picked the color of our uniforms (baby blue) and the flavors of pizza we'd all order and eat together (lots of meat). He was finishing up his doctorate in sociology in this new thing called social media. None of us really even knew what that was back then.

Jason and a couple of undergrads; Woyzeck, whom we called the Polish Sausage; and a guy whose name I can't remember but who had luscious black hair and a beauty spot like Cindy Crawford were all heading out to a criterion at the far edge of Brooklyn, on Jamaica Bay. Jason asked if I wanted to come and race the women's field. I said I'd come but not race, and so I followed them downtown on the subway, and then we biked over the Brooklyn Bridge and out to Floyd Bennett Field. Bennett Field was New York City's first municipal airport, built in 1930. Floyd Bennett was a naval aviator and Adm. Richard Byrd's pilot on the purported first flight to the North Pole. Despite the various medals of honor they received, it's now generally believed they had lied about making it to the North Pole. If it hadn't been for a nasty crash, they said they would have beat Lindbergh across the Atlantic too. For that day, though, Bennett Field was three runways oriented in a triangle and a sufficient course for a criterion. Cattails and weeds grew around the cracking pavement.

The guys got ready for their race, stretching and peeing in the reeds. Straddling his bike near me, where I sat in the grass, Jason pointed at the only other woman around; they must have canceled the women's race. She was thin and boyish, with short, mousy hair, and seemed awkward. A referee scolded her for not having a helmet on. Something about liability on the course. "Hey, Cherry, that dyke over there is looking your way, better watch out," Jason said.

"You're an ass," I replied.

"Well, you came out here to watch me, didn't you?"

I rolled my eyes. "I just want to see the race."

The men lined up then, and they were off. The problems with the course—its rough pavement and tight, triangular shape—became apparent after the pack made just its third or fourth pass around. There was a delay. Woyzeck and Beauty Mark emerged unscathed, but Jason came out later, with a bleeding gash across his calf and torn shorts. I could tell it hurt from his locked jaw, but the pain just seemed to amplify his cruel humor.

After the race was over, the four of us headed back home along Flatbush Avenue, until I felt a resistance and looked down between my legs. I was already at the back. "Hey, guys, wait up, I've got a flat." They stopped and turned around. Before I could pull out my kit, Jason had a new tube in his hand and had pulled the wheel off.

"Cherry, you are a fucking embarrassment," he said with surprising sincerity.

"I can do this myself, you know." I knew I wasn't an embarrassment. It was just a flat tire. But he proceeded to change the tube in a big hurry. I don't know what he found had impaled it or if he even took the time to look. I held up the frame, and he threaded the wheel back into the chain in what might have been a moment of intimacy, if he hadn't been so pissed off about it.

The repair accomplished, the guys mounted their saddles and headed off. Jason shouted, "Bye," and I could see a white patch of his ass visible through his torn shorts. Woyzeck looked back at me for a split second, and I just watched them go. I didn't feel like making chase, and they obviously didn't feel bound by either friendship or chivalry. I looked down at my hard plastic cycling shoes with clips on the soles and remembered how hard it had been to navigate the subway with its iron-tipped staircases. Then I swung my spandex-clad leg over my bike and stood for a moment on the sidewalk, looking around. Men and women were walking in colorful African textiles. Storefront windows were covered with stacks of cheap clothing and bright signs in Hangul. Curry wafted through the air. I had absolutely no idea where I was.

I didn't own a cell phone, and even if I had, this was long before phones had maps on them. I could just remember we'd come a ways down this avenue, so if I took it the other direction, eventually Manhattan would come back into view, and the Brooklyn Bridge, and I should be able to find the on-ramp again. Or should I head to the East River first and then just hug the water until the bridge? I remember thinking then and there that I just wanted to depend on myself. These guys weren't my friends. Even after I'd spend the night at Jason's, a few weeks later, that would still hold true. Later I'd go on to date a woman for a whole year who looked remarkably like that gal at the race. But that day I took a drink of water from my bottle, shifted into a comfortable gear, and rode the whole thirty miles home to Morningside Heights. I was young and really fit and starting to understand how things worked: mechanically, physically, hormonally.

Eventually, I gave up on those guys and the gals on the team, too, and just rode to and from Manhattan and Rockland County, New York, where I worked. I loved that ride, but I never did get comfortable riding over the George Washington Bridge, even when I did it every day. On a bike you sit far above the railing and have to accommodate other cyclists and pedestrians going both ways in a narrow space, more than two hundred feet above the Hudson River. I never have liked heights. A lot of pilots don't, you would be surprised. The route around the two towers that suspend the bridge bothered me the most, and I would hug the inside as best I could. That September, after the race at Bennett Field, I stopped one morning to look down the Hudson, and it was a beautiful morning, but something seemed strange. A few small planes and a helicopter were all flying up the river toward the bridge, like traffic had been diverted. After I dropped down onto the crumbling road of Palisades Park in Fort Lee, New Jersey, past some white-tailed deer, and climbed back up onto busy Route 9W and to our lab at the state line, I arrived to a changed world. And only one pair of clean clothes on 9/11. After one night sleeping on the floor of my office and another at a classmate's mother's house a few towns over, the GW Bridge reopened. I rode back home, and there were soldiers with assault rifles guarding the bike path now. Downtown would be on fire for another month. I didn't feel it right then, but five years later, I'd had enough of the crowded subway and dirty air. I'd received my degrees and was ready for a different kind of education. I read Seth Kantner's *Ordinary Wolves* and got on a plane to Alaska, for what I didn't know would be the rest of my life.

Now in Anchorage, almost two decades later, this year feels strangely similar, but my vantage point could hardly be more different. When the COVID-19 pandemic started, my first response was to pull out my old titanium racing bike, the yellow and red Serotta that I'd splurged on toward the end of grad school. Surely, with no travel out of state, I'd be putting in some miles on this thing. I zipped the dry rotten tires off the rims and labored to stretch the new ones on, so much so, I was actually laughing at myself. My husband was in the other room, and I might have asked him to help, but why? This was an important skill for self-sufficiency. I tightened my core, held my breath, and used all of the strength in my hands to push and pull each tire on. I wondered about those interns from last summer, Annie and Serena, and whether they'd listened to me and learned to change a tire by now. "You're engineers," I'd said. "You need to know how stuff works in real life, not just in a spreadsheet. IRL."

I can laugh now about Felix's catcalls, Happy's "coach" massages, and Jason's rejection. They mean nothing to me by now. Tiny flickers of memory jogged by the shadow of Serena's landlord. I remember the sound of Jason's radio playing a Yankees game on a Sunday afternoon while I watched him ejaculate precisely into his hand, like a machine squeezing an orange into a glass. For all of his intelligence and physical skill, he was just a weird man in his twenties, with no agility in his relationships. Now he's a dean of a college. This is the gift of middle age—my middle age: the way countless, senseless things start to add up to a strange body of experience. I had wonderful friendships in those years, too, but I can't forget how I showed these cycling guys more empathy than they deserved, and that person is still a part of me. Already inclined toward independence, their bad behavior pushed me even further. Now, so many years later, I understand better how things work. Not just bikes and airplanes but people too—men and women, and myself. I've received a physical education.

It's interesting how learning to ride a bike skillfully helps your body navigate space and time. As a kid, I was a ballet dancer, so I know nothing of the feeling of throwing a ball toward another person in an efficient and effective way. I only learned about all the ways in which a foot can bleed and a knee can bend and how many vertices can form along the curvature of arms. Like flying an airplane, riding a bike is a pas de deux with a machine. The term *mastery* has fallen out of fashion, for a good reason, but when you can minimize excess movement, perfectly transfer your power into the pedals, and endure whatever the environment has to offer, those add up to something both graceful and pleasing. And when those things on your ride aren't optimal, if you can still enjoy the scenery or get to your job or deliver someone's takeout food in Manhattan, under your own power, that's still an exceptional act. It's a rare kind of exceptionalism that almost anyone can access. When she was in her midfifties, my grandmother, who lived right on that MoPac Trail when it was still a train track, finally learned to ride a bike. It was always something she'd wanted to try. She was every bit as fearful as she was courageous. Maybe I got this from her.

Understanding my body, and the simple machines in my life, has given me courage. We say, in children's books, afterschool specials, and Girl Scout retreats, that we want women to have positive body images, mechanical skills, and financial independence. Those goals sound reasonable enough, but how does being so individualistic lead to all the team endeavors we also want women to participate in: marriage and motherhood, caretaking and careers? I think anyone can learn more self-reliance, and plenty of men don't know how to use a wrench either. But what, really, do you gain from physical confidence? There's so much more to life than using a wrench correctly or building better machines, but this essay isn't about those other things.

That day with the interns, Annie and Serena, we left both bikes at the office after all, and we drove to Merrill Field Airport. The guys at the office had really built up this experience, about how much fun they would have doing something so quintessentially Alaskan. We parked near the plane, but before we got out, Annie opened her mouth, and I could tell what she had to say was hard for her. "I actually don't think I'm going to fly with you; my Dad thinks it's too dangerous."

I felt ready for her fear. Shit, it *is* too dangerous. I always feel wary of taking passengers who don't really know what they've committed to. And to be truthful, age has started to sow doubt, and I wonder if it may be time to retire from aviation. Sometimes I think about all the places I could go on a bike if I wasn't spending time and money on airplanes. But this was not that moment.

"No problem," I said. "Just come over with Serena and me, and I'll show you both the plane, and if either of you or both of you don't feel comfortable, that's totally fine. We don't even have to tell anyone; I won't say a word." Annie smiled and said, "Sounds good." I'll give her time to think about it. I'll show her how it *works*.

I pushed my flight bag over my shoulder and gave them each a headset to carry, and we walked out onto the tarmac. I unlocked the plane, plugged in my headset, and stowed my bag. I unhooked the tie-downs on the wing struts and the tail, and then I told Annie and Serena to follow me as I did the preflight inspection and I would explain how everything worked and what I looked for on the inspection.

There on the Cessna, I sumped the fuel on the left wing tank and showed them how I look for water, which is heavier than gas. Water in the fuel can cause the engine to quit, as I've learned too well. I told them how the fuel is dyed blue, so we know it's the right octane. I made sure the luggage door was closed and locked. I felt the leading edges of the horizontal stabilizers for damage, and I made sure the elevators had all of their bolts and moved correctly. I explained that the airplane's lifting surfaces are the most important things to inspect. I made sure the vertical stabilizer looked right and that the rudder moved as it should. I felt for the bolts that connect the rudder to the tail. I sumped the right wing tank for water, and I reached in and showed them how the yoke, the airplane's steering wheel, controls the ailerons on the wings. I put the flaps down and reminded them about the shape of airfoils and the center of lift. The flaps help us drop down for landing slower, at a sharper angle. We looked at the tires and compared the hydraulic brakes to how various bike brakes work. I explained how the pilot's foot pedals work the brakes on the ground and the rudder in the air.

At the front of the plane, I carefully pulled the propeller through a few strokes and looked inside the cowling for bird nests. I checked the oil for its level and color and replaced the dipstick with a single, gentle turn. It will tighten more as the engine heats up. I reached inside the cockpit and drained the gascolator and explained that this is the lowest place that water can pool in the fuel system. I showed them the pitot tube, static ports, fuel vent, and stall horn. I pulled out a couple of floatation vests and showed them how to put them on. I described what happens in an emergency and what to do if we crash into the Knik Arm.

It's a grim final, but I asked if they have any questions about how the plane works. Heads shook no, and mouths smiled wide. "Well, what do you think? Annie, do you feel up for a ride?" She enthusiastically agreed. Serena, too, of course. They piled in the passenger seats, and I showed them how to work the seatbelts and headset jacks. "Annie, we've got a long taxi before takeoff, why don't you just text your dad and tell him we'll be gone for two hours and that you'll text him when you're back." She agreed, and we were off.

We didn't fly too far, just far enough to see a glacier in the distance and two of the rivers Annie had studied in her research project. It was late afternoon, and the summer air was choppy. Through the turbulence I talked about convection, thermals, and the afternoon storm clouds formed by so much evaporation. I didn't want them to be too afraid or barf in the plane, so we headed back to the airport. I called the tower, joined the pattern, and took in the beauty of Cook Inlet on an early-summer evening. I talked them through each step of the landing process: pulling the power back, trimming the elevator, flaps down, propeller in, more trim to just the right speed. Flare over the numbers, gentle touchdown. I opened the window for fresh air and called ground control as we taxied back to the parking spot. Serena enjoyed herself, but Annie was ecstatic. I took a selfie of all three of us in front of the tail and will remember that fondly. On the way home they peppered me with questions about lessons and licenses.

After they went back to Illinois and Georgia, respectively, I picked up the poor Terry. Maybe it was me who'd put Serena at risk on this bike. My coworker had called it a piece of junk. What nerve! This thing is a classic, built for a body like mine. Serena had taped a plastic clamshell to the handlebars to hold her phone while she rode. I was offended by the aesthetics of that. I pulled it off and put it in the garbage. Next I took the wheels off and put it in my car and drove to the bike shop, my own bike tools having been stolen the year before. "This bike needs some love," I told the mechanic. I didn't like the sales staff who worked at this shop; they always found a way to insult my intelligence in that bike shop–guy way. The mechanic, though, I liked. He was a big, heavy guy, a hand like a bear paw. He took the tiny handlebars from me and stroked the top tube. "Wow, look at this thing! An old Terry. Where did you find this?" I smiled. He understood.

"Up in Fairbanks."

"Cool! What should I do with her?"

"All new cables, please, and handlebar tape in Bianchi green. Bottom bracket if it needs it."

"Sounds good. I'll give you a call when she's ready."

"Thank you."

[Some names have been changed in this story for privacy.]

There Is No Tomorrow

BJØRN OLSON

The sting of pebbles peppering the back of my legs reminded me to be grateful that the wind was at our back. In front of me, my three companions clamped down on their brakes and fought to retain control of their expedition-loaded fat bikes when the powerful gust slammed us. We were three days into our Arctic expedition, riding over a lichen-encrusted mountain pass in the western Brooks Range, when wind from a nightmare dream began to blow. The next even more powerful gust flung us from our bikes.

"This is fucking incredible!" I yelled as I hefted my loaded bike upright and leaned hard into the wind. Wide-eyed smiles and nervous laughter greeted my comment.

The Beaufort Wind Scale labels wind speeds between fifty-six and sixty-three knots as a violent storm. Anything above sixty-four knots is a hurricane. For the next three days, the winds hovered between these two classifications. Simple tasks like adding or removing a jacket required methodical intention. To let go of a strap or sleeping pad, even for a second, meant risking it being blown out of reach, most likely never to be seen again.

Over a thousand miles to the south, in my cozy cabin in coastal Alaska, lives a large, shaded relief map of the state. It is a beautiful, well-designed map. It is a centerpiece fixture, a conversation starter, and a debate settler. This map is where many of our trip ideas first take seed.

In the cold, dark month of December, my life partner, Kim McNett, and I imagined an extensive, trailless, fat bike traverse across the top of Alaska. Staring at the map, our fingers traced previous wilderness cycling trips, some of which led us north above the latitude of the Arctic

Circle. An idea began to take shape, to pick up where we'd left off and attempt a summer fat bike and packraft trip in the Far North.

Starting in the Iñupiat Eskimo village of Point Hope, we conceived a route through mountains, along coastlines, passing through two villages (Point Lay and Wainwright), and terminating 450 miles later in the northernmost community in the United States—Utqiaġvik (formerly Barrow) and perhaps beyond. This would be our first fat bike trip entirely above the Arctic Circle.

The wind found us in the Lisburne Hills. This series of low-elevation mountains, the westernmost extent of the Brooks Range, reside entirely above the Arctic Circle and dramatically terminate as sheer cliffs and capes into the Chukchi Sea.

The treeless landscape of the western Brooks Range appeared ancient, and it was easy for me to imagine herds of mammoth, mastodon, and steppe bison roaming about, with Paleo-Arctic hunters in pursuit. As we rode over the mountain passes, my mind whirled. Despite the strong wind, I was in a bliss state. This was what I'd come for—raw, unadulterated Arctic wilderness. With the wind at our back, we were able to ride up and over the mountains. For two days we were treated to the best off-trail cycling I've ever experienced.

Long distances between villages, and thus resupply points, demanded heavy loads. Kim and I and our two traveling companions, Daniel and Alayne, who would join us as far as the first village of Point Lay, each carried ten days' worth of food as we set out from Point Hope. As a parting gift, our friend Ayagaaq, an Iñupiaq hunter, sent us off with traditional Native food: dried whitefish, bearded seal jerky, and raw muktuk—whale fat and skin. This rich food has sustained northern people for thousands of years. Our group graciously accepted the food and the added insurance it bought us.

We emerged out of the hills and onto a pebble beach some five miles east of Cape Lisburne. For some inexplicable reason, our two-way satellite tracker-texting device had been rapidly losing power. Our only chance of recharging the potentially lifesaving device would be to retreat to the cape, to Wevok—a Cold War–era radar site—in the hopes someone was there and that they had an outlet we could usurp for an hour.

"There is no tomorrow," one of the four permanent employees at Wevok told us. I assumed, at first, he meant that the sun never sets in the summer and never rises in winter and therefore there is no such thing as a tomorrow. As he continued, however, I realized he meant something different. "If you have a good day in the Arctic, do not waste it," he said. "Tomorrow the wind may be screaming, and whatever chore you needed done will have to wait for who knows how long." We didn't have the luxury of sitting out bad days, but his metaphor was good, and it rolled around in my mind for the entirety of the trip.

Days of painless travel flowed from one to the next as the terrain flattened and our routine settled in. Long hours of beach riding were punctuated with short paddles across deep channels of water, always making time to stop and observe the abundant and varied wildlife.

Through still water on a rare calm morning, I paddled one final forward stroke and let my packraft lazily drift the last few feet to shore. When my bow made contact, I stepped out onto a beach below the village of Point Lay and swatted at the mosquitoes buzzing around my head.

As we rode our bikes around and got our bearings, the village seemed energized. Four-wheelers pulled loaded trailers to and fro, kids were outside playing and riding bikes, and many people stood in front of their houses butchering and processing meat. "Welcome to Kali"—the Iñupiaq name for Point Lay—everyone said as we passed. The day before, the community had taken thirty-three beluga whales, and today was Nalukataq—the spring whaling festival—auspicious timing on our part.

People gathered outside the school and into the gymnasium; tray upon tray of food were being carried and set out for the upcoming feast. Kids flocked to us and our freakish looking oversized bikes. "Can I try?" they asked. "If my bike can withstand what I just put it through, I don't see how you can hurt it," Kim said, as she stabilized her bike for an enthusiastic little boy. "Me next. Me next," came the cacophony.

Five days of prepackaged food awaited us at the post office, which we'd sent from home two weeks earlier. As we reorganized the bags on our bikes to make room for the resupply, people from the village stopped to ask questions and offer advice. "Nalukataq is beginning soon. Come eat," they told us.

Inside the gymnasium we sat at one of the school cafeteria lunch tables that had been set up for the feast. Round after round of food was passed out, with elders respectfully being served first. We were treated to a delicious meal of traditional Native food—boiled beluga, bird soup, black and white muktuk, fry bread, and sweets. While eating, we received advice from Doug Rexford, the esteemed whaling captain, and others. Our biggest concern about the route ahead was finding fresh water. On our unrolled map, fingers full of wisdom and local knowledge pointed to our best options.

After the meal and before the dancing began, we were again surrounded by kids. They each in turn told us stories of Iñupiat lore, excitedly cutting one another off to tell their version of Silla, the Big Mouth Baby, or the Woman in White. Within these kids were the ancient stories, passed down through the millennia. In their capable care, Iñupiaq culture is in safekeeping.

"There are two kinds of Arctic problems," Arctic adventurer Vilhjalmur Stefansson once said, "the imaginary and the real. Of the two, the imaginary is the most real."

As we said goodbye to Alayne and Daniel in Point Lay, our imaginations had settled down some. Polar bears were not hiding behind every rock, and what appeared to be the most challenging terrain was behind us. We left the village a smaller team, armed with local knowledge and a resupply of food, our confidence renewed.

Two days later Kim and I crouched low behind our bikes as a herd of caribou steadily marched toward us on a narrow island. Earlier in the trip, we'd similarly encountered a brown bear. In that instance we were glad that the bear had stopped, caught our scent, turned tail, and ran, but now we hoped for the opposite. A medium-sized bull led the small herd to within a few yards of us. They stopped, sniffed the air, and casually ambled on their way.

Wildlife encounters permeated our expedition. We were treated to sightings of substantial beluga pods, a bowhead whale, spotted and bearded seals, brown bears, foxes, and rare bird sightings. Eventually, we reached a point in our trip where we no longer excitedly blurted out, "Spectacled eider!" every time we saw a flock. Traveling by human power has enriched my life in a way that money or material wealth could never purchase; the Arctic rewarded us generously.

On the far shore of Wainwright Inlet, we scouted around, looking for the narrowest place to cross the channel. For the first time since the Lisburne Hills, we'd been gratefully accompanied by a tailwind. As we prepared to make the final crossing before the village, the wind built, and the skies darkened. Not until everything was strapped onto our small, one-person, inflatable rafts did I grasp how strong it had become. We decided to risk it. Halfway through the crossing, I leaned hard to windward, paddled for everything I had, and regretted our decision.

Safely on the other side, I reflected on the idiom "Don't race back to the barn." Many adventurers, hunters, and other cold, hungry, or tired people have made the mistake of disregarding safety when they are near comfort or the finish line. Impatience can have terrible consequences. Fortune may favor the bold, but long life favors the prudent.

"My great-uncle used to live in that sod hut," a Wainwright hunter, with two field-dressed caribou draping over his four-wheeler, told us. He was pointing to a collapsing but intact house site. Since leaving Cape Lisburne, we'd seen several of these traditional huts and had always assumed that it had been hundreds of years since people last inhabited them. There, in Nunagiaq, just north of Wainwright, we listened to stories of this hunter's family and how life on the North Slope of Alaska used to be not that long ago. Few stories or pieces of trail advice are ever as impactful or memorable as those heard on the trail.

In the back of Peard Bay, I attempted to circumvent a short bluff by riding in front, through hub-deep water. As I rode, my bike became heavier and heavier from freshly eroded, floating chunks of loose peat, which glommed onto my spokes and drivetrain.

Roughly one-quarter of the land in the Northern Hemisphere is permafrost, and it is thickest in the Arctic. Trapped within permafrost is more than double the amount of carbon already in our atmosphere. As our planet rapidly warms, from our wholesale combustion of fossil fuels, the melting of permafrost is accelerating, releasing this trapped carbon into the atmosphere. This is known as a positive feedback loop. The outcome for Alaska, however, will be anything except positive.

As I cleaned the peat chunks from my bike, I looked ahead at the rapidly thawing landscape eroding into the sea and wondered how different it would look here in five or ten years . . . or even next month. I also wondered when Alaska and the rest of the nation would get serious about reducing our dependence on fossil fuels and mitigating climate change. Will we choose to act before reaching a critical tipping point? Again, the saying I'd heard in Wevok came to my mind: "There is no tomorrow." The time for action is now.

Past Peard Bay, we knew there was one more obstacle before reaching Utqiaġvik—the Skull Cliffs. We rode on until the sand and pebble beach turned to mudstone slabs and the walls of the cliff steepened above us. Although the elders in Wainwright had told us we wouldn't be able to ride in front, I convinced Kim to keep trying. Waves crashed under our feet as we jumped from one slab to another until we made it around the first headland. Looking ahead at the steep cliffs, with no shore below, we knew we'd have to change strategy.

That evening we camped in a beautiful sun-drenched valley, saving the rest of the Skull Cliffs for morning. As the wind died, the bugs came out, and we discussed our plans. Originally, we had hoped to continue traveling east out of Utqiaġvik. We'd begun to reconsider.

Before leaving home, we often looked at the map and wondered how we would approach the vast terrain—full of long bays, massive lakes, and wet tundra—between Utqiaġvik and Prudhoe Bay. This stretch would be the longest between resupply of the whole route, and so far, no one had offered any reassuring advice. "Maybe better for you in the spring, when there's still snow and the lakes are frozen," we heard more than once.

As we tightened the mosquito netting under our shelter and prepared to tuck in for the night, we resigned ourselves to a decision. The summit of Alaska, Utqiaġvik, would be the end of our route . . . for now.

Over the last ten years, the fat bike and packraft have rapidly evolved in form and functionality. Both instruments of human-powered wilderness exploration were originally conceived and developed in Alaska, but the efficiency and practicality of both have caught the imaginations of people worldwide. What can be done with a fat bike in conjunction with a lightweight, one-person packraft is still being discovered.

On past wilderness trips with the bike, I have been happy when we were able to ride anything more than half of the distance. On this trip, however, we were able to pedal more than 90 percent of the route. And often, the riding was fun and engaging.

Kim and I cheers'ed pizza slices together in the first restaurant we stumbled across in Utqiaġvik and continued to eat the whole pie like there was no tomorrow.

A Positively Memorable Mountain Bike Ride(ish)

ERIC TROYER

Optimism.

It drove gold seekers north during the gold rush. It convinced them they that they could succeed where others had not. It kept them striving, knee-deep in muck, when their chances for success were clearly fading.

Granted, some of that optimism was fueled by lies from hucksters and other scam artists.

But I am no huckster or scam artist. I swear!

Our group of six mountain bikers was not seeking gold. We sought a different kind of treasure—a coveted loop ride on mostly excellent trails. Sadly, like most of the gold rushers, we didn't find our treasure. And yes, I was the reason we were there, knee-deep in muck. But I didn't lie. I just misremembered.

Well, I misremembered, *and* I have a lot of optimism. It seems people will follow you anywhere if you have enough optimism. Fortunately, people will forgive you too.

Since about 2007, I have been one of the coleaders of the Tuesday Night Mountain Bike Rides for the Fairbanks Cycle Club. Affectionately known as Doug Rides—for ride founder Doug Burnside—the TNRs are held May through September. We ride different trails throughout the Fairbanks area. We set up a schedule over the winter, keeping most of the same rides but always experimenting with new trails and routes. (Experimenting, that's it! I didn't lie. We were experimenting. It was a group effort. Right, guys?)

Despite the rides being held on Tuesday nights and many of the riders having to work on Wednesdays, our rides have often been ambitious.

Until recently, we always had at least one ride on the schedule in the Chena River State Recreation Area. That's nearly an hour drive just to get to the start for a lot of the riders.

When the multiuse Compeau Trail was built in 2006 in the rec area, we were excited. It's a great trail to ride. Unfortunately, it's not a loop trail. We like loops.

We made the Compeau Trail work for a while. At about its ten-mile mark, it ties into a dozer line created in 2004 to protect nearby homes and property from wildfires. We followed the Compeau to the dozer line, now called the Mike Kelly Trail, and then followed that to Two Rivers Elementary School. But that route required a long car shuttle. We don't like shuttles. We dropped that ride.

But I liked the Compeau Trail—a lot. I was willing to do it as an out-and-back just for the many fun descents on the way back. But despite my optimism, I couldn't sell the other guys. I couldn't lie to them either. Could I?

No, of course not. Instead, I started remembering.

But first, some context. At eight miles long, the Compeau Trail mostly climbs for the first thirteen or fourteen miles before descending all the way down to the Colorado Creek Public Use Cabin. That's a long way for an out-and-back—thirty-six miles total—especially on a Tuesday night. But another trail, the Colorado Creek Trail, also accesses the cabin. That one is just under six miles long and ends at a trailhead just a mile and half along Chena Hot Springs Road from the Compeau Trailhead. I did the math. About twenty-four miles of great trail riding and just one and a half miles of pavement. Awesome!

Oh, did I call it the Colorado Creek Trail? That's what it used to be called. At least that's how I remember the name. It's now called the Colorado Creek Winter Trail. But that's just an addition of one little word.

Back to my remembering: I recalled that I rode that trail on my bike shortly after moving up to Fairbanks in 1989. As I pondered this new great loop ride, the calendar showed it was 2014. But really, how much would a trail have changed in twenty-some years?

And while I remembered that I had to push my bike on the trail, I remembered not pushing it much. The trail had been mostly rideable;

surely, it still was. And even if it involved some pushing, the whole "winter" trail was less than six miles long. It couldn't be that much pushing, right? And it was basically downhill. Easy peasy.

The more I thought about it, the more optimistic I became. This would be an awesome ride! Of course, I figured I should probably check it first before leading anyone on it. So, I made plans to do that. Well, I made plans to make plans. I never did get out there for a scoping mission. Optimism has a wonderful way of blurring silly little details like that.

I pitched the ride at our winter planning session. The guys had some doubts. It says *winter* trail, they said. Sure, I said, it's a *little* swampy, but I had ridden it before. It was mostly rideable. We'll be able to add the Compeau Trail to a ride *and* make it a loop. We put the ride on the 2015 summer schedule. (I could have made a killing as a salesman during the gold rush.)

Six of us came out for that ride. Dave (one of the other TNR coleaders) and I and four others, most of them regulars. We started off in high spirits. Mountain bikers tend to love the Compeau Trail. The first two miles include a lot of climbing, but it's all rideable. Then you follow along a ridge that trends upward, but the trail includes a lot of fun downhills even as you go up.

We got to the high point of the Compeau Trail in good time and had a blast descending down to the Colorado Creek Cabin. We were grinning. Things were going great!

We rode past the cabin to the start of the Colorado Creek Trail. (Whoops, I mean Colorado Creek *Winter* Trail.) One of the riders, I think it was Forrest, pointed out a sign that said, "Winter Use Only."

I shrugged. Sure, but that's for motorized vehicles, I said. We're on bikes, I said. No problem, I said. We rode on.

At first the trail was relatively dry and rideable. One might say it was an optimistic trail. It lured you in. No problem, it said. You can do this, it said.

Then the riding became a bit more challenging. But most of us were game to try the trickier sections. Lots of laughing as we challenged our skills or watched others fail in their attempts. Ron, in particular, was game to try the tricky sections and laugh when he failed. He helped keep the mood light.

But as the tricky sections increased, attempts to do them became fewer and fewer. Even Ron, Smiling Ron, quit trying. Soon everyone was just pushing their bikes. And there was some water. Okay, quite a bit of water. Swamp, really. But we knew there was going to be some of that. I had let the guys know. We laughed pushing through it. Well, most of us laughed. Good times!

Eventually, the guys started getting tired of pushing through swamp. Heck, even I got tired of the pushing. But my spirits were buoyed by what I saw ahead. I shared my optimism with the group.

See that ridge ahead of us? I said. We just have to push across this swampy valley, and when we get to the base of that ridge, we'll be on good trail again. Are you sure? they asked. Oh, yes, definitely! I insisted. Sure, I didn't remember that the swampy parts were so swampy or long, I admitted, but I definitely remember that the dry trail starts on that ridge. It's an awesome trail, I said.

We slogged on. Each mudhole, each squishy step forward, we focused on that ridge. The dry trail would be there. We knew it. After all, I had said so. With great optimism.

We got to the ridge. The trail was there! I was forgiven! Still, it was getting a bit late. The ride had taken longer than we figured. A lot longer. It was close to midnight already. Hardly anyone had brought lights. This was summer in Fairbanks, so it wouldn't get totally dark, but the trail along the base of the ridge was in forest, and it was darker in there.

Then one of the guys had a flat tire. But we shone one of the lights on the bike, put our heads together, dug into our gear and tools, and fixed it. Soon we were again riding on that great trail. That's the kind of camaraderie you enjoy when out riding with others.

It won't be long until we reach the road, I said. Cool, they said. My reputation was a bit tannin stained, but it had survived. I'm pretty sure they were thinking about how awesome I was.

Then the trail dropped back down into the swamp. We looked around. No other trails to be seen. I even backtracked a bit. Did we miss a turn-off? No turnoffs. Just a trail heading into the swamp. The guys looked at me. I wanted to look at someone else, but there was no one else.

Er, I don't remember this, I said. It's probably just a short section of swamp before the trail climbs back onto higher ground, I said. That's why I don't remember it. Sure, the guys said, their voices damp with doubt.

The wonderful thing about optimism is that you can lie to yourself without realizing it. And that goes a long way toward convincing others. Of course, what were they going to do—go back? Once you lead a group of guys far enough down the rabbit hole, the only way back is forward.

We pushed, slogged, waded, looking ahead for where the trail climbed back onto dry ground. We pushed, slogged, and waded. Pushed, slogged, and waded. At one point Dave said he hadn't seen a trail marker for a while. I hadn't either. But the light was dim. I peered into the gloom. The swampy trail was hard to tell from the swampy non-trail.

No, this is it, I told Dave. We're on the trail. Definitely.

Optimism has its own momentum. I kind of knew I was lying, but I wasn't really lying. I mean, I kind of knew we were on the trail, so that's pretty much the same as knowing it, right? And I knew that Chena Hot Springs Road lay somewhere to the south. And we weren't that far away from it. We were going south, right? I didn't mention any of that to Dave. No reason to dim his spirits any further.

Dave didn't look convinced. But what choice did he have? He had already bought the ticket I was selling, and he didn't have any better alternatives. We slogged on.

At one point we passed a tripod made of black spruce poles. That dimly rang a bell in my head but not enough for me to pull myself out of the head-down slogging. The laughing and joking had died out long before. Even Ron, Smiling Ron, was grim faced. We were now enduring. But we still had camaraderie. We were in this together! Well, sort of. We were in this together—because we believed Eric! Mutiny was a possibility.

I was at the back of the pushing pack when we passed a sign that said something about a historic site. That rang a bell in my head a little more loudly. I definitely recognized that sign, but from when, and what did it mean? A short slog later I heard water running. The rest of the guys were standing next to a stream. A broken-down cabin, a historic site, lay crumbling on the other side. The guys were talking about crossing the stream.

But that's when the bell starting ringing loudly in my head. The sign, the cabin, the stream. I recognized it all but from my winter trips. We were on the Chena Hot Springs Winter Trail.

I know where we are! I said.

I pointed back the way we had just come. We have to go that way.

They all looked at me with exhausted disbelief. Except Dave. Dave looked at me with disgust.

"You don't know where the f— you are!"

Dave was mad. My good buddy Dave. My good buddy who has always laughed as he has followed my optimism into swamps or otherwise unrideable trails. I had made Dave mad. I hadn't thought it possible. I guess there can be such a thing as too much optimism.

Dave is obsessed with historic Arctic exploration, especially the doomed Franklin expedition, the last stragglers of which resorted to cannibalism. Dave knows about when things go wrong, when there is no hope. We weren't that bad off. Were we?

I looked at the guys. They just stared at me. They stared at my hand pointing back down the trail/swamp we had just slogged through. No one moved. I knew we could ford the creek. But I was pretty sure it was chest-high at least, meaning we would get even more soaked than we already were. And I knew what lay beyond was more than two miles of swampy trail. I knew that by going back the way we had come, we would hit Stiles Creek Trail, a decent trail, in less than a mile. From there it was less than a mile to Chena Hot Springs Road. I knew it. No, really, I actually knew this. Really.

No one moved.

I turned around and started pushing my bike back the way we had come. It was a leader's gambit. I knew I couldn't convince the guys with my words. I just hoped they would follow me. I worried most about Dave. He was coleader of the rides. He could rally the crew against me. The threat of mutiny hung heavy in the air.

After several yards of pushing, I snuck a glance over my shoulder. They were following me! Everyone. Even Dave. I kept going. I knew I had to keep going until we reached the trail. The black spruce trees that surrounded us were small, but a few of them were tall enough. If someone had rope, there just might be some good ol' gold rush frontier justice. Or maybe Dave would convince them to start a fire and have some fresh, tasty backstrap. I was motivated to move.

We passed the tripod, which I now recognized as marking the Chena Hot Springs Winter Trail, which is also a part of the Yukon Quest Trail. It roughly parallels Chena Hot Springs Road, and I knew it would provide connection to Stiles Creek Trail. We hadn't seen the Quest Trail when we passed it the first time. It just looked like more swamp. Now it looked obvious. Well, not obvious. More like a wider cleared area in the swamp. Kind of like the Colorado Creek Trail. I mean, *Winter* Trail.

After not too much pushing, slogging, and wading, I pushed my bike onto the Stiles Creek Trail. A firm dirt trail. A rideable trail. A less-than-a-mile-from-the-trailhead-which-was-just-1.5-miles-down-Chena-Hot-Springs-Road-from-our-cars trail! I yelled in triumph.

One by one the guys pushed their bikes onto the trail. The relief was palpable. The guys even smiled at me. Well, some did. Eric actually knew what he was talking about!

We got back to the cars at 2:30 a.m., after more than six and a half hours of riding. Well, riding and such. The previous Doug Ride lateness record had been a 2:00 a.m. return to the cars. That one was due to getting lost. But we were never really lost on this ride, not really. Still, we smashed the old record. Even more so because that other late ride had started and ended on Goldstream Road. We were still about an hour drive from home.

But I kept the triumph of that record to myself. We would celebrate that later. One of the guys—a newer rider—had to be at work at 6:00 a.m. (He quit coming to the rides for some reason.)

As usual, we had some snacks and drinks when we got back to the cars. We didn't banter for long. Though we did banter. There was some laughter and joking, if a bit subdued. No one proposed flattening my car tires and making me bike home. It's amazing how forgiving people can be. It's part of what makes me optimistic about the human race.

Well, it did take about two years before I could get a hint of a smile from Forrest when I mentioned the ride, which I gleefully did whenever the chance arose. But Dave has never yelled at me again. Not even after I have led him into more swamps.

But people do learn. My new trail suggestions are now met with a healthy dose of skepticism. When was the last time you rode it? What do you mean by just a *little* swampy? Why should we believe anything you say?

But optimism prevails. I rode it not long ago, I say. The swampy section is mostly rideable, I say. I've learned my lesson, and I even doubt myself now, I say. And it seems that everyone has some optimism because the group believes me, sometimes.

I wonder how I would have fared as a gold rusher. Would I have continued on despite the setbacks that hit most stampeders? Would I have convinced others to follow me, knee-deep in muck, even if the chance of success was low?

Maybe. But I know of at least five guys who are happy they will never find out.

Back in Alaska to Share
the Story of the Roads

LAEL WILCOX

My dream was to ride all of the major roads in Alaska, and I did in 2017. I'm fourth-generation Alaskan. It's where I got into endurance riding on my mom's Specialized Ruby in between bartending shifts in 2014. Examining the map and fitting in the biggest rides I could on my two days off led me to the goal of riding them all, imagining what the 2D map could look like in real life and why the roads existed in the first place. Three years later I had a wide-open summer, and I was ready for an open-ended adventure. Four thousand five hundred miles took me past Wiseman to the north slope at Prudhoe Bay on the Arctic Ocean, through Chicken to Eagle on the Yukon River, to the three hot springs north of Fairbanks, into Denali National Park and across the Denali Highway to Paxson. I used *The Milepost*, the local guidebook that chronicles every mile of Alaskan road with conditions and services. If the road is listed in *The Milepost*, I had to ride it. About two-thirds were paved and a third high-quality dirt.

I relentlessly connected the dots, and when I reached the end of the road, I'd turn around and start pedaling back. I figured I wanted to ride all of the roads, but I didn't have to ride them both directions. I hitched with a French tourist circumnavigating the globe, with a pastor from Zimbabwe driving from home in Valdez to Anchorage to fly back to Africa to visit family. He sped and cornered like a race car driver. I got a lift from a bush plane pilot out of McCarthy and sat in the back of an ATV trailer with a fellow called Eight Ball who showed me his favorite lookout into Gates of the Arctic National Park. He told me not to tell anyone where it is, so I won't.

An ice road trucker named Colin took me back from Deadhorse.

230

I'd ridden through the night to get there. The cab of his truck had a full-sized bed in the back. I slept while he drove. After four hours we stopped for burgers at the Trucker's Café in Coldfoot. I slept another four hours to the entrance of the Dalton Highway. My mom met me there. She was also born in Alaska and had never been this far north. For this stretch our plan was to drive out to Manley Hot Springs together, stay at the Roadhouse, and I'd ride back. On the third of July, the bar was packed. The water coming from the sink was red with iron. There was no cell phone service, but there was a landline with an index card on the wall to call Gladys about the hot springs, so I did. She told me you can reserve the hot springs for $10 for an hour.

"How about tomorrow at 8:00 a.m.?"

"Nah, that's too early."

"9:00 a.m.?"

"Okay. You have to cross back over the wooden bridge to the log cabin on the left to pick up the key. Then back over the bridge, and the building is on the right. Make sure to lock the door behind you."

We follow the instructions. My mom turns the key on the door of a large shabby building.

"Oh my!"

The roof is covered in green vines. It's lush and humid. There are brightly colored tropical flowers and trees with broad leaves open to the sun streaming through the clear-paned roof. There's a sign that asks us not to pick the grapes, and we don't. It can be minus sixty degrees Fahrenheit (minus fifty-one Celsius) in Manley Hot Springs in the winter. The hot springs is a greenhouse, using thermal water to warm the building all through the winter to allow for this growth. I imagine coming in from the frigid winter cold into this oasis. There are three steaming concrete tubs with pots of hanging flowers over them. We soak.

Back outside we lock the door and return the key. I start pedaling east, and my mom meets me at the turnoff to Minto. I wasn't expecting another road, but if I see a sign to a destination, then I guess I just have to ride there. It's a long descent to the Tolovana River. Minto is a small Athabascan village. For the Fourth of July there's a boat race and games for the kids. As we pull up, a lady yells, "Clear out of the way!"

She throws a large handful of coins onto the dirt road and yells, "Go!"

Kids with face-painted cheeks scramble for the coins. They're laughing and cheering. We're out in front of the cafeteria. Inside they're serving plates of ribs and corn on the cob, cornbread and baked beans. We have a plate and a Coke. I get back on my bike. We head toward Fairbanks. Tomorrow we'll shoot for Circle on the Yukon River and the spur to Circle Hot Springs, only to find out they've been closed and abandoned for decades.

Every road in every era tells a story of history and change, of animals and people and life. On a different day, with different weather and different company, the experience would be wildly altered.

A few days later I return to Anchorage to work for a couple of weeks at The Bicycle Shop to save money to fund the next leg of the trip. I fall in love with Rue. Seeing her photos inspires me to take my own for the first time—they look so real and essential. I get my first camera. I want to show people a little of what I'm seeing—what it looks like to ride north of the Arctic Circle at summer solstice, to see a herd of musk ox near the pipeline and a red fox on the top of Atigun Pass. The snapshots are limited and don't capture the feeling of the place. Rue comes out for a few stretches of road. I'm grateful for the photos she takes and even more that she's with me for those rides.

Since I rode in 2017, I've been wanting to share the story of riding all of the roads.

I'm back in Alaska this summer with Rue to do better together. We've been here for just over a month—I rode an Everest challenge on Hatcher Pass and out to my folks' A-frame in Willow a couple times. We went bike camping with my sister's kids on the beach and out on the Denali National Park Road on a clear day. I traveled north to Chena Hot Springs with my parents, and then I rode home.

We're studying the map again, watching the weather and dreaming of all the places we can go. A big goal is to inspire others to start adventures from home. Seeing the road lines and the rides makes me want to connect all of the dots again. This time of year there are over twenty hours of official daylight in Anchorage. Farther north gets even more. There's time and light to fit it all in, and I'm so excited for what's ahead.

Nulato Hills

LUC MEHL

Biking Musk Ox Trails in Western Alaska

I first heard about the Nulato Hills at a wedding. Alaska is a big state, and I've spent weeks and months exploring it, so I was surprised to hear of an unfamiliar hiking destination in northwestern Alaska. Between bites of wedding cake, Andy painted a picture of good hiking on alpine ridges. How had the Nulato Hills escaped my notice?

I didn't bother to change out of my suit before finding the Nulato Hills on Google Earth that night. I would have been content looking up the Hills in the worn pages of my *Alaska Atlas and Gazetteer* in a less excited state. But if Andy's description was accurate, the alpine ridges didn't just sound hikeable; they sounded bikeable!

After growing up along the quiet banks of the Kuskokwim River, I seek every opportunity to leave Anchorage's crowded streets for less impacted areas. Indigenous Alaskans were good at living on the land without leaving signs of development, and traveling off the road system feels like a sample of how the natural world should look and feel. But I don't take the traditional approach to travel through the land. I'm a terrible shot and don't know which plants are poisonous. Instead, I stuff a backpack with freeze-dried dinners and use specialty equipment to support my journeys: inflatable packrafts, metal-edged skis, or carbon-framed bikes.

During my Google Earth exploration, what struck me was a nearly continuous ridge that stretched between the villages of Nulato and Unalakleet, a distance of one hundred miles. Based on the imagery and my years as a geology graduate student, I predicted that the ridge surface was a mixture of loose rock and spongy lichen, an ideal biking surface. I measured the vertical relief along the ridge to be forty thousand feet, or the equivalent of climbing Denali twice. That seemed like a lot, but maybe the gradual gain wouldn't be noticed on a bike? The ridge looked so benign—from outer space.

Nulato is a Koyukon village of about 250 people on the banks of the Yukon River. Even though Nulato is similar to my hometown of McGrath in many ways—geography, ecology, and the traditional subsistence lifestyle—it still sounded exotic to me. One difference is the Yukon River itself. The Kuskokwim is a big river, but the Yukon is huge—irrationally so. The headwaters of the Kuskokwim drain the northern Alaska Range. That makes sense; the water has nowhere else to go. But the headwaters of the Yukon are as close as fifteen miles from the ocean in southeastern Alaska. I can't help but wonder, "What are you thinking?! Why flow two thousand miles to the Bering Sea when you could turn around and flow fifteen miles into Lynn Canal?" I'm still waiting for a response.

The other aspect of Nulato that feels exotic is its rich history. Nulato is near the border between traditionally Koyukon and Iñupiat peoples, and before colonization the region hosted both trading and hostility. Colonization occurred earlier here than in other parts of Alaska due to the use of the Yukon as a marine highway to transport goods. A trading post was established in the 1830s, well before the gold rush traffic that permanently altered the traditional lifestyle. The city of McGrath was established much later, and it feels younger.

At the other end of the ridge, Unalakleet was a complete unknown to me, geographically and culturally. I have a sense of subsistence living in Interior Alaska, but as soon as ocean fish, marine mammals, and Iñupiat history come into the mix, I'm clueless. All I really knew about Unalakleet was that it was on the Iditarod Trail.

I convinced my adventure partner, Eric Parsons, that I had discovered a remote biking gem. We contacted the Nulato school principal, hoping for logistical support, and then shipped our bikes to the school in early September 2017.

Like many village kids, I grew up on pilot bread crackers, canned fruit cocktail, and Dinty Moore stew. One of the easiest ways to give thanks in a village is to bring fresh food. I asked the principal what they would appreciate and then packed a box of oranges, pineapples, watermelon, coffee, and creamer.

After the flight from Anchorage to Fairbanks, we boarded a small plane for the middle Yukon hub of Galena. Fifteen minutes into the flight, I woke Eric to see if he had a water bottle. I've never had to pee so badly in my life, and watching our slow progress on the pilot's GPS wasn't helping. I crawled to the back of the bathroom-less plane with Eric's bottle.

We spent our layover in Galena's one-room airport trying to confirm that our bike boxes had been delivered to Nulato. When we could not establish that the bikes had arrived, we hoped for the best and caught up on the news in outdated magazines. A pilot announced the flight to Nulato, and we crawled into a smaller plane for the fifteen-minute trip. I sat on the right side of the plane, eyes glued to the window, hoping to catch a glimpse of the Nulato Hills, but we never got close enough to verify that the ridge would be bikeable.

I don't know if it is dust from gravel airstrips or pollen from black spruce trees, but something about village airstrips feels like home. We stepped out of the plane, collected our luggage, and started walking to the school but were quickly offered a ride by Martha Turner. Martha laughed when we told her about our plan.

The school principal confirmed that our bikes had arrived and took the fresh food box off our hands. We assembled the bikes in front of teacher housing and threw the bike boxes in the dumpster. We wouldn't need those again . . . right?

In the early afternoon we rode three miles to the road's end at the Nulato River. The river was not a surprise; I had packed a floating rope that we could use to pendulum the bikes across the river. Fortunately, the river looked shallow enough to wade, saving us the hassle of working with the rope. I peeled off my clothes and gave Eric updates as I crossed. The river reached waist-deep, but it wasn't swift enough to knock me off my feet. I reached the far shore and dressed between bear tracks in the silt.

After the river crossing, we had seven miles of hard travel to reach the ridge. It took us ten hours of pushing, lifting, and throwing our bikes through a mix of wildfire scars and boreal forest. This was bad travel, and the only thing that made it manageable was Eric's positive attitude.

Growing up in rural Alaska taught me that things often go wrong or are harder than you expect. The snowmachine won't start, plastic snaps in the extreme cold, driftwood damages the fish wheel, and so on. I'm pretty good at staying positive during the hard parts, and I seek partners who are too. I had made no promises to Eric about the trip, but it was still a relief that he didn't blame me for severely misinterpreting the satellite imagery through the burn. I expected the mottled gray texture in the imagery to be rocky soil, when in fact, it turned out to be pick-up-stick piles of fallen trees. We were exhausted and relieved when we reached the edge of the burn around 10:00 p.m.

We set up our pyramid shelter (a one-pole floorless tent) by strapping a trekking pole to Eric's upright bike. My bike had to sleep outside. We boiled water to rehydrate our freeze-dried dinners and then passed out in our sleeping bags, too tired to debrief about the day. Things would either get better or not, and discussing them wouldn't change a thing.

We woke up dehydrated and sore. A peek out the tent door revealed a wall of fog, which didn't boost our optimism for the day. But we put the pedals on the bikes and were eager to earn some biking miles. The ridge dipped in and out of the tree line for the first miles, so we alternated between pushing our bikes, short downhill rides, and struggling through the brush. The bikeable sections were wonderful, and it didn't take much downhill to make the uphills worth the effort.

We were in the clouds and rain all day and yet didn't find any water sources. We spent part of the days soaking wet yet thirsty. We used catchment off the tent one night to collect seven liters of water, and when that was gone, we resorted to using fabric to collect water off the blueberry and dwarf birch leaves. The fabric sponge worked surprisingly well but not so well that we weren't dehydrated. We knew that if we got desperate, we could hike down any of the hills and find water on the valley floor, but our familiarity with the thick brush didn't make that option appealing. We opted to maintain a constant degree of dehydration.

We brought "plus bikes," the specialty equipment deemed most appropriate for this terrain. Eric had an Otso with 27.5+ (four inches) wheels and lent me his Surly ECR with 29+ (three inches) wheels. They were the right bikes for the job. The riding was best when we found musk ox trails—narrow strips through the tundra with firm ground. On either side of the musk ox trails, the tundra was saturated with water and spongy, easy enough to ride downhill but not as fast or fun. The contrast of white caribou lichen and small red leaves in the tundra made for beautiful descents, even with the fog dampening the light.

We saw only a few birds and two musk ox, or possibly the same musk ox twice. The first musk ox was in thick fog, unnoticed until we were only forty feet away. Even then, the musk ox was not at all concerned about us and gradually turned away. I've only seen a few in Alaska and still don't know what to think of them. Big enough to look like a grizzly bear, but aren't they just skinny goats under all that fur? We gave the musk ox a wide margin, not knowing how aggressive they might be.

The weather didn't improve, and we never got a clear view of the surrounding hills and valleys. What we could see left us wanting more—dark-green spruce hillsides dotted with bright-yellow birch canopies. The clouds felt thin, giving us hope that they might burn off, despite the weather forecast.

Our progress was significantly slower than planned, twelve miles instead of twenty-five miles each day on the ridge. We calculated that we needed at least four more days of food, assuming that the ridge would get more bikeable. The weather and lack of water compounded the factors working against us, so we admitted needing to turn back to Nulato. We spent a lot of time debating our options, even though it was obvious that we needed to turn around.

The clouds began to break as we turned around, rewarding us with the first real view from the ridge. We continued to steal water from the blueberry leaves and enjoyed rolling down each of the slopes we had pushed up. We took a better route off the ridge to avoid some of the burn and were rewarded with a surprisingly bikeable descent through tall grass and birch trees. Carrying our bikes through the remaining sections of the burn was hard but finite—this time we knew what to expect.

We received a warm welcome in Nulato—the locals were not surprised that we weren't able to ride bikes to Unalakleet in one week. But rather than ridicule us, they seemed to appreciate that we thought the Nulato Hills were worth visiting. The locals were surprised to hear that musk ox were in the area and explained that caribou used to migrate through but no longer. An older man told us that his mom used to hike through the hills, but he didn't explain why. I wish I'd been able to hear more about her journeys and why she made them.

Construction workers at the school helped us find cardboard and tape to build new bike boxes. We were still sealing the boxes when the Ravn agent pulled up in a pickup truck and said that the plane was about to land. It was disappointing to rush out of town, but after a week of camping wet, sleeping at home sounded wonderful.

I was careful not to drink too much water before the flight from Galena to Fairbanks, and we had just enough time to grab burgers during our layover in Fairbanks. Returning home at the end of a trip always feels abrupt. One night you are in a wet sleeping back spooning a bike, the next you are pulling curtains to block streetlights.

I love how much I learn while traveling through Alaska's wildlands—it is a large part of my motivation for these trips. The Nulato Hills taught me about the pitfalls of judging terrain from outer space (Google Earth) and the slow reality of trying to bike off-trail. But I had also learned how truly promising the hills are for hiking. If I could learn from my mistakes—carry more food, solve the lack-of-water problem—maybe I could return and finish the route to Unalakleet.

After a winter of developing a better strategy for the Nulato Hills, my wife, Sarah, and I returned the following June. Historical satellite imagery suggested that there would still be remnant pods of snow on the ridge in June, which would solve our water problems. And we brought packrafts instead of bikes so that we could float the second half of the journey, cutting out a cool approximately twenty thousand feet of vertical relief.

The burn was difficult to hike, even without bikes. We spent our first night at tree line near where Eric and I had camped and had familiar visitors—musk ox! This time we had the visibility to see more of the herd, maybe a dozen mixed adults and kids. After a week of admittedly harder than expected hiking on the ridge, we enjoyed a beautiful float to Unalakleet, treated by sights of ducklings tumbling down the banks, fish jumping, and swarms of swallows spiraling in and out of mud nests along the riverbank.

We arrived in Unalakleet on a sunny solstice and were invited to a celebration fit to make any city slicker want to stay for good. We spent an extra day in town walking the beach, buying treats from the AC grocery store, and questioning why we lived in the big city. The village kid in me wants to collect firewood and have a freezer full of moose. But if it weren't for my city friends and that wedding conversation with Andy, I never would have made these trips to the Nulato Hills. Alaska is a big state, and sometimes the best way to discover your next destination is to sit down with a slice of wedding cake and strike up a conversation.

Growing Old with My Bicycle   KATHLEEN McCOY

I don't remember a childhood bike. Certainly, my parents gave me one; I have a dim memory of wobbling along with my dad's hand firmly on my back, then a final shove as I went pedaling on my own. If that bike had colorful plastic handlebar streamers or a white wicker basket, I don't remember.

The bike I do recall is the one I bought for myself in 1978. My friend Isabelle and I, postcollege and both working for the State of California in downtown Los Angeles, dreamed up an escape. She wanted to visit her mom's and dad's relatives in Germany and Hungary, and maybe we'd visit mine in Ireland.

We bought new, blue Motobecane touring bikes with yellow panniers and handlebar pouches with clear plastic map windows. The bikes were $400, and the accessories added another $100. The shop owner, hearing our plans, decided we needed some training. He took us on long rides around Los Angeles so we knew how to snap into pedals, maintain cadence, and get up hills.

We quit our jobs and headed for Strasbourg, where we'd signed up to study French for eight hours a day, five days a week, for eight weeks. It was a chance to acclimate. We were with young people from all over the world at the university's summer session.

That was forty years ago, and details have faded. But I know it was delightful! Fresh bread, cheese, farm tomatoes, good coffee. A little wine here and there. New friends from Mexico and Japan.

After our language classes ended, Isabelle and I hit the road. We wanted for nothing, whether we slept in a rural train station with only chocolate bars for dinner or rented a tiny, dirty room in Paris for the night. We were free and on our own. We made it through Switzerland, into Germany, and eventually to Budapest on the Danube. Isabelle's family celebrated us with good food and good times.

Isabelle fell in love with a French lawyer, Jean Marc. When I left to go back to the United States, she stayed and married and set about perfecting her French. I finally faced adulthood and started the work I'd do for decades—journalism and newspapering.

I also married, and my husband and I went to visit Jean Marc and Isabelle, still in Strasbourg. I brought my Motobecane, and he borrowed Jean Marc's bike. We cycled through the Dordogne. We lived like kings—8 francs to the U.S. dollar at the time. For the rest of our lives, my husband has yearned to go back and repeat this vacation. Maybe this time on e-bikes?

At any rate, the Motobecane weathered its European adventures well. It came with me to Alaska in 1981, though for years I really didn't ride much. Newspapering requires a car to get out and report. In fact, it wasn't until my twenty-six years of newspapering ended and I took a job at a university that I began my bike commuting life. Parking was expensive and tight on campus, but a partnership with public transit meant a free bus pass. The buses had bike racks. For eight years I put my bike on the rack each morning—rain, shine, sleet, hail—and I rode it home at night along the Anchorage Chester Creek Trail.

To be honest, I was intimidated at first. It was one thing to bike home in the long summer twilight along a tree-lined paved trail. But as fall and darkness and cold came on, the prospect grew intimidating.

I remember going to a free talk at REI on winter biking. A tiny woman led the seminar, and she described her gear and her clothing. I quickly realized the Motobecane would be the wrong kind of bike for all-weather riding. I pondered my daughter's old high school bike, an inexpensive hybrid. What if I put studded tires on that?

Still, what about the darkness? Was it a safe thing to do?

I raised my hand: "How late do you go down on the trail at night?"

This tiny person (she was the height of an average seventh grader) thought a minute, shook her head back and forth weighing the answer, and finally said, "I wouldn't go down later than ten o'clock at night."

Oh! Here I'd been thinking 6:00 p.m. might be too late. Apparently not.

An office mate of mine biked from Mountain View each day. He's the one who really gave me the courage to go for it. He knew some practical stuff: like the day of a big snowfall, you'll be pushing your bike home. But by the next day there'd be a narrow foot traffic trail, nicely packed down, that you could navigate. It was a balancing act: get out of that narrow groove, and snow pulled you and your bike over.

He alerted me that there were no lights from the university to Goose Lake, but after that you'd be traveling on lighted ski trails. Once I passed Westchester Lagoon in west Anchorage, I was traveling in the dark again. But then I was close to home.

I bought myself an $80 rechargeable headlamp that attached by Velcro to my bike helmet. I learned that wearing gloves inside thin single-layer mittens was almost enough to keep my hands warm. I have great circulation, so although I had cold feet, cold hands, cold butt, and cold face many, many times, I was warm, even hot, by the time I hit C Street.

The trail from C Street to I Street was perhaps the most intimidating. There were dog walkers and skiers here and there, but it was a long, lonely stretch. As the years passed, though, the number of bikers kept increasing. There was a kind of camaraderie to be out there pumping along in ten degrees or zero or sixteen.

I never had a bad experience on the trail home. I came upon moose about a half dozen times and rerouted up to city streets to get past the problem. And out on the Coastal Trail, winds could drift over the trail dramatically. I remember a municipal worker out there with a little backhoe trying to open the trail up again for people like me. We were the only two there.

When I would hit the Lagoon, I could feel my shoulders relax a bit. For one thing a big evergreen along the trail was always decorated, all the way to the top, with holiday lights. It cheered me up to spot it, then pedal past. Soon I was in Coastal Trail darkness, but now, so close to home, I knew I could make it.

Finally, I'd pump up the last hill to my house, slide off my bike, and open the gate to the backyard. I'd put my bike in the shed and head to the kitchen. My husband always let our dog out to greet me. She'd frisk and bark and welcome me home. Once in the steamy kitchen, my glasses would fog up, and I'd remember to turn off my headlamp before blinding my husband.

I felt good. Sweaty and good. I'd strip out of those biking clothes into soft sweats and then pour myself a glass of wine and get ready for supper. Let the evening begin.

I'm sixty-eight now. My husband is seventy-five. COVID-19 put a crimp in our plans to visit Europe in the fall of 2020. My bike commuting days are about three years behind me, but I'd be game still to try for some e-bike touring in the Dordogne in a few years. What do you think?

The Magic Bus on the Stampede   TOM MORAN

For a place marked by tragedy, the Stampede Trail is a hell of a fun ride.

On this January day, Jay and I both ride fat bikes, but we scarcely need them: the sparse snow on the trail is packed so hard that we may as well be riding on pavement. The approaching dawn streaks the gray sky to the south, and we exult in the ease of the journey as Jay pedals his Fatback and I my Surly Pugsley westward through the northern reaches of the Alaska Range.

The trail slices through scraggly black spruce trees and half-buried clumps of brown grass. It is anonymous, silent, and indistinguishable from a hundred other winter tracks scattered across the Alaskan wilds. Except that this is the Stampede. And twenty-plus miles in the distance rests a decaying International Harvester that has improbably morphed into the closest thing the Last Frontier has to a pilgrimage site.

We're bound for the Magic Bus.

Chris McCandless's much-publicized trajectory has largely been cemented in our collective memory and, for many of us, our high school curricula. But for the unacquainted: fleeing his privileged suburban youth in search of raw experience, McCandless drifted around the West for two years, hitching rides and suffering odd jobs before embarking on his "Great Alaskan Adventure." The intense and idealistic twenty-four-year-old walked down the punchy snow of the Stampede Trail in April 1992 carrying a rifle and ten pounds of rice, determined to live off the land—which he was able to do for most of the summer, basing himself out of a long-abandoned bus. But he eventually succumbed to starvation (possibly hurried along by poisonous potato seeds or maybe mushrooms, depending on who you ask), and his emaciated corpse was discovered that September by hunters.

His story would end there were it not for journalist Jon Krakauer, who saw echoes of himself in the rebellious youth and eloquently recounted McCandless's rovings, first for *Outside* magazine and later in the book and film *Into the Wild*. In the years since, the Stampede Trail—an unassuming route through a notch in the northern reaches of Denali National Park—has become a destination for hundreds, if not thousands, of individuals inspired by McCandless's peregrinations.

Jay, like most Alaskans I know, is not one of them. In fact, for the purposes of this essay, he's not even sure he wants to be Jay. "I might demand a pseudonym for this," he states, half-jokingly, as we cruise down the gentle downhill that marks the first few miles of the Stampede. While I'm as excited about the destination as I am the journey, Jay sees the rusting hulk of Fairbanks bus 142 as an incidental, an excuse to crank out fifty-odd miles on an unseasonably warm midwinter day.

When we park at the end of the maintained road at around 8:00 a.m., we still have more than two hours until sunrise, and it's already close to twenty degrees out—about sixteen degrees warmer than the local average for January. We're halfway through one of the warmest and driest winters in Alaska's history and are concerned that the trail might be an unbroken, uneven, unrideable mess. Thanks to their wide tires that can "float" on snow, fat bikes are a fun and fast way of traversing broken-in routes—but unless a critical mass of local snowmobilers or dog mushers have preceded us on the trail, we're facing a twenty-five-mile push.

But we're in luck: while the exposed grass clumps beside the trail make it look more like a mid-April thaw than the depths of January, the Stampede itself is a ribbon of flat white hardpack. Hats, boots, and jackets on, hands in pogies, we pedal swiftly off into the dim.

Before long, hats are gone and sleeves rolled up. But the high temperatures carry hazards as well: forty-five minutes in, the trail detours to circumvent open water on the Savage River, and we're unsure whether even the reroute will be safe to traverse. When we do reach the river, we find the surface frozen from shore to shore, but that doesn't stop Jay from hustling across. "Let's not stop here," he says as we briefly halt between the banks. "I could hear rocks tumbling around in there."

The Stampede follows the fertile river valley through a serene birch and aspen forest before rising onto a plateau and dropping back down to its most noteworthy obstacle: the Teklanika River. This was McCandless's Rubicon: he forded it on his outbound hike during low April water, but when he tried to return in early July, it was engorged by rain and snowmelt, cutting off his route to civilization and sealing his fate.

Swift, deep, and wide, the Teklanika has turned back countless McCandless acolytes, stranded many more, and in 2010 took the life of a French backpacker, who drowned trying to cross on a rope that prior visitors had (loosely) strung across. The sheer number of times troopers and park rangers have rescued ill-prepared hikers on the Stampede doubtless goes a long way toward explaining the antipathy many locals feel toward McCandless, Krakauer, and the bus itself, which some would just as soon see burned or towed out to the highway.

Almost all McCandless pilgrims, of course, come during summer. For Jay and I, the "Tek" is nothing more than a landmark affirming our swift progress. We cross the broad expanse of the river, briefly examine some shelf ice hanging over the waterway's far bank, and continue on through low hills.

We cross frozen streams and steadily climb through a dense forest. As we emerge onto a broad vein of tundra, we get our first glimpse of the heart of the Alaska Range, rising purple and white above the lowlands to the south. If the weather were clear, we would see Denali, North America's tallest mountain, rising about eighty miles to our southwest, but on this overcast day, all we can distinguish are foothills, backlit by the rosy dawn, fading into mist.

We have not encountered anyone else on the trail, but we are not alone. As we pedal through the tundra, Jay turns to me and makes a hand gesture suggesting big teeth. "You see that?" he asks as I pull up even, pointing to a stand of trees to the south. "There's a wolf or a dog over there—it just darted off into the woods." In this spot, surrounded by protected wilderness but frequented by mushers, either seems possible, but a few minutes of careful scanning doesn't result in another sighting.

We do, however, discover what the canine might have been chasing: a little ways ahead, three caribou range to the south of the trail. Shortly afterward, ten more of the handsome animals cross the Stampede a quarter mile ahead, then another half dozen come into view. Just fifteen or so miles to the south, hundreds of thousands of visitors a year board Denali National Park buses for a chance to spot caribou and other wildlife in the distance, and I remind myself how lucky I am to have access to the spectacle year-round.

The closer we get to Fairbanks 142, the more taxing the trail becomes. Signs of traffic have dwindled after the Teklanika, and slanted ice crosses portions of the track, making for slow and cautious biking on our studless tires. More significantly, on the tundra snowmobilers and mushers are no longer confined to a narrow corridor. Their tracks diverge into parallels, each with a fraction of the use that has so effectively beaten down the Stampede thus far. The trails are punchy, tussocked, and uneven, the riding jarring and slow. We deflate our tires to increase their surface area; we steer slowly and deliberately, but a few times we simply have to get off and walk.

We reenter the forest, round a bend, and suddenly Fairbanks 142 looms in front of us, rusting amicably beside a small clearing. Even though I know it's coming, the Magic Bus still takes me by surprise, in part due to its incongruous presence so far from pavement (it was towed here in the 1960s as worker housing for a road that was never completed) and in part because it's a peculiar sensation to arrive at a scene you recognize from a book cover. The miles that took McCandless four days have disappeared beneath our tires in less than five hours.

It's safe to say that Jay and I don't see eye to eye on Chris McCandless. I first read *Into the Wild* years before I moved to Alaska, and I saw a lot of myself in the restless young man stifled by his upbringing and uninterested in the tidy paths laid out for him. Like McCandless, I lit out for the territories, and while my adventures have been less all-consuming than his, I feel like I understand his motivations. Though my fifteen years in Alaska—and maybe just fifteen more years on Earth—have tempered my sympathy, I still think of McCandless as a character to admire for the strength of his convictions, regardless of his tragic finale.

But Jay grew up in Alaska. To him McCandless showed symptoms of mental illness and bears more than a fleeting resemblance to the wild-eyed young men he saw filter through his hometown of Skagway, looking for adventure or redemption in a wilderness they didn't understand or respect. "Not all there," Jay says about them, and I have spent long enough in Alaska not so much to agree with him as to know what he means.

On the other hand, Jay and I do agree on this: whether McCandless was delusional or visionary, his impromptu memorial leaves much to be desired. Whatever dilapidated state that Fairbanks 142 was in when McCandless took up residence in 1992, the steady stream of disciples (and detractors) in the last two decades has taken even more of a toll on the vehicle.

The green paint job is rusting in spots, in others fading to a soft yellow. Most of the windows are either gone or broken. Bullet holes pock the body, and someone's used a shotgun to obliterate the "142" above the driver's side door. Inside are a barrel stove, two cots, a set of drawers, and a debris field of trash. There are old tarps, dirty pants and socks and gloves and shirts. A frozen pair of sneakers hangs off the steering column, two rusty saws lie on the floor nearby, and a hatchet is frozen in the ground outside. A store-brand tent ineffectively hangs over some broken-out windows. Clutter is everywhere, including outside, where fifty-five-gallon drums and other flotsam crowd the clearing.

When Krakauer voyaged to the bus in 1993, evidence of McCandless abounded. Today most of his meager possessions have presumably been taken for souvenirs and his graffiti subsumed beneath that of the many who followed. In addition to several logbooks full of visitors' stories, every inch of the vehicle seems to be scrawled with memorials, which occupy much of Jay's and my attention. There are apropos quotations from Tolstoy, Thoreau, Stegner, Kerouac. Pithy sentiments abound: "Never stop exploring," "Live before you die," "Bound for glory!" (And conversely, "Stupid people die fast.") Names come from multiple states and every continent, a majority of them European, most dating from the last five years.

Jay doesn't detest or denigrate McCandless; he just feels sorry for him. But he has no such sympathy for the artistes. He breaks out laughing at a particularly baroque inscription: "To my honey bee, you are my cosmic angel of love. Always and forever, we'll have Alaska."

If people consider this site sacred, Jay wonders aloud, why do so many deface it? "Say we were visiting Golgotha, out of the Bible," he offers. "What if there was stupid graffiti like, 'Honey bee, we'll always have Golgotha?' I rest my case."

As much as I sympathize with those who seek out the magic of the Magic Bus, I admit he's got a point: this is no way to treat a shrine. On the other hand, all of the attention and abuse in evidence underscore the lasting power of the story that ended on the Stampede. And more than two decades and countless ravages later, it is still a spot that lingers in the memory. It is impossible to forget that a man slowly wasted away here, right here, in the cot that still occupies the rear of the vehicle. Even surrounded by bright white, even with daylight streaming in through the knocked-out windows, it feels like a dark and oppressive place. When Krakauer visited the bus, no one slept inside, and I admit, I wouldn't either.

The Stampede Trail dead-ends at the Sushana River just past the bus; while the route continues to the west for miles, it's a thick maze of alder in summer and unbroken in the winter. Like the doomed wanderer before us, we've reached the end of the road.

Jay and I are not generally given to philosophical discussions, so I am surprised when, stopping for a quick energy bar during our return trip, he brings up the spiritual implications of the McCandless hajji. He's startled and depressed by the almost religious fervor he saw in the graffiti and logbooks, since he doesn't believe McCandless ever did anything worth emulating—coupled with the fact, he notes, that the Stampede Trail is hardly an untrammeled wilderness destination by Alaskan standards.

Jay's got me there. We're less than thirty miles from a busy highway. Half as far south of us, thousands of daily Denali National Park visitors cross the Teklanika safely ensconced in buses of their own. Even in the summer, Jay knows we could negotiate the mud and brush of the Stampede on foot and safely cross the rivers with our packrafts. "I just anticipate that while it's not a nice trail, it's probably not all that hard," he says. For Jay, a veteran of multiple Iditarod Trail Invitational bike races and countless other trips into the Alaskan wild, the Stampede is hardly the sort of adventure worth dying over.

Perhaps he's right. But I still debate him, taking the rare middle ground: McCandless should be considered in light of his journey, not just his destination. Isn't it possible, I ask, to acknowledge the validity of his quest, despite the fatal errors of his methods? Can't the same man be both courageous and foolhardy? Is there no credit for the attempt? I'm not sure I'm making a dent in Jay's opinions, until finally, as darkness begins its early descent, he unexpectedly relents. "Fine," he says. "I'll read the book."

We continue on in companionable silence as the sun sets—about five hours after it came up—and the world shrinks to the comforting glow of our headlights. The darkness scarcely dents the temperature, and Jay rides with bare hands outside of his pogies as we sweat up the long, slow incline back to the trail's start. Soon we hear dogs barking and see a row of red lights on the horizon, a wind farm on the far side of the highway. Ten hours after setting out for Fairbanks 142, we arrive hungry and exhausted back at the car, load up our bikes, and roar off toward Fairbanks and home. We are happy to have made the journey, but we are just as grateful for the return.

Tell 'Em about It

EARL PETERSON

An Alaska Cyclist at Large

I have a friend and longtime cycling buddy on the East Coast, in the northern part of the Deep South. Every other year we get together and cycle someplace more convenient to him than Alaska. Don (a name changed to cloak the slow in anonymity) has more paved roads within fifty miles of his house than we have within this the largest state in the nation. He can generally ride all twelve months of the year, on his *road* bike. When the weather gets inclement, he leaves his road bike in the garage and, if he really feels like riding, gets out his *other* bike, his mountain bike, and braves a little dirt or (*gasp*) mud in his local nature preserve. Out in the wild he saw a deer last year. It ran away, thankfully. And goodness, if it ever snows, Don cycles vicariously through one or another cycling magazine he subscribes to, from an easy chair, of course.

Two years ago, for our biannual cycling trip, we met up in Colorado for some organized stage riding in the Rockies west of Denver. At the end of the first stage, about thirty yards past the finish line, just beyond a line of aquamarine Portacans, Don and I left our bikes in the bike paddock to be guarded by minimum-wage security guards hired by the organizers. Eighteen-fifty an hour split between two guys in Kmart shirts with sewn-on badges, to watch over maybe a half million dollars' worth of carbon and rubber and finely machined Italian and Japanese gears. Hmmmm. Somehow it made sense at the time. Next to the paddock in a brewery serving up libations and post-ride recovery noshes, about a hundred of us psyclists (psycho cyclists, according to my wife) gathered to swap lies and ribald tales of glory, not to mention the occasional phone or local room number.

In our array of wildly colorful three-pocketed jerseys and Lycra shorts that embarrass your hips and make it look like you're carrying a dump in your rear, with a locally brewed ale in one hand and a protein bar in the other, we gathered. Most of us still wore our biking shoes, hard-soled shoes with awkward cleats across the balls of our feet that turn walking into a minor exercise in silly walks.[1] Worse yet, we were all fresh off of eighty miles of riding up and down some of Colorado's finest alpine roads under the summer sun; Don was certain that we went over Nose Bleed Peak by way of Heart Attack Pass. To a guy like Don, who may average twenty-five miles for a training ride with an overall gain of maybe fifty feet at an elevation of three hundred feet above sea level, the Rockies surely was a lung-sucking, oxygen-starved adventure.[2] But for this Alaska-based cyclist, the same twenty-five-mile training ride gains almost half a mile in elevation, when I can actually ride it, of course, so no complaints were heard from this rider as we ordered another round. In our sweaty but eye-catchingly bright-colored kits, in a corner of the biergarten where we could eyeball our likely most expensive possessions being guarded by rental guards in the bike paddock, we rounded out a group of about ten psyclists.

Without exception we all wore part of our cycling histories on our breasts and backs. A word about cycling jerseys before we go too much further, because jerseys are a major identifier in the sport. Your jersey is who you are. Now, there are shirts and uniforms for every sport engaged in by men and women around the world, but cycling is unique in that when you win a professional race, your trophy *is a jersey*. You win the Tour de France, you win the Maillot Jaune, the yellow jersey. You win the sprint title, you win the green jersey. You are the King of the Mountains, you win the polka dot jersey. You are the reigning world cycling champion, you win the rainbow jersey, a jersey awarded for over ninety years and the rainbow colors of which no professional or serious amateur cyclist will adorn on jersey or bicycle without actually winning it, in a time-honored tradition, or superstition.[3] Heck, even individual national champions in cycling have garish jerseys that somehow incorporate their national flag into the color scheme. Among mere mortal psyclists, and certainly the ones who over the years may never have delved into better cycling through chemistry, we wear, in descending order, jerseys of our local club, our state, other races and rides we've done, and the college(s) from which we graduated. Which brings me back to our jerseys, telling others who we are, in some way conveying our origins or personal histories or past riding experiences. And they aren't cheap, no sir. A decent club jersey will start at $70 or $80,[4] probably because it's made of some NASA-designed material made to suck the air ahead of the rider and blow it out the back, it's tight enough to show that you have a mole on your side by your left sixth rib, and it has a color scheme that's a cross between Picasso and Mondrian while seemingly being designed by Dior or Armani. A psyclist's pants are embarrassing and his or her black shoes difficult to walk in. Gloves are padded and helmets mandatory, but a psyclist's jersey tells a story about its bearer. In our newly formed post-ride recovery group, our jerseys were our introductory name badges.

The one-upmanship got started.

Texas A&M: Hey, Alaska, join us! We were just talking about great cycling adventures; you must have some stories to tell!

Alaska: Thanks! Make a space for two, please.

Seattle to Portland 2017: No problem. Iowa, can you slide over just a smidge?

Alaska: Cheers!

And there was much clinking of glasses around the circle of new friends.

State of California: That's the first Alaska jersey I've seen today. You come here just for this?

Alaska: Yup. And to get a break from snow.

Texas A&M: Ha, ha—not in June, you can't fool me.

Alaska: Well, aren't you cleverer than your jersey would let on!

And there were a few snickers heard round the circle.

DeKane Cyclery: What's it like riding up there? The scenery must be fantastic!

Alaska: Yeah, I guess so. I suppose, though, that since we ride in it all the time, we don't really notice. I mean, face it, most of the time we are all staring eight feet in front of our front tire, am I right?

Santa Cruz Cycling Club: Yeah, sure, I get ya. Many of my rides involve going up and down the PCH,[5] and if a pod of whales danced by on their flukes, I probably wouldn't notice.

And there was much nodding of heads.

Hotter'N Hell 100: You get much wildlife on your rides up there?

Virginia Is for Lovers: Of course he does! It isn't just the usual deer and dogs like for the rest of us. Tell 'em.

Texas A&M: You wanna talk about deer—I was riding out in the Texas Hill Country, by a place called Vanderpool, and once ran a deer along a road fence line ahead of me for almost two miles. The fence was too high for it to jump it. I actually stopped. I felt sorry for it, tryin' to escape and all.

Seattle to Portland 2017: You actually stopped a ride because of a scared deer?

University of Iowa: Are you kidding? It's more like he probably couldn't keep up with the "scared" little deer, and it got away when he pooped out!

And there was much laughter.

DeKane Cyclery: Speaking of wildlife, did anyone notice those chirping like groundhogs or whatever they were skittering around the rocks above the tree line today? What are those?

Alaska: Marmots.

DeKane Cyclery: Marmots, huh? You have those in Alaska?

Alaska: Yes, but mainly in the mountains in the north, above the Arctic Circle. Certainly no biking that far north. But we have our fair share of wildlife.

Santa Cruz Cycling Club: Virginia implied no deer. Really?

Alaska: Not whitetail deer, like the Aggie there was talking about, probably like you have in California. On the other hand, let's talk about moose. Talk about a road hazard!

Virginia Is for Lovers: Tell 'em!

Alaska: An adult moose will stand over six feet tall at the shoulder and weigh over a thousand pounds, and big and heavy doesn't mean slow. They will charge you and stomp you, especially if it's a cow with a calf. Just this summer a cyclist in Anchorage was charged by a mother moose and taken off his bicycle.[6] I was cycling with my usual Sunday guys a couple of weeks ago, and on the grass by our finishing road in, there were a cow and calf grazing on saplings. Our first guy passed, alerting her, and the mother left her calf at the tree line and came and stood in the roadway, daring us to pass. We found another way to go—no one was willing to risk a thousand pounds of angry mama moose.

State of California: Really? They don't spook and run like a deer?

Alaska: No, they spook and charge like a tank. The rest of the time they wander aimlessly and can go anywhere. There was even one I saw in downtown Fairbanks a few winters ago. Very much something to be alert for when biking.

Virginia Is for Lovers: And is that your only worry?

Alaska: No.

University of Iowa: Getting clobbered by a moose isn't your worst fear?

Santa Cruz Cycling Club: Wait! Let me guess . . . getting eaten by a polar bear?

Virginia Is for Lovers: Oh, so close! Tell them!

Alaska: Not polar bears, no, but black bears and grizzly bears, yes.

Texas A & M: Now hold on a minute there, Alaska. Bears?

Alaska: Bears. You spook a bear, you won't just get charged, you'll be lunch! The only saving grace is that if you alert them first, they tend to be skittish and shy away. Unless, of course, it is a sow with a cub. Then you're just dead.

DeKane Cyclery: You're making that up!

Virginia Is for Lovers: No he's not. I went to visit him in the summer, and we raced in a stage race in Anchorage. One of the stages was in a residential neighborhood on the southeast side of the city. There were about thirty of us in one heat, and in the middle of the race, the middle of the freaking race, a black bear runs across the road, behind him and in front of me![7]

University of Iowa: You're kidding!

Alaska: No, he's not. I saw the bear along the bushes on the right, just coming out as I passed. I guess it bolted across the road behind me.

Santa Cruz Cycling Club: Did they stop the race?

Alaska: No, why would they? The bear, it was a black bear, just ran across the road, into the backyard of some house. There are lots of black bears in some areas. Just make noise, and they tend to scare off before you even see them.

Texas A & M: What about grizzlies?

Alaska: Different story there. A grizzly will maul you. A grizzly will kill you. About a decade ago there was a twenty-four-hour mountain bike race in Anchorage, and one of the racers, a teenager, came around a corner in the forest and must have surprised a grizzly because she was mauled and left for dead. She was found by other racers and was saved, but it was pretty bad.[8] That was in Anchorage. Closer to my home in Fairbanks, about five years ago, a grizzly moved into the western suburbs, and everyone was on edge. No one wanted to be the one guy who surprised that bear.

Virginia Is for Lovers: But you kept riding, though, didn't you?

Alaska: Hey, the road season is too short not to ride whenever the weather is halfway decent.

And there was much nodding of heads.

Alaska: You just have to be prepared and keep one eye on the road and one eye on nature.

Hotter'N Hell 100: How do you prepare for a grizzly bear?

Alaska: Remember, you don't have to be faster than the bear, you just have to be faster than the guy riding next to you!

And there was chuckling heard all around.

Alaska: To start with, a good canister of bear spray fits in a water cage. I've known some road cyclists to carry it but more mountain bikers than roadies. That can be a first line of defense. I have also been known to bring something with a little more oomph than that.

Virginia Is for Lovers: Such as . . .

Alaska: I have a hammerless, featherlite .44-caliber that fits perfectly in the middle pocket of any jersey I own. It holds five jacketed rounds. Plenty of oomph to deter a bear and make an escape.

State of California: What do you mean "hammerless"?

Alaska: The hammer is the part that you cock; it strikes the back of the bullet, sending it on its way. It has a hammer but internal. The advantage to not having an external hammer is that it can be drawn out without catching on something like a pocket. Makes for a faster draw, which I figure is an advantage when potentially facing a startled grizzly.

DeKane Cyclery: Smart. Ever have an occasion to test that premise?

Alaska: No, but I don't care to find out what happens if I don't have it.

Texas A&M: You packing now?

Alaska: Well . . .

And there were gasps all round as Alaska reached behind to his center pocket.

Alaska: . . . no. Just getting my phone, to show y'all a picture of the moose and the calf I last encountered.

And sighs of relief or amazement were heard as the phone was passed around.

Alaska: I see red fox a few times on rides during the summer. And a couple of wolves, but that was in the national park. There are reports of wolves along the eastern border with Canada that will watch cyclists along the highway, but I've never heard of anything like the cyclist who was attacked by a wolf on the Alaska Highway in the Yukon. I guess he was lucky to not get mauled.[9]

Virginia Is for Lovers: So, after that, anyone want to share a deer or a dog story?

Seattle to Portland 2017: Nope.

Santa Cruz Cycling Club: I'd only embarrass myself, thank you.

State of California: Pass.

University of Iowa: My loose cow story pales in comparison.

And everyone looked about awkwardly and sipped their beers.

Alaska: Well, I'll break the ice. Great weather today, eh?

Hotter'N Hell 100: You said it brother. When I rode this here Texas century it literally was a hundred degrees. Nothing tougher than riding North Texas for a hundred miles in the heat in August!

Texas A & M: Hell yeah, pardner! I'm with y'all! That's hot, but it's a dry heat. Last year I did the Katy Flatland Century in July outside of Houston. Almost a hundred degrees, with an equal humidity!

University of Iowa: You know, the Ride Across Iowa can get pretty toasty, too, being in July and all. I rode it two years ago, and every day it was ninety degrees plus, and it was plenty humid, you betcha. Heat and humidity, makes for good sweet corn and tough biking.

Virginia Is for Lovers: Tell us. What about riding in Alaska?

Alaska: Well, I can tell you that I've never seen a hundred degrees anywhere in Alaska. The highest high anywhere is like one hundred degrees in Fort Yukon a hundred years ago.[10] In my home of Fairbanks, the record high is ninety-six degrees, half a century ago.[11] In the summer, for the most part, we rarely make it to eighty, and then we feel like we're dying.

Seattle to Portland 2017: Yes, but you have one bonus over all of us.

Peterson

Alaska: What's that?

Seattle to Portland 2017: In the summer it's never dark.

State of California: What do you mean never dark?

Alaska: We're up by the Arctic Circle. Between Mother's Day and mid-August, it doesn't get dark. The sun goes down, like goes below the horizon, but just barely as it swings around the top of the globe. But it stays light, like daylight light. We can ride at midnight, we can ride at 5:00 a.m., and any time in between.

DeKane Cyclery: Yeah, but what's the riding season? I can get in from March to November on the road in Illinois. The rest of the year sucks.

University of Iowa: Same in Iowa.

Texas A&M: In Southeast Texas we can ride the road just about all year long. It gets a little chilly in December and January, but as long as it's above freezing and there's no ice, I'll get out and ride. How about you, Alaska, what's your season? June to July?

And snickers were again heard round the circle of psyclists.

Alaska: If it was, that would be a waste of a lot of good summer daylight, don't you think? No, I bike year-round.

Hotter'N Hell 100: Nah, I gotta call BS on that. No way.

Virginia Is for Lovers: Don't let your skinny tires be a reflection of narrow minds! Tell 'em.

Seattle to Portland 2017: He's not riding on 18s all year guys.[12] Even I know that.

Alaska: He's right, but yeah, some of us ride all year round. The road season is May 1 to October 1, give or take. Mountain biking, say April 1 to November 1. If you've got studded tires for your mountain bike, you can go March 1 all the way into mid-November, depending upon the snow. November to March, it's fat tire season.

Texas A&M: Fat tire season?

Virginia Is for Lovers: That's right Aggie, go check it out on the internet. Fat tire bikes. The tires are four and a half inches wide and studded like a car tire, with aluminum rims on carbon or aluminum frames, shocks like mountain bikes, and gearing you wouldn't believe. A single ring up front, maybe twenty-five teeth, and eleven gears in the back, the largest maybe forty teeth. Special insulated covers over the handlebars, called pogies, and disc brakes front and back. Damn things float over the snow, though not exactly at breakneck speed. And not cheap with that kind of buildup. Costs as much as a decent used car![13]

Santa Cruz Cycling Club: I've seen fat tires on beach bikes.

State of California: Yup, makes riding in the sand look easy.

Alaska: And riding in the snow. Look, the opposite of our long, sunny days are our dark and cold winters, and I for one am not crazy about sweating all over an indoor trainer. November through March, we're out on fat tire bikes, on the streets, the bike paths, and through the forests. It's great!

Hotter'N Hell 100: Yeah, but it's gotta be cold. And dark.

Alaska: Well, yes, it is that. But that doesn't stop us from riding . . . fat tire riding. In fact, on the winter solstice we make a point of riding from sunrise to sunset, all day.

Texas A&M: When is that?

University of Iowa: You must have been at the top of your class in Aggieland! December 21, you idiot. Solstice! How long is all day?

Alaska: Three hours and forty minutes. It's not that long, though a local running club runs for that same time. It sounds more impressive to say sunrise to sunset.

Seattle to Portland 2017: That's less than half the time it took for today's ride!

Hotter'N Hell 100: And how far did you go in that time?

Alaska: Thirty miles.

State of California: That's like a regular Wednesday after-work quickie, but we knock that out in an hour and a half!

Virginia Is for Lovers: Yeah, but it's not the time or the miles. Alaska, what's the operative number here?

Alaska: A hundred.

Texas A&M: A hundred what?

Alaska: Degrees, as in, about a hundred degrees colder than now and way more than that compared to those Texas rides.

DeKane Cyclery: Twenty *below* zero? You're kidding me!

Alaska: No kidding there, DeKane. With an average low in December and January in the negative teens and records below negative forty, ain't nothing to be twenty or thirty below for a bike ride.[14] Below about minus ten, it kinda feels all the same anyhow.

State of California: How do you keep from catching frostbite or, worse yet, hypothermia?

Alaska: Dress in layers. Start with insulated waterproof cycling boots with wool socks, long johns, and insulated GORE-TEX pants, usually three layers up top, down gloves with liners, wool cap under a lined helmet, face mask, sometimes goggles. No exposed skin, that's for sure.

Texas A&M: It's the Michelin Man on a bike!

And the laughter returned.

Alaska: Maybe, but beyond the layers, the other key is to never stop moving; don't let the cold soak in. Keep my phone fully charged in an interior pocket so the battery doesn't drain from the cold, in case I need to call in help. Ain't nothing casual about riding at thirty below. Safety first.

Hotter'N Hell 100: I thought you said twenty below.

Alaska: I did. Coldest I've been out in is negative forty, about seven or eight years ago in January. Only went out for an hour, just to say I did it. Truth is, it's just painful at that temperature. It actually hurts to breathe—the air is so cold. And the tires squeak in the snow when it's negative degrees, a sound I'd bet none of you know.

Texas A&M: And I'd bet none of us want to. Any takers?

And if shaking heads could make a sound, a rumble would have been heard.

Alaska: Tell you what. Any of you want to come up, my house is open to you. We have a little winter race north of Fairbanks called the White Mountains 100.[15] The race is run around mid-March, so you're not dealing with crazy negative temperatures, and the length of day is approaching twelve hours, it being about spring equinox. Entry into the race is by lottery, but if you score a ticket, any of you can crash at my place before and after, and if I'm not in the race, I'll help support you in it. You come race the White Mountains, and then you'll have something to talk about at a post-ride kegger!

And eight minds simultaneously contemplated how to convince significant others and bosses that they needed time off in March to ride a bicycle over a hundred miles of snow-covered trail in the mountains in north-central Alaska. Followed by sips of lager again.

Rainbow Jersey: Hi! Got room for one more? What a ride today, eh?

You guys must be fast, looks like you've been here a while. Are you guys fast? I got this shirt online—I think it was Peter Sagan's.[16] Pretty cool, huh? Too bad the autograph washed out in the laundry. Anyone want to see a picture of him signing one like this? What are you guys talking about? Great day for riding, huh? Anyone here from Jersey? I'm from Jersey, can you guess what exit? What are you guys drinking? Could I go for a diet soda or what, know what I'm saying? Anyone seen sodas around here?

Virginia Is for Lovers: You ask a lot of questions for not being Peter Sagan. What is this, the Spanish Inquisition?[17]

And there was deliberate silence.

Rainbow Jersey: Okay . . . excuse me, I think I see someone over there . . .

Seattle to Portland 2017: Good save, Virginia.

Virginia Is for Lovers: Yeah, well . . .

Texas A&M: Anyone hungry? I'm about ready for something of more substance than these appetizers.

Hotter'N Hell 100: Ya know, I could go for a burger. Shall we?

Texas A&M: Sounds good. California?

State of California: Sure, why not. Santa Cruz, how about it?

Santa Cruz Cycling Club: I'll find a chicken alternative wherever you go. I'm in.

University of Iowa: I can't seem to shift into twelfth. I think I'd better work on my rear derailleur for a bit. I wouldn't mind help. It's worth a round on me, any takers?

Seattle to Portland 2017: I took a course at bike school. It's probably just a quick adjustment, let me take a look at it.

DeKane Cyclery: I use to work in a bike shop. Buy us both beers, and I'll fix it.

University of Iowa: Done deal.

Nice to meet you. Amazing rides. Good luck tomorrow. Maybe we'll see you out there tomorrow. Nice chatting with you. Love your jersey. Thanks, we'll see you. You guys ready? Take care. Okay, my bike's over here. Want to change shoes first? See you guys. Bye.

And then there were two.

I didn't get anyone's phone number that night. I listened to Don snore in the rarified altitude of the Colorado Rockies. For having the highest mountain in North America,[18] most of Alaska sits at five hundred feet above sea level, give or take. But Colorado's rarified air didn't seem to affect me. With Don it was another thing, a night of sawing wood as a result. The next day was going to be a moderate trek of eighty-five miles, over two passes, and at least one of us would be reasonably well rested. When the snoring got to be too much around 3:00 a.m., I rousted myself from bed and performed preventative maintenance on my bike, putting light lubrication on the chain and gears, checking the nuts and bolts for tightness and the tires for the right air pressure. I didn't want a mechanical problem on the road tomorrow. Like most organized rides of decent size, there would be mechanics at the start and end as well as at the rest stops and a couple cruising the route to help with mechanical issues that any rider might experience along the way. They would only be a last resort to fix a problem for me, if I kept on top of things. Like most of my riding buddies in the forty-ninth state, we all had to be handy with a bike multitool, capable of disassembling and reassembling a bike on the side of the road, not to mention most repairs of minor breakdowns on the fly, because bike shops are few and far between in the 907,[19] and out on the road, light traffic makes for nice riding, but light traffic also means less chances for help if one has equipment failure. Satisfied that my bike was ready to roll in a few hours, I tried my best to ignore the snoring next door and did catch a few hours of sleep before I had to go back in the saddle again.

Over the next four days, over hundreds of Colorado miles and over four more après-ride refreshment sessions, I swapped the same stories about moose and bears and fat tire bikes with pogies, all in response to the general theme behind each inquiry: the surprise that the bicycle even exists in Alaska. Rest assured, bicycling is alive and well in America's trans-Arctic playground, and to survive it all year round, Alaskan psyclists are tougher for it. And we're happy to share ribald tales of Alaskan cycling, no need for even little white lies, wherever we go. When we're Outside,[20] not worrying about moose and frostbite, just ask, and we'll tell 'em.

Notes

1. A gratuitous but obligatory nod to Monty Python. Shameless really.
2. Next year, Don, we'll join a group that cycles the Pacific Coast Highway, ten feet above sea level—you'll love it.
3. Not unlike NHL players who by tradition will not touch the Stanley Cup unless they have won it.
4. I have button-down dress shirts that cost less!
5. Pacific Coast Highway. Lucky Californians, a great road in a decent climate though sometimes a little too much traffic.
6. "Moose Protecting 2 Calves Charges Cyclist on Alaska Bike Trail," *Global News*, May 22, 2018, https://globalnews.ca/video/4224569/moose -protecting-2-calves-charges-cyclist-on-alaska-bike-trail.
7. I told you he was slow.
8. "Bear Mauls Girl during Mountain Bike Race: Grizzly Suspected in Attack along Trail during 24-Hour Event in Alaska," Associated Press, June 29, 2008.
9. Jacqueline Ronson, "Cyclist Narrowly Escapes Wolf Attack," *Yukon News*, July 12, 2013, https://www.yukon-news.com/news/cyclist-narrowly -escapes-wolf-attack.
10. "Local Climate in Alaska," National Weather Service, accessed April 13, 2022, https://www.weather.gov/afg/localClimate.
11. "Alaska Record High and Low Temperatures," Plantmaps.com, accessed April 13, 2022, https://www.plantmaps.com/en/us/climate/extremes/f /alaska-record-high-low-temperatures.
12. Short for eighteen-millimeter-wide tires, skinny high-pressure road and track tires, great for dry smooth pavement, crappy on anything else. Not favored by even pro riders now. Standard racing tires have moved to the twenty-five-millimeter-wide range.
13. I don't have a decent used car; all my money is in bikes. Don has two bikes—one road, one mountain. I have a road bike, a backup road bike, a gravel bike, a mountain bike, a fat tire bike, and a plain ol' out-riding- with-my-kids leisure bike.
14. U.S. Climate Data, accessed April 13, 2022, https://www.usclimatedata .com/climate/fairbanks/alaska/united-states/usak0083.
15. White Mountains 100 Race, EnduranceNorth.org, accessed April 13, 2022, http://wm100.endurancenorth.org.

16. Peter Sagan won the World Road Race Championships three years running, 2015–17, among other accomplishments. Replicas of his jerseys, including championship jerseys, abound on the internet.

17. Shameless again. See note 1.

18. Denali, formerly known as Mount McKinley, at twenty-three thousand feet, is the tallest peak north of the Panama Canal. Amazing to behold, definitely not bike friendly.

19. Biggest state in the nation, used to have four time zones, now just two, but hey, still only one area code.

20. A term for the rest of the United States outside of Alaska.

8. Ridgetop tundra in the Nulato Hills, Alaska.
Photo by Luc Mehl.

9. Trekking through downfall from forest fire in the
Nulato Hills, Alaska. Photo by Luc Mehl.

10. Route finding through an old burn scar.
Photo by Luc Mehl.

11. Lael Wilcox and friend riding in Denali National Park. Photo by Rugile Kaladyte.

12. Bikes at a cabin near Willow, Alaska.
Photo by Rugile Kaladyte.

13. Lael Wilcox on the Tony Knowles Coastal Trail in Anchorage. Photo by Rugile Kaladyte.

14. (*opposite top*) Lael Wilcox and family bike camping at the beach. Photo by Rugile Kaladyte.

15. (*opposite bottom*) Lael Wilcox at Hatcher Pass, Alaska. Photo by Rugile Kaladyte.

16. (*opposite top*) Clint Hodges III on the Iditarod Trail
    Invitational. Photo by Nicholas Carman. Courtesy of
    Clint Hodges III.

17. (*opposite bottom*) Clint Hodges III riding single-track
    in Anchorage. Photo by Kate Ginsbach. Courtesy of
    Clint Hodges III.

18. (*above*) Clint Hodges III riding on fresh snow. Photo
    by Kurt Refsnider. Courtesy of Clint Hodges III.

Magnetek's Fresh Fade

spit polish a glacier

0:38 / 0:56

19. (*above*) M. C. MoHagani Magnetek employs a beach cruiser in this music video called "Fresh Fade." Courtesy of the artist.

20. (*opposite top*) Cyclist Heather Best at Cooper Pass, Alaska. Photo by Jeff Oatley.

21. (*opposite bottom*) Self-portrait on the trail. Photo by Jeff Oatley.

22. Paddling on the Chukchi Sea with bike in tow.
Photo by Bjørn Olson.

23. Hunter and bike. Photo by Bjørn Olson.

24. Kids riding our bikes. Photo by Bjørn Olson.

25. Cycling through arctic fog. Photo by Bjørn Olson.

26. Pausing on the tundra. Photo by Bjørn Olson.

Acknowledgments

First of all, I want to thank Frank for being a thoughtful and generous mentor. Thanks to his wife, Margo Klass, and friend Kes Woodward for their help and support in finalizing the project after Frank's death. Thanks to all of the intrepid writers who poured their time, energy, and hearts into these pieces, many during the difficult time of the pandemic. Thanks to Dermot Cole for helping Frank and I with the permissions and archival material after Terrence's death. I want to acknowledge Lucy McCarthy for discussions and a class project she did in the mid-1980s that may have helped Terrence with his original book. Thanks to Terrence for teaching me in a wonderful class on the Literature of Polar Exploration and for encouraging me and my creative writing.

Thanks to Robert Liebermann for telling me about Cole's original *Wheels on Ice* book and for the (always) entertaining discussions. Thank you to Martha Amore, Indra Arriaga Delgado, Heather Aruffo, and Rosemary McGuire for giving me a literary community. Thanks to Patrick Farrell for connecting me with Charlie Kelly and helping me understand the cycling ecosystem outside Alaska. Thanks to cartographer Erin Greb, copy editor Elizabeth Gratch, and the wonderful staff at the University of Nebraska Press for their help in preparing the publication. Finally, thanks to my husband, Bob Busey, for his patience and understanding during this project.

—Jessica Cherry

Source Acknowledgments

Some pieces have been revised, combined, or renamed since original publication. Posts on personal blogs are not listed here.

Buettner, Dan. "Biking the Haul Road." *Anchorage Daily News*, October 5, 1986.

Cherry, Jessica. "Physical Education." *Sport Literate* 14, no. 2 (Fall 2021): 64–73.

Cole, Terrence, ed. *Wheels on Ice: Bicycling in Alaska, 1898–1908*. Anchorage: Alaska Northwest Publishing Company, 1985. Also published as a "book insert" called "Wheels on Ice: A Collection of Gold Rush Tales by Men Who Mushed with Bicycles Instead of Dogs" in *Alaska Journal: History and Arts of the North* 15, no. 1 (Winter 1985): 1–64.

Dial, Roman. "Hellbiking in Alaska." In *Bicycle: The Image and the Dream*, edited by Nick Sanders. London: Talman Company / Red Bus, 1991.

———. "Hell on Ice." *Mountain Biking UK*, November 1993.

———. "Hell Ride!" *Anchorage Daily News*, May 9, 1993.

———. "The Incredible Journey." *Mountain Biking*, February 1994.

Finkel, Michael. "Rough-Terrain Unicycling." *Atlantic* 141, no. 4 (April 1997).

Hirschberg, Max. "My Bicycle Trip Down the Yukon." *Alaska* 44, no. 2 (February 1978): 27.

James, David. "Last Ride of the Season." *Anchorage Press*, November 2, 2020.

Jesson, Ed. "From Dawson to Nome on a Bicycle." Edited by Ruth Reat. *Pacific Northwest Quarterly* 47, no. 3 (Fall 1956): 65–74.

Kelly, Charlie. "Iditabike, 1987." In *Fat Tire Flyer: Repack and the Birth of Mountain Biking*, edited by Charlie Kelly. Boulder CO: VeloPress, 2014.

Moran, Tom. "Fatbiking to the Magic Bus." *Bicycle Quarterly* 14, no. 4 (Winter 2015): 6–13.

Olson, Bjørn. "Group Fat-Bikes and Packrafts across Arctic." *Arctic Sounder*, July 29, 2017.

——— . "Whaling Festival a Welcome Respite for Arctic Cyclists." *Arctic Sounder*, August 4, 2017.

Romano-Lax, Andromeda. "Killer Hill." *Anchorage Press*, August 13, 2008.

Sherwonit, Bill. "Pribilofs by Bike." *Anchorage Daily News*, July 24, 1994. A slightly different version of this story originally appeared in the *Anchorage Daily News* Sunday magazine, *We Alaskans*, in July 1994.

"Thrilling Trip from Point Barrow to Nome of Levie, the Famous Yukon Wheelman." *Nome Gold Digger*, January 16, 1901.

Wilcox, Lael. "Back in Alaska to Share the Story of the Roads: Lael Wilcox Rides Alaska." *Radavist*, June 23, 2020. https://theradavist.com/2020/06/back-in-alaska-to-share-the-story-of-the-roads-lael-wilcox-rides-alaska.

Contributors

MARTHA AMORE lives in Alaska with her family and teaches writing at the University of Alaska Anchorage. She holds a master of fine arts degree in fiction and a doctorate in interdisciplinary studies in psychology and English. Winner of a Rasmuson Individual Artist Award, she is a contributing editor of the University of Alaska Press anthology *Building Fires in the Snow: A Collection of Alaska LGBTQ Short Fiction and Poetry*, which was a finalist for a LAMBDA Literary Award. Her collection of short fiction, *In the Quiet Season & Other Stories*, was published in 2018. She is currently hard at work on a new book.

DAN BUETTNER is a National Geographic Fellow and author of five books on longevity and happiness. He discovered the five places in the world—dubbed Blue Zones—where people live the longest, healthiest lives. His books, *The Blue Zones: Lessons for Living Longer from the People Who've Lived the Longest*; *Thrive: Finding Happiness the Blue Zones Way*; *The Blue Zones Solution: Eating and Living like the World's Healthiest People*; and *The Blue Zones of Happiness*, were all national best sellers. Buettner has appeared on *The Today Show*, *Oprah*, NBC *Nightly News*, and *Good Morning America* and has been the keynote speaker at TEDMED, Bill Clinton's Health Matters Initiative, and Google Zeitgeist. His speech in January 2018 at the World Economic Forum in Davos was chosen as "one of the best of Davos." Buettner also holds three Guinness World Records in distance cycling.

JESSICA CHERRY is a geoscientist, writer, aerial photographer, and commercial airplane pilot living in Anchorage, Alaska. She writes a literary column for the alt-weekly *Anchorage Press* and is at work on a scientific aviation-themed memoir. She's a three-time graduate of Columbia University in New York City, and her scientific research has been featured in *Science*, *Nature*, and the *New*

York Times. Her favorite ride is along Turnagain Arm on a road bike when the Beluga whales are passing through.

TERRENCE COLE was a professor of northern studies and history and director of the Office of Public History at the University of Alaska Fairbanks. He studied geography, northern studies, and history at UAF and earned a doctorate in American history at the University of Washington. He returned to his alma mater in 1988 to teach and pursue his passion about polar exploration. Students twice chose him as Outstanding Teacher of the Year. He also received the Emil Usibelli Teaching Award, the Edith Bullock Service Award, and the governor's Distinguished Service to the Humanities Award. He wrote five books on Alaska history and was awarded the 2011 Alaska Historian of the Year for *Fighting for the Forty-Ninth Star: C. W. Snedden and the Long Struggle for Alaska Statehood.* Terrence and his twin brother, Dermot, were the recipients of the Fairbanks 2011 Distinguished Citizens of the Year. Terrence loved to talk about history and politics and lead historical bike tours around Fairbanks.

CORINNA COOK is the author of *Leavetakings,* an essay collection. She is a former Fulbright fellow, an Alaska Literary Award recipient, and a Rasmuson Foundation awardee. Corinna's essays appear in *Flyway, Alaska Quarterly Review, Alaska* magazine, and elsewhere; her journalism appears in *Yukon North of Ordinary,* among others; and her critical articles appear in *Assay, New Writing,* and *Essay Daily.* Corinna holds a PhD degree in English and creative writing from the University of Missouri. More at corinnacook.com.

ALYS CULHANE'S areas of recreational interest are long-distance horse trekking, bicycle touring, and sea kayaking. Alys is currently working on a book titled "When You Come to a Fork in the Road, Pick It Up" and compiling an anthology titled "Women Who Run with Horses." She and her husband, Pete Praetorius, will soon begin work on the third edition of the *Alaska Bicycle Touring Guide.* Culhane is also the volunteer co-coordinator of the Bright Lights Book Project. She and Pete currently live in Palmer, Alaska. Alys's greatest claim to fame is having completed the Iditabike, in reverse.

ROMAN DIAL met his wife, Peggy, while living in Fairbanks from 1977 to 1988. In Alaska he and his friends have hellbiked across the Wrangells from Nabesna to McCarthy; the Brooks Range from Kaktovik to Arctic Village; the Kenai from Hope to Homer across the Harding Icefield; the Talkeetnas from Eureka Roadhouse to Talkeetna; the Chugach from McCarthy to Cordova; the Lost Coast from Cordova to Glacier Bay; and the Alaska Range from Canada to

Lake Clark. A professor at Alaska Pacific University, he lives in Anchorage with Peggy and their Icelandic sheepdog, Poppy. He's authored two books, *Packrafting!* and *The Adventurer's Son*.

MICHAEL FINKEL is the best-selling author of *The Stranger in the Woods* and *True Story*, which was adapted into a motion picture. He lives with his family in the western United States and southern France.

ERIC FLANDERS is a full-time endurance athlete, Schnauzer dad, race organizer, and *littérateur* based out of Anchorage. Eric holds a BA degree in religious studies from Arizona State University, where he found it hard to be pious, and an MA degree in English from University of Alaska Anchorage, where he has taught composition. Reared in the louche, humid confines of the northern Midwest, he would eventually migrate to higher latitudes, mostly to avoid the sweats. He now considers himself part of the local wildlife and can be viewed locally wherever the trail tilts up. Feed him if you see him!

MAX HIRSCHBERG came to Alaska from Ohio in 1900 at the age of nineteen. He made the ride to Nome by bicycle in the same year, a trip that took two and half months. He died in 1964.

CLINTON HODGES III was born and raised in Anchorage. He continues to reside there and works in construction, likes to ride bikes a long way, and has recently picked up packrafting. He has two half-brothers, Mike and Joe, who live in Alaska, and Clint's father and stepmother live in the desert next to the Colorado River. Clint looks forward to seeing you on the trails and would love to tell you a story.

DAVID A. JAMES is a freelance writer living in Fairbanks. His work has appeared in numerous Alaska publications, including the *Anchorage Daily News*, *Fairbanks Daily News-Miner*, *Anchorage Press*, *Alaska* magazine, and others.

First arriving in Alaska in 1896 to prospect for gold in the Cook Inlet region of southern Alaska, **EDWARD R. JESSON** made his way to the Yukon after the Klondike Gold Strike and began running a trading post at Star City. In 1900 he acquired a bicycle, and when news landed of a new discovery on Alaska's western shore, he rode more than a thousand miles from Dawson City to Nome, becoming one of the early pioneers of long-distance bicycle travel.

From California, **CHARLIE KELLY** is one of the inventors of mountain biking and the founder and editor of the magazine *Fat Tire Flyer*. He has written for *Bicycling* and *Mountain Bike Magazine* (where he also served as an editor) and wrote the books *Richard's Mountain Bike Book* and *Fat Tire Flyer: Repack and the Birth of Mountain Biking*.

Growing up in an old farmhouse near Lake Erie meant playing in snow and wind. GAIL KOEPF had three brothers, so her playmates contributed to her "tomboy" inclinations. Gail's first bike was a very used adult balloon tire tank that had two-by-four pieces strapped on the pedals so she could reach the seat. Later, degrees in geography and forestry led her to Alaska, a job with the Forest Service, and her future husband, Rocky Reifenstuhl. Rocky grew to be quite the biker and competitor as Gail raised their two daughters and happily joined in the fun once they were old enough to stay with friends. The 1991 Iditasport was Gail's second year doing the winter endurance bike race.

RACHAEL KVAPIL began writing in the mid-1980s as a form of self-entertainment and later as part of the high school newspaper staff. She graduated with a degree in journalism from the University of Alaska Fairbanks, working as a local reporter until she opened her marketing company in the early 2000s. Rachael has spent her life commuting on a bike, recently racing after discovering triathlons and fat bikes. Her most significant biking accomplishments include Ironman Coeur d'Alene, the Susitna 100, and the White Mountains 100. She served as the Fairbanks Cycle Club president from 2015 to 2020.

CORRINE LEISTIKOW moved to Fairbanks at age thirty. She is a family physician who encourages her patients to be physically active. She met her husband, a lifetime Alaskan, in the Golden Heart City, and together they have raised two children, encouraging them to hike, ski, and bike with them. Her passion is being physically active in the great outdoors. She and her husband chronicle their adventures at their blog, *Not Quite over the Hill*, https://notquiteoverthehillcorrineanderic.blogspot.com.

Joining Edward R. Jesson and Max Hirschberg, H. B. LEVIE was one of the first and earliest riders to make the trip from Dawson City to Nome in the winter of 1900. A year later he rode from Point Barrow to Nome.

M. C. MOHAGANI MAGNETEK (pronounced: *emcee mahogany magnetic*) resides in Anchorage, at her Wonder Woman Wonderdome, aka Camp Magnetek. She is a prolific writer who is cooler than ice water, highly educated in anthropology, English, creative writing, and forensic science. A coast guard veteran, community organizer, and human rights advocate, she is world renowned, nationally recognized, and locally accepted as the undisputed people's champ because she believes poetry is therapeutic. Some of her published works include "Shhh Be

Quiet," *Building Fires in the Snow* (2016); "Acrimonious Black Woman Sparks Climate Change Debate with the President," *Alaska Women Speak* (2019); and "Girlfriend, What's Your Recipe for Lemonade," *Woman Scream: The International Poetry Anthology of Female Voices* (2020). Her first novel is *The Mad Fantastic, 2098* (2020).

KATHLEEN MCCOY has worked as a journalist in Alaska for more than thirty years. After a year at the *Nome Nugget* in 1981, she joined the *Anchorage Daily News* as a writer and editor and eventually oversaw the Sunday magazine, *We Alaskans*, and fourteen feature sections as well as new media and audience interactivity. After a 2007 sabbatical at Stanford University's John S. Knight Mid-Career Fellowship Program, she accepted a position as an electronic media specialist and storyteller at the University of Alaska Anchorage. Her radio days began when KSKA launched a new community radio program, *Hometown Alaska*, and she joined as an inaugural host. She earned concurrent bachelor's degrees from the University of California, Berkeley, in journalism and rhetoric.

LUC MEHL grew up in McGrath, Alaska, a village with only fifteen miles of dirt roads. What little biking he did was on the airport runway. In 2015 Luc biked the Iditarod trail from his home in McGrath to his home in Anchorage, which sparked an interest in biking in other parts of remote Alaska. In 2017 he joined Eric Parsons on an ambitious bike mission to the Nulato Hills on the Yukon River. Luc works as an advocate for conservation, safety, and stewardship in Alaska. You can find Luc's other stories at thingstolucat.com.

TOM MORAN'S bike exploits include two solo crossings of the United States and tours in Iceland, East Asia, Cuba, Bolivia, and the Balkans as well as plenty of adventures closer to his home in Fairbanks. When he's not biking, running, hiking, skiing, or packrafting, he works at the University of Alaska Fairbanks.

JEFF OATLEY was born in Lansing, Michigan, in 1969. He grew up there until his family moved to Madison, Alabama, when he was a teenager. In April 2000 he moved to Fairbanks, where he still lives. Oatley has been riding bikes for fifty years and still rides as much as he can. Sometimes that's a whole bunch. Sometimes it's not as much as he'd like.

BJØRN OLSON is a lifelong Alaskan and a wilderness adventurer. Over the last fifteen years, he has devoted a large part of his energy to exploring as much of Alaska by fat bike and packraft as means allow. He was inspired at an early age by Roman Dial's and Roger Cowell's extreme cycling exploits. Some of Olson's "firsts" with the fat bike include riding down the Kuskokwim River from

Stony River to Bethel; Homer to Seldovia with fat bike and packraft; Hope to Homer with fat bike and packraft; Williamsport (Cook Inlet) to Bristol Bay with fat bike and packraft; Homer to Port Graham with fat bike and packraft; Knik to Kotzebue; Nome to Kivalina with fat bike; Point Hope to Utqiaġvik (Barrow) with fat bike and packraft; Nome to Nome via the Imurik Basin with fat bike and packraft; Kotzebue to Selawik with fat bike; Deadhorse to Utqiaġvik (incomplete) with fat bike; and Kotzebue to Point Hope with fat bike and packraft.

EARL PETERSON is a judge in the Fairbanks Superior Court. Judge Peterson has been an Alaska resident for more than ten years and has practiced law for twenty-five years. He graduated from Chicago Kent College of Law in 1995 and enjoys road cycling.

DON REARDEN is a screenwriter and poet and the author of the critically acclaimed novel *The Raven's Gift,* which made the Washington Post Notable List for Fiction. He grew up in Southwest Alaska and teaches writing as a professor at the University of Alaska.

ROCKY REIFENSTUHL lived in Fairbanks, where he was raised by daughters, Alex and Kirsten, and his wife, Gail (Gail has won Iditasport nine times in all its divisions: bike, foot, snowshoe, triathlon, and ski). As of 2000, Rocky had been human-powered racing for twenty-three years, had won the 100-mile, 200-mile, or 350-mile bike race versions seven times, and had numerous medals for biking championships, at state, national, and world venues. In 2000 Rocky and brother Steve finished first in the Iditasport Extreme foot division. Rocky wrote nearly one hundred geology publications as well as stories for *Velonews, Bicycling, Mountain Bike Action, Alaska, Mushing,* and *Bike* magazines. Rocky passed away in 2014 at age sixty-one. Steve Reifenstuhl lives in Sitka and in 2000 had won the Iditarod Trail Invitational, Alaska Ultrasport, three times and held the foot record (four days, fifteen hours: 350 miles).

ANDROMEDA ROMANO-LAX is the author of five novels and a travel narrative. She now lives on a small island in British Columbia, Canada, in an area of hilly roads and trails great for running and cycling. Follow her on Instagram at @romanolax.

Anchorage nature writer **BILL SHERWONIT** is a widely published essayist and the author of more than a dozen books, including *Living with Wildness: An Alaskan Odyssey* and *Animal Stories: Encounters with Alaska's Wildlife.*

DANIEL SMITH is an Alaskan amateur adventurer specializing in hiking, biking, and packrafting trips around the state with his best friend, Teresa. When not outside, he might be writing, drawing, or teaching his middle school English students. He currently lives in Unalaska.

FRANK SOOS, a native of Virginia, is the author of *Unified Field Theory*, which won the 1997 Flannery O'Connor Award for Short Fiction. He is also the author of *The Getting Place*; *Unpleasantries: Considerations of Difficult Questions*; *Bamboo Fly Rod Suite*; *Early Yet*; and, with Margo Klass, *Double Moon: Constructions and Conversations*. He was a professor emeritus of English at the University of Alaska Fairbanks. A touring cyclist since the 1970s, Frank liked nothing more than loading up his panniers and heading out on the road. Tragically, Frank died in a cycling accident during this book's production. He is remembered by his many friends and students as a thoughtful and generous person.

ERIC TROYER loves to do too many things, including writing, volunteering, playing guitar, biking, skiing, running, and a variety of other human-powered outdoor activities. He was born to an outdoor-loving family and has lived in Alaska his entire life, exploring the state's wild areas. He studied at the University of Alaska Anchorage and got a degree in journalism from the University of Montana in Missoula. He worked for two Alaska newspapers—the *Mat-Su Frontiersman* and *Fairbanks Daily News-Miner*—and tried his hand at elementary school teaching before becoming a full-time stay-at-home dad, volunteer, and freelance writer.

Born and raised in Anchorage, **LAEL WILCOX** is an ultra-endurance bike racer and rider, traveling all over the world to compete and explore. In 2017 she completed a passion project to ride all of the major roads in Alaska, her effort to get to know her home state and see it all from the seat of her bicycle.